VESPER FLIGHTS

VESPER FLIGHTS

NEW AND COLLECTED ESSAYS

HELEN MACDONALD

THORNDIKE PRESS
A part of Gale, a Cengage Company

Copyright © 2020 by Helen Macdonald.
Some of these pieces have appeared in different form in the *New York Times Magazine, New Statesman* and elsewhere.
Thorndike Press, a part of Gale, a Cengage Company.

ALL RIGHTS RESERVED
Thorndike Press® Large Print Core.
The text of this Large Print edition is unabridged.
Other aspects of the book may vary from the original edition.
Set in 16 pt. Plantin.

**LIBRARY OF CONGRESS CIP DATA ON FILE.
CATALOGUING IN PUBLICATION FOR THIS BOOK
IS AVAILABLE FROM THE LIBRARY OF CONGRESS.**

ISBN-13: 978-1-4328-8486-4 (hardcover alk. paper)

Published in 2021 by arrangement with Grove/Atlantic, Inc.

Printed in Mexico
Print Number: 01   Print Year: 2021

CONTENTS

INTRODUCTION

Back in the sixteenth century, a curious craze began to spread through the halls, palaces and houses of Europe. It was a type of collection kept often in ornate wooden cases, and it was known as a *Wunderkammer,* a Cabinet of Curiosities, although the direct translation from the German captures better its purpose: cabinet of wonders. It was expected that people should pick up and handle the objects in these cases; feel their textures, their weights, their particular strangenesses. Nothing was kept behind glass, as in a modern museum or gallery. More importantly, perhaps, neither were these collections organised according to the museological classifications of today. *Wunderkammern* held natural and artificial things together on shelves in close conjunction: pieces of coral; fossils; ethnographic artefacts; cloaks; miniature paintings; musical instruments; mirrors; preserved speci-

7

mens of birds and fish; insects; rocks; feathers. The wonder these collections kindled came in part from the ways in which their disparate contents spoke to one another of their similarities and differences in form, their beauties and manifest obscurities. I hope that this book works a little like a *Wunderkammer.* It is full of strange things and it is concerned with the quality of wonder.

Someone once told me that every writer has a subject that underlies everything they write. It can be love or death, betrayal or belonging, home or hope or exile. I choose to think that my subject is love, and most specifically love for the glittering world of non-human life around us. Before I was a writer I was a historian of science, which was an eye-opening occupation. We tend to think of science as unalloyed, objective truth, but of course the questions it has asked of the world have quietly and often invisibly been inflected by history, culture and society. Working as a historian of science revealed to me how we have always unconsciously and inevitably viewed the natural world as a mirror of ourselves, reflecting our own world-view and our own needs, thoughts and hopes. Many of the essays here are exercises in interrogating such human ascriptions and assumptions. Most of all I hope my work is about a thing that seems to me of the deepest possible importance in our present-day historical moment: finding ways to recognise and love difference. The attempt to see through eyes that are not your own. To understand that your way of looking at the world is not the only one. To think what it might mean to love those that are not like you. To rejoice in the complexity of things.

Science encourages us to reflect upon the size of our lives in relation to the vastness of the universe or the bewildering multitudes of microbes that exist inside our bodies. And it reveals to us a planet that is beautifully and insistently not human. It was science that taught me how the flights of tens of millions of migrating birds across Europe and Africa, lines on the map drawn in lines of feather and starlight and bone, are stranger and more astonishing than I could ever have imagined, for these creatures navigate by visualising the Earth's magnetic field through detecting quantum entanglement taking place in the receptor cells of their eyes. What science does is what I would like more literature to do too: show us that we are living in an exquisitely complicated world that is not all about us.

It does not belong to us alone. It never has done.

These are terrible times for the environment. Now more than ever before, we need to look long and hard at how we view and interact with the natural world. We're living through the world's sixth great extinction, one caused by us. The landscapes around us grow emptier and quieter each passing year. We need hard science to establish the rate and scale of these declines, to work out why it is occurring and what mitigation strategies can be brought into play. But we need literature, too; we need to communicate what the losses mean. I think of the wood warbler, a small citrus-coloured bird fast disappearing from British forests. It is one thing to show the statistical facts about this species' decline. It is another thing to communicate to people what wood warblers are, and what that loss means, when your experience of a wood that is made of light and leaves and song becomes something less complex, less magical, just *less,* once the warblers have gone. Literature can teach us the qualitative texture of the world. And we need it to. We need to communicate the value of things, so that more of us might fight to save them.

NESTS

When I was small, I decided I wanted to be a naturalist. And so I slowly amassed a nature collection, and arranged it across my bedroom sills and shelves as a visible display of all the small expertises I'd gathered from the pages of books. There were galls, feathers, seeds, pine cones, loose single wings of small tortoiseshells or peacock butterflies picked from spiders' webs; the severed wings of dead birds, spread and pinned on to cardboard to dry; the skulls of small creatures; pellets – tawny owl, barn owl, kestrel – and old birds' nests. One was a chaffinch nest I could balance in the palm of my hand, a thing of horsehair and moss, pale scabs of lichen and moulted pigeon feathers; another was a song-thrush nest woven of straw and soft twigs with a flaking inner cup moulded from clay. But those nests never felt as if they fitted with the rest of my beloved collection. It wasn't that they

11

conjured the passing of time, of birds flown, of life in death. Those intuitions are something you learn to feel much later in life. It was partly because they made me feel an emotion I couldn't name, and mostly because I felt I shouldn't possess them at all. Nests were all about eggs, and eggs were something I knew I shouldn't ever collect. Even when I came across a white half-shell picked free of twigs by a pigeon and dropped on a lawn, a moral imperative stilled my hand. I could never bring myself to take it home.

Naturalists in the nineteenth and early twentieth centuries routinely collected birds' eggs, and most children who grew up in semi-rural or rural surroundings in the 1940s and '50s have done it too. 'We only used to take one from each nest,' a woman friend told me, abashed. 'Everyone did it.' It's simply an accident of history that people two decades older than me have nature knowledges I do not possess. So many of them, having spent their childhoods bird's-nesting, still see a furze bush and think, *Linnet,* and can't help but assess the ability of last year's laid hedge to hold a chaffinch or robin's nest. They possess different wordless intuitions from me, ones relating to how one holds the landscape between head and eye and heart and hand. In my own history of the countryside, nests weren't things that were made to be found. They were carefully maintained blind spots, redacted lines in familiar texts. But even so, they had special salience when I was very young. For children, woods and fields and gardens are full of discrete, magical places: tunnels and dens and refuges in which you can hide and feel safe. I knew, when I was small, what nests were about. They were secrets.

I followed the flights of blackbirds and tits and thrushes and nuthatches through my garden. And every spring their nests changed how I felt about home. To have the presence of these birds shrunk down to that one point of attachment, the nest, made me anxious. It raised questions of vulnerability, made me worry about predatory crows and cats; made the garden a place of threat, not safety. Though I never searched for nests, I'd find them all the same. I'd be sitting at the kitchen window eating a bowl of Weetabix and I'd spot a dunnock flit into the forsythia, a mouse-sized bird, all streaks and spots and whispers. I knew I should look away, but I'd hold my breath at my transgression and track the almost imperceptible movement of leaves as the disappeared bird hopped up and across through twigs to its nest. Then I'd see the blur of wings as the bird slipped free of the hedge and was gone. And once I'd determined where it was, and saw that the adults were gone, I needed to know. Most of the nests I found were higher than my head, so I'd reach my hand up and curl my fingers until their tips touched what might be warm, glossy smoothness. Or the unbearable fragility of small flesh. I knew I was an intruder. Nests were like bruises: things I couldn't help but touch, even though I didn't want them to be there. They challenged everything that birds meant for me. I loved them most because they seemed free. Sensing danger, sensing a trap, sensing any kind of imposition, they could fly away. Watching birds, I felt I shared in their freedom. But nests and eggs tied birds down. They made them vulnerable.

The old books on birds that lined my childhood shelves described nests as 'bird homes'. This confused me. How could a nest be a home? Back then I thought of homes as fixed, eternal, dependable refuges. Nests were not like that: they were seasonal secrets to be used and abandoned. But then birds challenged my understanding of the nature of home in so many ways. Some spent the year at sea, or entirely in the air, and felt earth or rock beneath their feet only to make nests and lay eggs that tied them to land. This was all a deeper mystery. It was a story about the way lives should go that was somehow like – but not anything like – the one I'd been handed as a child. You grow up, you get married, you get a house, you have children. I didn't know where birds fitted into all this. I didn't know where I did. It was a narrative that even then gave me pause.

I think differently of home now: it's a place you carry within you, not simply a fixed location. Perhaps birds taught me that, or took me some of the way there. Some birds' nests are homes because they seem indivisible from the birds that make them. Rooks are rookeries – birds of feathers and bone that are also massed assemblages of twigs in February trees. House martins peering from the entrances of their nests under summer gables are beings of wings and mouths and eyes but also all the architecture of gathered mud. But some birds' nests seem so far from nests at all that the word itself drifts and almost loses purchase. The form of one such nest is: chips of old rock and bones and hardened guano, where the overhang supplies shade. The form of another is: a raft of weeds that rises and falls with the ebb and flow of water. Another: a dark space under roof tiles where you can crawl on your mouse feet and your wings drag like feathered blades the colour of carbon steel. Peregrine. Grebe. Swift.

Nests increasingly fascinate me. These days I wonder about how they seem to be one kind of entity when they contain eggs and a different kind of entity when they contain chicks. How nests and eggs are good things to think about when considering matters of individuality, and the concepts of same, and different, and series. How the form of a nest is part of the phenotype of a particular bird species, but how local conditions foster beautiful idiosyncrasies. How we humans are intrigued when birds make nests out of things that belong to us: house finches lining their nests with cigarette butts, nests of Bullock's orioles fashioned from twine, kites decorating their tree platforms with underwear stolen from washing lines. A friend of mine found a ferruginous hawk's nest wrought almost entirely from lengths of wire. It's satisfying to consider the incorporation of human detritus into the creations of birds, but it is troubling, too. What have they made out of what we have made of this world? Our world intersects with theirs and our habitations are strangely shared. We have

16

long rejoiced at birds building nests in unusual places. We love the robin rearing chicks in an old teapot, a hen blackbird sitting tightly on a nest tucked above the stop bulb on a traffic light: these are nests that gesture towards hope, as birds use our things for their own ends, making our technologies redundant, slowed down, static, full of meaning that is no longer entirely our own.

But that is what nests are. Their meaning is always woven from things that are partly bird and partly human, and as the cup or wall of a nest is raised, it raises, too, questions about our own lives. Do birds plan like us, or think like us, or really know how to make knots, or slap beaks full of mud in series, or is this merely instinct? Does the structure they're making begin with some abstract form, a mental image, to which the bird plans, rather than thinking, step by step, *There, that is where that goes*? These are questions that pull on us. We make things according to plans, but all of us also have that sense of where things should go. We feel it when we arrange objects on mantelpieces, or furniture in rooms. Artists feel it when they construct collages, when they sculpt, when they bring pigment to bear on a surface, knowing that the dark

17

smear of paint just here provides or provokes a sense of balance or conflict when viewed in relation to the other marks upon the scene. What is it in us? We are fascinated by the difference between skill and instinct, just as we police the differences between art and craft. If pigment is smeared on to a guillemot's eggshell as it rotates before being laid in drip-splashes that resemble in their exuberance and finesse the paintings of Abstract Expressionists, what is our delight in those patterns saying about us? I think of that need to collect that sometimes is billionaires hoarding de Koonings and Pollocks and sometimes tradesmen hiding plastic margarine tubs full of exquisitely marked red-backed shrike eggs beneath beds and floorboards.

We see our own notions of home and family in the creatures around us; we process and consider and judge, and prove the truth of our own assumptions back to us from a hall of twigs and mud and shells and feathered mirrors. In science, too, the questions we ask are commonly woven this way. I think of Niko Tinbergen's eminence in the field of ethology – and remember, too, his patient attention to the way ritualised gestures appeased aggression in colonies of nesting gulls, and how they related to his anxieties about the relationship between overcrowded cities and human violence. I think of the young Julian Huxley, full of all the sexual confusion of youth, spending one spring watching the courtship of great crested grebes, speculating on mutual sexual selection and ritualised behaviour. And I see interwar anxieties about marriage in Henry Eliot Howard's work on bird behaviour; he puzzles over the concept of territory, of nest building, of extra-pair copulations, and is desperately keen to understand the reasons behind the sexual attractiveness of particular females who lure males from their established mates. And, in literature, too, everywhere. Nesting birds naturalising the English class system in T. H. White's *The Once and Future King,* where seabird-nesting cliffs of auks and kittiwakes make 'an innumerable crowd of fish-wives on the largest grandstand in the world', exclaiming phrases like 'Is me hat on straight?' and 'Crikey, this isn't 'arf a do!' while White's skeins of aristocratic pink-footed geese pass high over the slum, singing Scandinavian goose-themed sagas as they fly north.

Friends of mine who grew up in marginal rural communities mostly have little truck with the mainstream rules of nature appreciation and the laws that enforce them.

Most of them hunt with longdogs. Some of them are poachers. Some have collected eggs. Some of them probably still do, though I don't get to hear about that. Most have limited financial or social capital, and their claim on the landscape around them is through local field knowledge, rather than literal possession. Egg collecting in this tradition makes me wonder about the terms of ownership, investment and access to pleasure that economically deprived communities are allowed to have in the natural world. I think of Billy, the boy in Barry Hines' *A Kestrel for a Knave,* who refuses to play football, refuses to work down the mine, rejects all the models of masculinity he's given. What opportunities for tenderness does he have? He strokes the backs of baby thrushes in their nest. He keeps a kestrel that he loves. What kinds of beauties can be possessed? If you are a landowner, you get the whole compass of the watered-silk sky and the hedges and the livestock and everything in it. But if you're a factory worker? There's the rub. Egg collecting requires skill, bravery in the field, hard-won knowledge of the natural world. It can become an obsession for minds gripped with stilled beauty. It is a practice that halts time. The collectors grant themselves the power to withhold new lives and new generations. And egg collecting is also, at the same time, one in the eye for the elite and all their rules about what is and what is not an acceptable way to relate to nature.

Egg collecting was especially derided in the cultures of natural history operating during and after the Second World War. At that time, British birds were laden with new significance. They were what the nation was made of, what we were fighting for. In this milieu, species with a perilous foothold on British soil, such as avocets, little ringed plovers and ospreys, had their rarity bound up with imperilled nationhood. Thus, the theft of their eggs was seen as an act akin to treason. And protecting the birds from the depredations of collectors seemed analogous to military service. Again and again, in books and films of this period, injured servicemen who have proved their bravery on the field of battle now show their love for their country by protecting rare birds trying to raise families. 1949's *The Awl Birds* by J. K. Stanford, for example, where the threatened nest belongs to avocets, or Kenneth Allsop's *Adventure Lit Their Star*, published the same year, where it belongs to little ringed plovers. The historian of science Sophia Davis has written on how the villains of these books are egg collectors, routinely described as 'vermin' and 'a menace to England', and how the nests in their pages are guarded by heroes with the fate of the nation close to their heart. Indeed, gangs of egg protectors guarding the nests of rare birds were a true-life legacy of the war. After years in a German POW camp, the ornithologist George Waterston sat with his colleagues by the first Scottish osprey nest for fifty years and kept it under observation through the telescopic sights of rifles. And in the 1950s, J. K. Stanford wrote of his own experiences guarding avocets. 'Keyed up by the general air of secrecy,' he reminisced, 'we sat till long after dusk, prepared for anything, even an amphibious raid by armed oologists.' Egg collectors today tend to be seen as beings in the grip of hopeless addiction, simultaneously suffering from great moral failings. These characterisations were firmly codified in the cultures of post-war ornithology as threats to the body politic.

Eggs and war; possession and hope and home. In the 1990s, years after my natural historical collection was disassembled and my childhood home was gone, I worked at a falcon-breeding centre in Wales. In one room were banks of expensive incubators containing falcon eggs. Through the glass, their shells were the mottled browns of walnut, of tea-stains, of onion skins. This was before the advent of newer incubators that mimic the press of a brood patch through hot air-filled plastic pouches. These were forced-air incubators with eggs on wire racks. We weighed them each day, and as the embryo moved towards hatching, we'd candle them: place them on a light and scribe the outline of the shadow against the bright air-cell with a soft graphite pencil, so that as the days passed the eggshell was ringed with repeated lines that resembled tides or wide-grained wood. But I always left the incubation room feeling unaccountably upset, with a vague, disquieting sense of vertigo. It was a familiar emotion I couldn't quite name. I finally worked out what it was one rainy Sunday afternoon. Leafing through my parents' albums I found a photograph of me a few days after my birth, a frail and skinny thing, one arm ringed with a medical bracelet and bathed in stark electric light. I was in an incubator, for I was exceedingly premature. My twin brother did not survive his birth. And that early loss, followed by weeks of white light lying alone on a blanket in a Perspex box, had done something wrong to me that

23

echoed with a room full of eggs in forced-air boxes, held in moist air and moved by wire. Now I could put a name to the upset I felt. It was loneliness.

That was when I recognised the particular power of eggs to raise questions of human hurt and harm. That was why, I realised, the nests in my childhood collection made me uncomfortable; they reached back to a time in my life when the world was nothing but surviving isolation. And then. And then there was a day. One day when, quite by surprise, I discovered that if I held a falcon egg close to my mouth and made soft cluck-ing noises, a chick that was ready to hatch would call back. And there I stood, in the temperature-controlled room. I spoke through the shell to something that had not yet known light or air, but would soon take in the revealed coil and furl of a west-coast breeze and cloud of a hillside in one easy glide at sixty miles an hour, and spire up on sharp wings to soar high enough to see the distant, glittering Atlantic. I spoke through an egg and wept.

NOTHING LIKE A PIG

I'm baffled. My boyfriend and I are standing up against a short barbed-wire fence shaded by sweet chestnut leaves. Woods are quiet in autumn: just the sifting hush of a small wind above and a robin making dripping-water noises from a holly bush.

I'm not quite sure what to expect because I'm not sure why I'm here. The boy said he'd show me something I'd never seen before in the woods, which made me raise an eyebrow. But here we are. He whistles and calls, whistles again. Nothing happens. Then it happens: a short, collapsing moment as sixty or seventy yards away something walks fast between trees, and then the boar. The boar. The boar.

When I saw *Jurassic Park* in the cinema something unexpected happened when the first dinosaur came on screen: I felt a huge, hopeful pressure in my chest and my eyes filled with tears. It was miraculous: a thing

I'd seen representations of since I was a child had come alive. Something like that was happening now and it was just as affecting. I've seen pictures of boars all my life: razor-backed beasts on Greek pottery, sixteenth-century woodcuts, trophy photographs of twenty-first-century hunters kneeling over them with rifles, ink drawings of the Erymanthian boar in my book of Greek legends. There are animals that are mythological by virtue of being imaginary: basilisks, dragons, unicorns. There are animals that were once just as mythologically rich, but have had so much exposure to us now that their earlier meanings have become swamped with new ones: lions, tigers, cheetahs, leopards, bears. They've been given modern stories. For me, boars still exist inside those older stories, are still emblematic, still rich and passing strange. And now here one was, called into the real world.

This creature was not what I expected, despite its slap of familiarity. It had the forward-menacing shoulders of a baboon and the brute strength and black hide of a bear. But it was not really anything like a bear, and what surprised me most of all was that it was nothing like a pig. As the beast trotted up to us, a miracle of muscle and bristle and heft, I turned to the boy, and said, surprised, 'It's nothing like a pig!' With great satisfaction he grinned and said, 'No. They're really not.'

For the first time in centuries, free-roaming wild boars are thriving in British woods, descendants of animals bred for meat that escaped from captivity or were released on purpose. Adaptable and resilient, wild boars are also increasing in number across continental Europe and in places far from their natural range, which spans Eurasia from Britain to Japan. From the first introduction of boars to New Hampshire in the 1890s, boar-like wild pigs have now been reported in at least forty-five states in the United States. In Britain, they have strongholds in Sussex, Kent and the Forest of Dean in Gloucestershire, an ancient hunting preserve that stood in for an alien planet in the movie *The Force Awakens*. Sixty farm-reared animals were secretly and illegally dumped there in 2004; eleven years later, night-time thermal-imaging surveys suggested the population has grown to more than a thousand.

I lived near the forest some years ago and I went looking for them. My motives were more than just natural-historical curiosity: their presence made me feel I was stepping into something like the wildwood of ancient times. I never saw them, but I did come across signs of their presence: deep ruts and broken ground on woodland paths and grassy roadsides where they'd rooted for food. Boars are landscape engineers that alter the ecology of their woodlands. Wallowing holes fill with rainwater and become ponds for dragonfly larvae, seeds and burrs caught on their coats are spread wide, and their rooting on the forest floor shapes the diversity of woodland plant communities.

Knowing that boars lived in the forest I walked through also charged the English countryside with a new and unusual possibility: danger. Boars, particularly farrowing sows protecting their young, can be aggressive, and will charge and attack intruders. Since the boars' return to the Forest of Dean, there've been reports of walkers being chased, dogs gored, horses newly nervous upon familiar paths. As I walked, I found myself paying a different quality of attention to my surroundings than I ever had before, listening apprehensively for the faintest sounds and scanning for signs of movement in the undergrowth. It made the forest a wilder place but in a sense a far more normal one, for conflict between humans and dangerous wildlife is commonplace in much of the world, from elephants trampling crops in India and Africa to alligators in Florida dining on pet dogs. In Britain, wolves, bears, lynxes and boars were long ago hunted to extinction, and we have forgotten what this is like.

The boar I met up against the fence wasn't a threat. It was a captive boar, one of a few kept by a local gamekeeper and safely behind wire, but it provoked intense introspection about my place in the world. This creature was one of the semi-legendary beasts charging straight out of the medieval literature I'd read at university, the quarry hunted in *Sir Gawain and the Green Knight* and Malory's *Le Morte d'Arthur,* creatures renowned for their formidable ferocity and power. In medieval romances, boars were seen as a challenge to masculinity and hunting them a test of endurance and bravery. When we meet animals for the first time, we expect them to conform to the stories we've heard about them. But there is always, always a gap. The boar was still a surprise. Animals are.

We have a long history of territorial anxiety over wild animals intruding on our spaces. The seventeenth-century English garden writer William Lawson advised his readers of the tools they'd need to keep their properties free of marauding beasts: a 'fayre and swift greyhound, a stone-bowe, gunne, and if neede require, an apple with a hooke for a Deere'. Concerns about the danger of Gloucestershire boars have led to efforts by the Forestry Commission to reduce their population in the Forest of Dean: three hundred and sixty-one were shot in 2014 and 2015, despite anti-hunting activists attempting to get in the way of hunters to prevent the cull. The controversy over how to manage English wild-boar populations points to the contradictory ways that we understand animals and their social uses. Wolves can be depredators of livestock or icons of pristine wilderness; spotted owls can be intrinsically important inhabitants of old-growth forests or nuisances that inhibit logging and livelihoods. These creatures become stand-ins for our own battles over social and economic resources.

When animals become so rare that their impact on humans is negligible, their ability to generate new meanings lessens, and it is then that they come to stand for another human notion: our moral failings in our relationship to the natural world. The world has lost half its wildlife in my own lifetime. Climate change, habitat loss, pollution, pesticides and persecution have meant that vertebrate species are dying out over a hundred times as fast as they would in a world without humans. The single boar appearing from behind the trees felt like a token of hope; it made me wonder if our damage to the natural world might not be irreversible, that creatures that are endangered or locally extinct might one day reappear.

So many things were affecting about this encounter: not just the calling-forth of an animal icon into flesh, but the realisation that there is a particular form of intelligence in the world that is boar-intelligence, boar-sentience. And being considered by a mind that is not human forces you to reconsider the limits of your own. As the boar looked up at me, it was obvious that my knowledge of boars was limited, and only now, face to snout with a real one, its eyes fixed on mine, did I wonder what a boar really was and, oddly, what it thought of me. I had fitted the boar into my medievalist memories, but my friend, who was once a boxer, admired its physique. Talked of its cutlass-curved, razor-sharp tusks. Its small legs and hindquarters that work to steer the huge muscular bulk of the front end. Its manifest, frightening power.

As he spoke, the boar pressed itself up

against the fence and sniffed loudly through its wet nostrils. Rashly, I moved my hand towards it. It looked up, flat-faced, with red boar eyes considering, and sniffed again. I drew my hand away. Then, after a while, I lowered it again. The boar stood. It allowed me to push my fingers gently into its arched black back. It felt like a hairbrush with too many bristles and backed with thick muscle, not wood. There was wool underneath the hair. 'He'll be getting his winter coat soon,' said the boy. 'Six-inch guard hairs.' I scratched the beast's broad hump and felt, as the seconds passed, that some tiny skein of aggression in his heart was starting to thrum. I have learned not to distrust intuitions like this. Suddenly we both decided that this was enough, my heart skipping, he grunting and feinting.

Wandering off, he sank on to his knees, nose to the ground, then, with infinite luxury, sat and rolled on to his side. Ripples ran down his hide. I was entranced. For all my interest in this creature, the boar had become bored with me and simply walked away.

INSPECTOR CALLS

I've a territorial, defensive soul. There's nothing like a visit from the landlord to put me on the back foot and then some. After most of the night cleaning the house I was spilling with contagious rage. I'd even considered burning the bastard building to the ground. It seemed a logical means of preventing any complaints about coffee rings on the Ercol dining table.

By eleven, things are calmer. I'm upstairs marking essays at my desk. The air is soothing, the window open upon cool grey. A red Ford draws up outside and a man and woman get out. The prospective tenants have an eight-year-old son, and he is autistic, my landlord told me. There's no sign of him. But these are parents; they're moving with the almost imperceptible restraint of manner born of care so he must be in the back of the car. Yes. And as he climbs out my heart folds and falls, not because he is wearing a stripy red and orange jumper but because he is grasping in each hand a model sea lion.

Downstairs the grown-ups are talking, and the boy is bouncing about in the semi-darkness of the hall. He is totally bored. I look down at his hands. Each of the sea lions has chips of missing paint about its nose where it has interacted with the other, or with something hard, and I ask him if he wants to see my parrot. His eyebrows rise and he waits. A brief, wordless OK from his parents, and we ascend the stairs. He counts each step out loud. And we stop in front of the cage. The bird and the boy stare at each other.

They love each other. The bird loves the boy because he is entirely full of joyous, manifest amazement. The boy just loves the bird. And the bird does that chops-fluffed-little-flirting twitch of the head, and the boy does it back. And soon the bird and the boy are both swaying sideways, backwards and forwards, dancing at each other, although the boy has to shift his grip on the plastic sea lions to cover both ears with his palms, because the bird is so delighted he's screech-ing at the top of his lungs.

'It is *loud*!' says the boy.

'That's because he is happy,' I say. 'He

likes dancing with you.'

And then, after a few moments, I tell him that I like his sea lions very much.

He frowns as if he's assuming upon himself the responsibility of my being one of the elect.

'Lots of people think they are . . .' he pauses contemptuously, *'seals.'*

'But of course they are sea lions!' I say.

'Yes,' he says.

We glory in the importance of accurate classification.

His parents come into the room. They have decided the house is too small for them and their son. So much for my week of cleaning purgatory.

His mother looks anxious. 'Come on, Antek! We are going now.'

There is, suddenly, one of the most beautiful moments of human–animal interaction I have ever seen. Antek nods his head gravely at the parrot, and the parrot makes a deep, courteous bow in return.

A minute later I hear the front door open, and just before they cross the threshold, I can hear clicking that I suspect might be the collision of sea lions' noses, and then Antek makes an announcement. 'I am going to sleep in the room with the parrot, when we live here,' he says. Such hard words to hear, uttered with such certainty, in the hall.

FIELD GUIDES

From a high lookout near a spectacular three-tiered waterfall in Australia's Blue Mountains National Park, the peaks in the far distance reflect sunshine scattered through a haze of aromatic eucalyptus terpenes; the light has turned them a bleached and dusty blue. At my feet the land falls away into a virgin forest of graceful, pale-barked trees that stretches as far as the eye can see. Further up the slope are leggy shrubs with flowers resembling bright plastic hair curlers: banksias, I think. When a small bird appears in the foliage below I fix it in my binoculars. White, black and acid yellow with eyes like tiny silver coins, it's wiping its down-curved beak on a branch of a shrub with strappy leaves. I don't know what the shrub is, and I'm not sure what the bird is, either. I think it's a honeyeater, but I don't know what anything is, not precisely. Not here. The air smells faintly of old paper and something a little like jet fuel. I feel lost and very far from home.

I grew up in a house full of natural-history field guides, everything from Locket and Millidge's 1951 two-volume guide to British spiders, with its hairy, many-eyed line drawings, to illustrated books on trees, fungi, orchids, fishes and snails. These books were the unquestioned authorities of my childhood. I marvelled at the names entomologists had given to moths – the figure of eighty, the dingy mocha, the dentated pug – and tried to match their descriptions to the drab living specimens I found on the walls of the porch on cool summer mornings. The process of working out what things were often felt like trying to solve a recalcitrant crossword puzzle, particularly when it involved learning technical terms like *scopulae* and *thalli.* The more animals and plants I learned, the larger, more complex and yet more familiar the world around me became.

It was a long time before I understood that even the simplest of field guides are far from transparent windows on to nature. You need to learn how to read them against the messiness of reality. Out in the field, birds and insects are so often seen briefly, at a distance, in low light or half-obscured by foliage; they do not resemble the tabular arrangements of paintings in guides, where similar species are brought together on a plain background on the same page, all facing one way and bathed in bright, shadowless light so they may be easily compared. To use field guides successfully, you must learn to ask the right questions of the living organism in front of you: assess its size and habitat, disassemble it into relevant details (tail length, leg length, particular patterns of wing cases or scales or plumage), check each against images of similar species, read the accompanying text, squint at tiny maps showing the animal's usual geographical range, then look back to the image again, refining your identification until you have fixed it to your satisfaction.

The process of identifying animals in this way has a fascinating history, for field guides have closely tracked changes in the ways we interact with nature. Until the early years of the twentieth century, bird guides, for example, mostly came in two kinds. Some were moralised, anthropomorphic life histories, like Florence Merriam's 1889 *Birds Through an Opera-Glass,* which described the bluebird as having a 'model temper' while the catbird possessed a 'lazy self-indulgence'. 'If he were a man,' she wrote of the latter, 'you feel confident that he would sit in shirt sleeves at home and go on the street without a collar.' The other kind of guide was the technical volume for ornithological collectors. In those days birds were often identified only after being shot, so such guides focused on fine details of plumage and soft parts. 'Web between bases of inner and middle toes,' runs the description of the semipalmated plover in Chapman's 1912 edition of his *Color Key to North American Birds*. But with the rise of recreational birdwatching following the First World War, when the morality of killing birds was increasingly questioned and the advent of inexpensive binoculars brought birds into visual range, such details were of limited use. A new way to identify birds was needed.

The first of the modern field guides was Roger Tory Peterson's 1934 *Field Guide to the Birds*. It was inspired partly by a chapter in the popular 1903 children's book *Two Little Savages,* written by Ernest Thompson Seton, first chief scout of the Boy Scouts of America. In it, a nature-minded boy despairs of learning the birds from books that require you to hold them dead in your hands. He decides instead to make 'far-sketches' of the ducks he sees in the distance and arrange them into a 'duck chart' that shows the characteristic 'blots and streaks that are their labels . . . like the uniforms of soldiers'. Peterson's paintings, like Seton's charts, tabulated and simplified birds, and he went further, adding small black lines on the page that pointed to distinctive characteristics that were most easily visible: the black band on the end of a crested caracara's tail, the 'ink-dipped' wings of the flying kittiwake.

When he was a young man in the 1920s, Peterson was a member of the Bronx County Bird Club, a group of competitive, iconoclastic young naturalists. In the days before portable guides, field identification aids could take unusual forms: one club founder carried around an envelope containing coloured plates cut from a copy of E. H. Eaton's lavish but unwieldy ornithological guide *Birds of New York* that he had found in a trash can. The group was mentored by Ludlow Griscom, a stern, exacting teacher who became renowned for inventing the technique of identifying a bird instantly in the field, even when flying. 'All the thousands of fragments we know about birds – locality, season, habitat, voice, actions, field marks and likelihood of occurrence – flash across the mirrors of the mind and fall into place – and we have the name of the bird,' Peterson later explained of Griscom's method. This split-second, *gestalt* ability to recognise a species built from combining book knowledge with long field experience became the mark of ornithological expertise, and was at the heart of a growing culture of competitive bird-spotting that lives on today. For there's an immense intellectual pleasure involved in making identifications, and each time you learn to recognise a new species of animal or plant, the natural world becomes a more complicated and remarkable place, pulling intricate variety out of a background blur of nameless grey and green.

Today, electronic field guides are becoming increasingly popular, and photo-recognition apps like Leafsnap and Merlin Bird ID let you identify species without the skills required to use field guides. They can do what print guides cannot: play animal sounds and songs, for example. But they also make it harder to learn those things we unconsciously absorb from field guides: family resemblances among species, or their places in the taxonomic order. When I was growing up, the materiality of these guides, their weight and beauty, was part of their attraction. I spent hours staring at their coloured plates of butterflies and birds, distinguishing each from each and fixing the painted images in my mind. The first time I saw a silver-spotted skipper butterfly basking on bare chalk on high downland pasture, I instantly knew the name of this dusty-golden dart with pale, ragged patches on its wings. Field guides made possible the joy of encountering a thing I already knew but had never seen before.

Back in my hotel room, I pull two Australian field guides from the bottom of my suitcase, eager to find out what it was that I had seen. Flicking through the first, I find a page of honeyeaters: nine birds arranged on a pale green background. That striking pattern of white and yellow and black is found in two species, but those round silver eyes are distinctive. I check against the distribution maps and the short description on the facing page. What I saw was a New Holland honeyeater. And turning to the plant guide, which describes only a few hundred of the thirty thousand different plant species found in Australia, I decide, tentatively, that the shrub it sat on was probably a waratah, and the banksias I saw by the path were hairpin banksias, with their 'protruding, wiry, hooked styles'. These species are well known here, but for me they are small triumphs. Now I know three things. A few hours ago, I looked over a valley at sunset and knew nothing at all.

TEKELS PARK

I shouldn't do the thing I do, because motorway driving requires you to keep your eyes on the road. I shouldn't do it also because pulling at your heart on purpose is a compulsion as particular and disconcerting as pressing on a healing bruise. But I do it anyway, and it's safer to do it these days, because this stretch is being transformed into a smart motorway, so the long slope of the M3 as it falls towards Camberley is packed with speed cameras and 50 mph signs, and when I'm driving there on my way somewhere else I can slide my car into the outside lane to bring me closer and slower to the section of fence I'm searching for, running west and high under skies white as old ice.

Perhaps a hundred thousand vehicles pass this place each day. Back in the mid 1970s I could lie awake in the small hours and hear a single motorbike speeding west or east: a long, yawning *burr* that dopplered into memory and replayed itself in dreams. But like snow, traffic noise thickens with time. By the time I was ten I could stand by Europe's second largest waterfall, listen to it roar, and think, simply, *it sounds like the motorway when it's raining.*

I shouldn't look. I always look. My eyes catch on the place where the zoetrope flicker of pines behind the fence gives way to a patch of sky with the black peak of a redwood tree against it and the cradled mathematical branches of a monkey puzzle, and my head blooms with an apprehension of lost space, because I know *exactly* all the land around those trees, or at least what it was like thirty years ago. And then the place has passed, and I drive on, letting out the breath I'd been holding for the last thousand feet or so, as if by not breathing I could still everything – movement, time, all of the dust and feet that rise and fall in a life.

Here's an early memory. A ridiculous one, but true. I learned to speed-read by trying to decipher military warning signs that bordered the roadside on my way to primary school. KEEP OUT was simple, but DANGER – UNEXPLODED ORDNANCE took me months. I needed to read the words *all at once,* because my mother's car was moving

46

and the signs were very close. Each weekday morning I'd stare out of the window as the army land approached and wait for the words to appear so I'd have another chance at them. And the feeling I had then, of wanting to apprehend something important that was passing by me very fast: that's the feeling I have now when I look for the place behind the motorway fence where I grew up.

I was five in my first summer in the Park. It was 1976. Cape daisies bloomed and died in the flowerbeds, and pine cones in the trees behind the house crackled and split through endless indigo afternoons. Standpipes, orange squash, dry lawns, and a conversation in which the matter of *drought* was explained to me. That's when I realised for the first time that not every year was the same, or perhaps that there were such things as years at all. My parents had bought this little white house in Camberley, Surrey, on a 50-acre walled estate owned by the Theosophical Society. They knew nothing about Theosophy but they liked the house, and they liked the estate too. There'd been a castle here once, or Squire Tekel's early nineteenth-century approximation of one, all faux-gothic battlements and arrow slits, peacocks and carriages. After it burned

47

down the Theosophists bought the grounds in 1929 for £2,600 and set about turning it into a place for them to live and work. Residing here was a privilege, the residents were told. A privilege for service. Members built their own houses, bought tents for a campsite and a second-hand Nissen hut from the Army to put there too. They grew food in the walled kitchen garden; opened a vegetarian guesthouse. In the 1960s, after leaseholders were granted the right to purchase the freeholds of their properties, outsiders like us slowly began to populate the place.

Theosophy had been banned in Nazi Germany, so many of our neighbours were refugees from the war, and others were the black sheep of good families: elderly women, mostly, who had refused the roles society had reserved for them: the quiet Lolly Willowes of Surrey Heath. One wore ancient Egyptian jewellery she'd been given by Howard Carter; another kept a great auk egg in a drawer. Spies, scientists, concert pianists, members of the Esoteric Society, the Round Table, the Liberal Catholic Church, the Co-Masonic Order. One former resident sent his beard clippings back from Nepal to be burned on the estate bonfire. On discovering that I had gone to

Cambridge, another, years later, inquired of me where I had stabled my horse – for he'd had dreadful trouble finding livery for his hunter while a student there in the 1930s. Everyone had lives and pasts of such luminous eccentricity that my notion of what was, and wasn't, normal took a battering from which it's never recovered. I am thankful for that, and for the women in particular, for giving me models for living a life.

But most of all I'm thankful for the other freedoms I had there. After school I'd make a sandwich, grab my Zeiss Jena 8x30 Jenoptem binoculars and strike out for my favourite places. There were ivy-covered walls and specimen trees, redwoods planted to commemorate the death of Lord Wellington – they called them Wellingtonias back then, of course they did – and creosoted summerhouses with fly-specked windows. 'Arthur Conan Doyle liked to sit here,' I was told, of the smallest summerhouse beneath the sparse shade of a balsam poplar, the one with original prints of the Cottingley Fairies hanging on its cream-washed walls. There was a round, shallow pond on the Italianate terraces that held an intermittently-broken fountain, smooth newts and great diving beetles, and from which vespertilionid bats dipped to drink at

49

night; a 9-acre meadow with decaying stables on one side, acres and acres of Scots pine, and damp paths obscured by bracken, rhododendrons, swamp laurels with piped-icing flowerbuds, and there were roads that went nowhere, for when the motorway was built on land compulsorily purchased from the Theosophists in the 1950s, it cut the estate in two. I loved those roads. Bare feet on the rotting tarmac down by the straight avenue of sessile oaks that ended in drifts of leaves and a new desire path that curved right to trace the perimeter of the motorway fence. One dead-end lane at the back of the Park had 10-foot sandy banks I'd scramble up towards the vast grey beech carved with hearts and dates and initials, and I was awed by the notion that anyone had found this tree, because I'd never seen anyone near it, ever, and one afternoon I dug up a rotted leather drawstring bag from the humus beneath it that spilled threepenny bits into my hands. There had been glow-worms here, and snipe, and ponds, before the motorway came, I was told. Everything on the other side was already houses.

I was allowed to roam unchallenged be-cause everyone here knew me – though they'd have quiet words with my parents after they'd yet again spotted me knee-deep in the middle of the pond looking for newts, or walking past the guesthouse with a big grass snake, two feet of supple khaki and gold twined about my arms. Reg the gardener took me for rides on his tractor-trailer, and we'd putter down the road singing music-hall songs he'd taught me:

It's the same the whole world over
It's the poor what gets the blame
It's the rich what gets the pleasure
Ain't it all a bloomin' shame?

And while Reg rolled a cigarette I'd race off to explore the bracken and scrub in the back woods, where rhododendrons had grown to near-trees with branches shaped by ancient prunings. They were *superb* to climb when I was small: frames of right-angled kinks and acute wooden curves I could hoist myself into and up, and sit inside a canopy of dark leaves that clicked and pattered with tiny rhododendron leaf hoppers that on closer inspection resembled the brightest of bestiary dragons. In the back woods too was the wood ants' nest, that glittering, shifting particulate mound which moved from year to year and reeked of formic acid. You could turn blue flowers pink if you tossed them on the top before the ants carried them away, and for a while I'd prepare skeletons of the dead birds I found by folding them carefully in little cages of wire mesh and lodging them on top of the nest. When I pulled them free weeks later they'd been reduced to clean white bone that never quite stopped smelling of ants.

Almost by accident I'd been granted this childhood of freedom and privilege, partly through a quirk of location, partly through my parents' trust in the safety of this place, and I lived in the familiar setting of so many of my children's books, from *The Secret Garden* to *Mistress Masham's Repose,* though I wasn't half as posh as their protagonists. I was a state-school kid running free in crumbling formal parkland that might have been written on paper as metaphor for the contracting Empire, or a wilder life, or social transgression, or any number of dreams of escape forged in the imagination of writers years before I was born.

I didn't know how unusual my freedom was, but I knew what it had given me. It had turned me into a naturalist. And for a new naturalist like me, the nine-acre meadow was the best place of all. So much of what was there must have arrived in hay brought for long-dead horses, as seeds from lowland meadows: scabious, knapweed, trefoil, harebell, lady's bedstraw, quaking grass, vetches, diverse other grasses and herbage. And butterflies, too, marooned in this small patch of the nineteenth century: common blues, small skippers, grizzled skippers, marbled whites, small coppers, and grasshoppers that sang all summer and pinged away from my feet. The other side of the meadow was different, and more what you'd expect on acidic soil: a low sea of sheep's sorrel, stars of heath bedstraw, white moths, small heaths, anthills and wavy hair grass brushed with fog by the sun. I knew that meadow intimately. It was richer, more interesting, had more stories to tell than any other environment in my life. I'd press my face in the grass to watch insects the size of the dot over an 'i' moving in the earthy tangle where the difference between stems and roots grew obscure. Or turn over and prospect for birds in the thick cumulus rubble of the sky.

So many of our stories about nature are about testing ourselves against it, setting ourselves against it, defining our humanity against it. But this was nothing like that at all. It was a child's way of looking at nature: one seeking intimacy and companionship. When I learned the names of these creatures from field guides it was because I needed to know them the same way I had to know the names of my classmates at school. Their diverse lives expanded what I considered as home way beyond the walls of my house. They made the natural world seem a place of complex and beautiful safety. They felt like family.

When you are small, the things you see around you promise you they'll continue as they are forever, and you measure life in days and weeks, not years. So when the mowers came one day in early August to cut the meadow as they had done every year since the meadow was made, and I saw what was happening, I burned with terrified outrage. There was no time to think about what I was doing. I ran. I stumbled. I sat in front of the mower to make it stop, then mutely, passively, held my ground in front of the bewildered driver, who came down to quite reasonably ask me what the hell I was doing, and I ran home crying. I didn't understand how hay meadows work. All I saw was destruction. How could I know that the mower's job was to hold history in suspension, keeping the meadow exactly where it was against the encroachment of heather and birch and time?

Every year the meadow grew back and

thrived and was as rich as ever, right up until we left the Park in the 1990s. A decade later, I returned on a grey summer afternoon, nervous of what I would find. Driving up Tekels Avenue the passing scenery possessed the disconcerting, diffuse, off-scale and uncanny closeness of things in dreams. I was frightened by what I might see when the car crested the curve down to the field. But there the meadow was: impossible, miraculous, still crowded with life.

Then I went back in my forties, less scared now, more certain of myself and what I would find when I got there. But I was wrong. Someone who thought meadows should look like football pitches had treated it like a lawn and mowed it repeatedly for several years until the exuberant moving life I'd known and loved was gone. The meadow now looked how that man thought it should look: blank and neat and flat and easy to walk upon. I cried when I saw it: a woman weeping not for her childhood, not really, but for everything that had been erased from this place.

Losing the meadow is not like losing the other things that have gone from my childhood: Mac Fisheries, Vesta paella, spacehoppers, school lunches, *Magic Roundabout* toys, boiled sugar lollipops when I'd finished my meals in roadside café chains on holiday trunk roads. You can mourn the casualties of fast capitalism for your own generation, but you know they've merely been replaced with other programmes, other media, other things to see and buy. I can't do that with the meadow. I can't reduce it to nostalgia *simpliciter*. When habitats are destroyed what is lost are exquisite ecological complexities and all the lives that make them what they are. Their loss is not about us, even though when that meadow disappeared, part of me disappeared, too, or rather, passed from existence into a memory that even now batters inside my chest. *Look,* I can't say to anyone. *Look at the beauty here. Look at everything that is.* I can only write about what it was.

When Henry Green started writing his autobiography in the late 1930s it was because he expected to die in the oncoming war, and felt he did not have the luxury of time to write a novel. 'That is my excuse,' he wrote: 'that we who may not have time to write anything else must do what we now can.' He said more. He said, 'We should be taking stock.' I take stock. During this sixth extinction we who may not have time to do anything else must write what we now can, to take stock. When I sat on the verge that day and wept I told myself over and over again that he was a nice man, that perhaps he had simply not known what was there. Had not known what was there. And I thought something that I was talking about with a friend just the other day: that the world is full of people busily making things into how they think the world ought to be, and burning huge parts of it to the ground, utterly and accidentally destroying things in the process without even knowing they are doing so. And that any of us might be doing that without knowing it, any of us, all the time.

A few years ago the Park was sold to a property developer. Today when I drive past the fence the pull on my heart is partly a wrench of recognition when I see those trees, knowing they are the standing ghosts of my childhood. But it's also the knowledge that with care, attention, and a modicum of love and skill, the meadow could be incorporated into the site plan and turned into something very like it had been only a few years ago. The pull on my heart is also the pain of knowing that this is possible, but that it is very unlikely. Centuries of habitat loss and the slow attenuation of our lived, everyday knowledge of the natural world make it harder and harder to have faith that the way things are going can ever be reversed.

We so often think of the past as something like a nature reserve: a discrete, bounded place we can visit in our imaginations to make us feel better. I wonder how we could learn to recognise that the past is always working on us and through us, and that diversity in all its forms, human and natural, is strength. That messy stretches of species-rich vegetation with all their attendant invertebrate life are better, just *better,* than the eerie, impoverished silence of modern planting schemes and fields. I wonder how we might learn to align our aesthetic and moral landscapes to fit that intuition. I wonder. I think of the meadow. Those clouds of butterflies have met with local extinction, but held in that soil is a bank of seeds that will hang on. They will hang on for a very long time. And when I drive past the fence these days, staring out at 50 mph, I know that what I am looking for, beyond the fence, is a place that draws me because it exists neither wholly in the past, nor in the present, but is caught in a space in between, and that space is a place which gestures towards the future and whose little hurts are hope.

HIGH-RISE

Dusk is falling over Midtown Manhattan on this chilly evening in early May. I've been googling the weather forecast all day, and pull out my phone to check it once again as I walk down Fifth Avenue. *North-northeasterly winds and clear skies.* Good.

At the Empire State Building the line snakes around the block, and because I'm the only person in it wearing a pair of binoculars around my neck, I feel a little self-conscious. I inch forward for the next hour, up escalators, through marble halls, past walls of soft gold wallpaper, before squeezing into a crowded elevator and emerging on the eighty-sixth floor. At over a thousand feet above the city, there's a strong breeze and a spectacular sea of lights spilling far below.

Behind the tourists pressed against the perimeter fence there's a man leaning back against the wall. Above him the Stars and

Stripes flap languidly in the night air. I can't see his face in the gloom, but I know this is the man I've come to meet because he's holding a pair of binoculars that look far better than mine, and his face is upturned to sky. There's an urgency to the way he stands that reminds me of people I've seen at skeet shoots waiting for the trap to fire the next target. He's tense with anticipation.

This is Andrew Farnsworth, a soft-spoken researcher at the Cornell Laboratory of Ornithology, and I'm joining him here in hope of seeing a wildlife phenomenon that twice a year sweeps almost unseen above the city: the seasonal night flights of migrating birds. It's an absurdly incongruous place for a nature-viewing expedition. Apart from the familiar exceptions – pigeons, rats, mice, sparrows – we tend to think of wild creatures as living far from the city's margins, and nature as the city's polar opposite. It's easy to see why. The only natural things visible from this height are a faint scatter of stars above and the livid bruise of the Hudson running through the clutter of lights below. Everything else is us: the flash of aircraft, the tilt of bright smartphones, the illuminated grids of windows and streets.

Skyscrapers are at their most perfect at

night, full-fledged dreams of modernity that erase nature and replace it with a new landscape wrought of artifice, a cartography of steel and glass and light. But people live in them for the same reason that they travel to wild places: to escape the city. The highest buildings raise you above the mess and chaos of life at street level; they also raise you into something else. The sky may seem like an empty place, just as we once thought the deep ocean to be a lifeless void. But like the ocean, this is a vast habitat full of life – bats and birds, flying insects, spiders, windblown seeds, microbes, drifting spores. The more I stare at the city across miles of dusty, uplit air, the more I begin to think of these super-tall buildings as machines that work like deep-sea submersibles, transporting us to inaccessible realms we cannot otherwise explore. Inside them, the air is calm and clean and temperate. Outside is a tumultuous world teeming with unexpected biological abundance, and we are standing in its midst.

Above us, LED bulbs around the base of the spire cast a soft halo of pale light up into the darkness. An incandescent blur of white skips across it. Through binoculars it resolves into a noctuid moth, wings flapping as it climbs vertically towards the tower. No one fully understands how moths like these orient themselves while migrating; there's speculation that they might navigate by sensing Earth's magnetic fields. This one is flying upward in search of the right airflow that will allow it to travel where it wants to go.

Wind-borne migration is an arthropod speciality, allowing creatures like aphids, wasps, lacewings, beetles, moths and tiny spiders hoisted on strands of electrostatically charged silk to travel distances ranging from tens to hundreds of miles. These drifting creatures are colonisers, pioneers looking for new places to live, and they'll make a home wherever they find one. Place a rose bush out on the arid environment of a top-floor balcony and soon wind-borne sap-sucking aphids will cluster on its stems, followed by the tiny wasps that parasitise them.

Insects travel above us in extraordinary numbers. In Britain, the research scientist Jason Chapman uses radar systems aimed into the atmosphere to study their high-altitude movements. Over seven and a half billion can pass over a square mile of English farmland in a single month – about 5,500 pounds of biomass. Chapman thinks the number passing over New York City may be even higher, because this is a gateway to a continent, not a small island surrounded by cold seas, and summers here are generally hotter. Once you get above six hundred and fifty feet, he says, you're lofted into a realm where the distinction between city and countryside has little or no meaning at all.

During the day, chimney swifts feast on these vast drifts of life; during the night, so do the city's resident and migrating bats, and nighthawks with white-flagged wings. On days with north-west winds in late summer and early fall, birds, bats and migrant dragonflies all feed on rich concentrations of insects caused by powerful downdraughts and eddies around the city's high-rise buildings, just as fish swarm to feed where currents congregate plankton in the ocean.

It's not just insects up there. The tallest buildings, like the Empire State, One World Trade Center and other new supertowers, project into airspace that birds have used for millennia. The city lies on the Atlantic Flyway, the route used by hundreds of millions of birds to fly north every spring to their breeding grounds and back again in the fall. Most small songbirds tend to travel between three and four thousand feet from the ground, but they vary their altitude depending on the weather. Larger birds fly higher, and some, like shorebirds, may well pass over the city at ten to twelve thousand feet. Up here we'll be able to see only a fraction of what is moving past us: even the tallest buildings dip into only the shallows of the sky.

Though you can see migrating raptors soaring at altitudes well over eight hundred feet above the city during the day, most species of diurnal birds migrate after nightfall. It's safer. Temperatures are cooler, and there are fewer predators around. Fewer, not none. Just before I arrived, Farnsworth saw a peregrine falcon drifting ominously around the building. Peregrines frequently hunt at night here. From high-rise lookout perches, they launch flights into the darkness to grab birds and bats. In more natural habitats, falcons cache the bodies of birds they've killed among crevices in cliffs. The ones here tuck their kills into ledges on high-rises, including the Empire State. For a falcon, a skyscraper is simply a cliff: it brings the same prospects, the same high winds, the same opportunities to stash a takeout meal.

We stare out into the dark, willing life into view. Minutes pass. Farnsworth points. 'There!' he says. High above us is a suspicion of movement, right at the edge of vision where the sky dissolves into dusty chaos. I swing my binoculars up to my eyes. Three pale pairs of beating wings, flying north-north-east in close formation. Black-crowned night herons. I've only ever seen them hunched on branches or crouched low by lakes and ponds, and it's astounding to see them wrenched so far from their familiar context. I wonder how high they are. 'Those are pretty large,' Farnsworth says. 'When you look up into the light, everything looks bigger than it is, and closer than it is.' He estimates that the herons are about three hundred feet above us, so they're about one and a half thousand feet from ground level. We watch them vanish into darkness.

I feel less like a naturalist here and more like an amateur astronomer waiting for a meteor shower, squinting expectantly into the darkness. I try a new tactic: focusing my binoculars on infinity and pointing them straight upwards. Through the lenses, birds invisible to the naked eye swim into view, and there are birds above them, and birds higher still. It strikes me that we are seeing a lot of birds. An awful lot of birds.

For every larger bird I see, thirty or more songbirds pass over. They are very small. Watching their passage is almost too moving to bear. They resemble stars, embers, slow tracer fire. Even through binoculars those at higher altitudes are tiny, ghostly points of light. I know that they have loose-clenched toes tucked to their chests, bright eyes, thin bones and a will to fly north that pulls them onward night after night. Most of them spent yesterday in central or southern New Jersey before ascending into darkness. Larger birds keep flying until dawn. The warblers tend to come earlier to earth, dropping like stones into patches of habitat further north to rest and feed over the following day. Some, like yellow-rumped warblers, began their long journeys in the south-eastern states. Others, like rose-breasted grosbeaks, have made their way up from Central America.

Something tugs at my heart. I'll never see any of these birds again. If I weren't this high, and the birds weren't briefly illuminated by this column of light cast by a building thrown up through the Depression years to celebrate earthly power and capital confidence, I'd never have seen them at all.

Farnsworth pulls out a smartphone. Unlike everyone else holding screens up here, he's looking at radar images from Fort Dix in New Jersey, part of a National Weather Service radar network that provides near-continuous coverage of airspace over the continental USA. 'It's definitely a heavy migration night tonight,' he says. 'When you see those kinds of patterns on radar, in particular, those greens,' he explains, 'you're talking about one thousand to two thousand birds per cubic mile potentially, which is almost as dense as it gets. So it's a big night.' After days of bad weather for birds wanting to fly north, with low cloud and winds in the wrong direction, a bottleneck of migrants built up, and now the sky is full of them. I watch the pixellation blossom on the animated radar map, a blue-and-green dendritic flower billowing out over the whole East Coast. 'This is biological stuff that's up in the atmosphere,' Farnsworth says, pointing one finger to the screen. 'It's all biology.'

Meteorologists have long known that you can detect animal life by radar. Just after the Second World War, British radar scientists and Royal Air Force technicians puzzled over mysterious plots and patterns that appeared on their screens. They knew they weren't aircraft and christened them 'angels' before finally concluding that they were flocks of moving birds. 'That was their contamination, right?' Farnsworth says of radar meteorologists. 'They wanted to filter all that stuff out. Now the biologists want to do the reverse.' Farnsworth is one pioneer of a new multidisciplinary science, fit for an era in which weather radar has become so sensitive it can detect a single bumblebee over thirty miles away. It's called aeroecology, and it uses sophisticated remote-sensing technologies like radar, acoustics and tracking devices to study ecological patterns and relationships in the skies. 'The whole notion of the aerosphere and airspace as habitat is not something that has come into the collective psyche until recently,' Farnsworth says. And this new science is helping us understand how climate change, skyscrapers, wind turbines, light pollution and aviation affect the creatures that live and move above us.

At ten o'clock, cirrus clouds slide overhead like oil poured on water. Ten minutes later, the sky is clear again, and the birds are still flying. We move to the east side of the observation deck. A saxophonist begins to play, and in concert with this unlikely soundtrack we begin to see birds far closer than before. One, in particular. Though it is overexposed in the light, we detect a smear of black at its chest and a distinctive pattern on its tail: a male yellow-rumped warbler. It flickers past and disappears around the corner of the building. A little while later, we see another flying the same way. Then another. It dawns on us that this is the same bird, circling. Another one joins it, both now drawn helplessly towards and around the light, reeling about the spire as if caught on invisible strings. Watching them dampens our exuberant mood. The spire is lit with pulsing rivulets of climbing colour like a candle tonight to mark the building's eighty-fifth anniversary. And these birds have been attracted to it, pulled off course, their exquisite navigational machinery overwhelmed by light, leaving them confused and in considerable danger. After being mesmerised in this way, some birds drag themselves free and continue their journey. Others don't.

New York is among the brightest cities in the world after Las Vegas, only one node in a flood of artificial illumination that runs from Boston down to Washington. We cherish our cities for their appearance at night, but it takes a terrible toll on migrating songbirds: you can find them dead or exhausted at the foot of high-rise buildings all over America. Disoriented by light and reflections on glass, they crash into obstacles, fly into windows, spiral down to the ground. More than a hundred thousand die each year in New York City alone. Thomas

King, of the New York pest-control company M&M Environmental, has had calls from residents of high-rise buildings asking him to deal with the birds colliding with their windows during migration season. He tells them that there's no solution, but they can talk to their building manager about turning off the lights. It helps. Programmes like New York City Audubon's 'Lights Out New York' have encouraged many high-rise owners to do the same, saving both energy and avian lives.

Every year the 'Tribute in Light' shines twin blue beams into the Manhattan night as a memorial to the lives lost on September 11. They rise four miles into the air and are visible sixty miles from the city. On peak migration nights songbirds spiral down towards them, calling, pulled from the sky, so many circling in the light they look like glittering, whirling specks of paper caught in the wind. On one night last year, so many were caught in the beams that the few pixels representing the 'Tribute' site glowed super-bright on the radar maps. Farnsworth was there with the Audubon team that got the lights shut off intermittently to prevent casualties. They switched off the 'Tribute' eight times that night for about twenty minutes at a time, releasing the trapped birds to return to their journey. Each time the lights went back on, a new sweep of birds was drawn in – the twin towers made ghosts of light visited over and over by winged travellers intermittently freed into darkness before a crowd rushed in to take their place. Farnsworth is a lead scientist in BirdCast, a project that combines a variety of methods – weather data, flight calls, radar, observers on the ground – to predict the movements of migrating birds throughout the continental United States and forecast big nights like this that might require emergency lights-out action.

The flow of birds over the observation deck continues, but it's getting late. I make my farewell, take the elevator back down the building and wander uphill to my apartment. Though it's long past midnight, I'm wide awake. Part of what high-rise buildings are designed to do is change the way we see. To bring us different views of the world, views intimately linked with prospect and power – to make the invisible visible. The birds I saw were mostly unidentifiable streaks of light, like thin retinal scratches or splashes of luminous paint on a dark ground. As I look up from street level, the blank sky above seems a very different place, deep and coursing with life.

Two days later, I decide to walk in Central Park, and find it full of newer migrants that arrived here at night and stayed to rest and feed. A black-and-white warbler tacking along a slanted tree trunk deep in the Ramble, a yellow-rumped warbler sallying forth into the bright spring air to grab flies, a black-throated blue warbler so neat and spry he looks like a folded pocket handkerchief. These songbirds are familiar creatures with familiar meanings. It's hard to reconcile them with the remote lights I witnessed in the sky.

Living in a high-rise building bars you from certain ways of interacting with the natural world. You can't put out feeders to watch robins and chickadees in your garden. But you are set in another part of their habitual world, a nocturne of ice crystals and cloud and wind and darkness. High-rise buildings, symbols of mastery over nature, can work as bridges towards a more complete understanding of the natural world – stitching the sky to the ground, nature to the city. For days afterwards, my dreams are full of songbirds, the familiar ones from woods and backyards, but also points of moving light, little astronauts, travellers using the stars to navigate, having fallen to Earth for a little while before picking themselves up and moving on.

The Human Flock

Under heavy rain the lakes have turned to phosphorescent steel. Pygmy cormorants hunch on dead trees. Twelve of us stand on the shore. Some have set out spotting scopes on tripods on the grass, others carry binoculars. Silently we stand in wait for the Hungarian dusk. As the sun slips behind the expanse of water the air grows colder. We strain our ears until – there it is – we hear a faint noise like baying hounds or discordant bugles, at first hardly discernible through the wind rattling the reeds before it grows into an unearthly clamour. 'Here they come!' someone whispers. Overhead, a long, wavering chevron of beating wings is inked across the darkening sky. Behind it flow others, and there are others behind them, all passing overhead in ever-increasing waves, filling the air with a barrage of noise and beauty.

The birds above us are long-necked,

graceful Eurasian cranes. Every autumn more than a hundred thousand of them stop off on their southward migration from Russia and Northern Europe to spend a few weeks in the Hortobágy region of northeastern Hungary, feeding on maize left in the fields after harvest. Every night they fly to roost in huge numbers in the safety of shallow fish-farm lakes, attracting wildlife tourists who come here to witness the spectacle of their evening flights. Similarly impressive congregations can be seen in other places. In Nebraska, more than half a million sandhill cranes fatten up in cornfields before continuing their spring migration; in Quebec, watchers are awed by blizzards of snow geese blotting out the sky as they rise from the Saint-François River. In Britain, clouds of wintering starlings flying to their roosts draw crowds of all ages.

Standing close to vast masses of birds affects everyone differently: some people laugh, some cry, others shake their heads or utter profanities. Language fails in the face of immense flocks of beating wings. But our brains are built to wrest familiar meaning from the confusions of the world, and watching the cranes at dusk I see them first turn into strings of musical notation, then mathematical patterns. The snaking lines synchronise so that each bird raises its wings a fraction before the one behind it, each moving flock resolving itself into a filmstrip showing a single bird stretched through time. It is an astonishing illusion that makes me blink in surprise. But then, part of the allure of flocking birds is their ability to create bewildering optical effects. I remember my amazement as a child watching thousands of wading birds, knots, flying against a cool grey sky, vanish and reappear in an instant as the birds turned their counter-shaded bodies in the air. Perhaps the best-known example is the hosts of European starlings that assemble in the sky before they roost. We call them murmurations, but the Danish term, *sort sol,* is better: black sun. It captures their almost celestial strangeness. Standing on the Suffolk coast a few years ago, I saw a far-flung mist of starlings turn in a split second into an ominous sphere like a dark planet hanging over the marshes. Everyone around me gasped audibly before it exploded in a maelstrom of wings.

Though the rapid dynamism of flocking birds is a large part of their beauty, news sites and magazines often publish still photographs of murmurations that look like other things: sharks, mushrooms, dinosaurs. In 2015, an image of one flock over New

York City shifting into the shape of Vladimir Putin's face went viral, though it may have been fake. It's not difficult, when presented with such a strange phenomenon, to believe in signs and wonders. The changing shape of starling flocks comes from each bird copying the motions of the six or seven others around it with extreme rapidity; their reaction time is less than a tenth of a second. Turns can propagate through a cloud of birds at speeds approaching ninety miles per hour, making murmurations look from a distance like a single pulsing, living organism. In a 1799 notebook entry, Samuel Taylor Coleridge wrote of a murmuration that shaped itself into various forms and moved 'like a body unindued with voluntary power'. Sometimes they seem uncannily like an alien, groping entity, living sand or smoke moving through a suite of topological changes. Murmurations are thrilling, but they can also provoke an emotion akin to fear.

And fear is in large part why many of these flocks exist. Cranes, for example, roost in shallow water because it is safer than sleeping on the ground; and the sheer profusion of beating wings makes it hard for predators to focus on any single starling in a murmuration. No starling wants to be on the edge of the flock, or among the first to land. Anne Goodenough, who runs the Royal Society of Biology and University of Gloucestershire international starling survey, speculates that murmurations may act as signposts to invite other starlings to join a specific roost and increase its size – in cold weather, large roosts keep birds warm. But in the air, fear is the factor shaping the flocks, pressing and contorting them as they fly. A dark, shivering wave running through a mass of starlings is often a response to a raptor diving into the flock in search of a meal.

It is nearly dark now at the Hortobágy fishponds, and my ears ring with the cacophony of calling cranes. There is boiling confusion over the lake as flocks come from all directions to join the mass on the water that now looks like stippled, particulate fog. White-fronted geese are pouring in, too, tumbling and sideslipping from the sky through swathes of other wings. Suddenly it is almost too much to bear. I feel uncomfortably disoriented. Big flocks of birds can do this. Birders have described the experience of watching flocks of rooks at nightfall as so confusing and noisy that it produces in the viewer something close to motion sickness.

In search of something solid, I peer

through a spotting scope focused on the far side of the lake. In the circle of the viewfinder, the confusion resolves into individual birds. It's so dark that their colour has leached away. I am watching stately groups of cranes in greyscale, landing, drinking, shaking their loose feathers, greeting one another and getting on with the business of finding a place to sleep. The switch in recognition is eerie: I go from seeing rushing patterns in the sky to the realisation that they are made of thousands of beating hearts and eyes and fragile frames of feather and bone. I watch the cranes scratching their beaks with their toes and think of how the starling flocks that pour into reed beds like grain turn all of a sudden into birds perching on bowed stems, bright-eyed, their feathers spangled with white spots that glow like small stars. I marvel at how confusion can be resolved by focusing on the things from which it is made. The magic of the flocks is this simple switch between geometry and family.

As I stand there watching the cranes, my mind turns to human matters. The village we'd stayed in the previous night had felt so much like my home in the fens. It had the same damp, underwater air, chickens roaming around backyards, poplars, piles of winter firewood. Before I came here I'd asked a few British friends who'd spent time in Hungary what it was like, and several said that the strangest thing about it was how much it felt like home. It's painful to recall that now. It has been nagging away at me all the time I've been here, the razor-wire fence the government has erected more than a hundred miles south of here to stop Syrian refugees walking across the border from Serbia; the thought of crowds moving slowly north-east as the cranes move south-west. Watching the flock has brought home to me how easy it is to react to the idea of masses of refugees with the same visceral apprehension with which we greet a cloud of moving starlings or tumbling geese, to view it as a singular entity, strange and uncontrollable and chaotic. But the crowds coming over the border are people just like us. Perhaps too much like us. We do not want to imagine what it would be like to have our familiar places reduced to ruins. In the face of fear, we are all starlings, a group, a flock, made of a million souls seeking safety. I love the flock not simply for its biological exuberance, but for the way it has prompted me to pick similarity out of strangeness, for the way its chaos was transformed, on reflection, to individuals and small family groups wanting the simplest things: freedom from fear, food, a place to safely sleep.

THE STUDENT'S TALE

There's a window and the rattle of a taxi and grapes on the table, black ones, sweet ones, and the taxi is also black and there's a woman inside it, a charity worker who befriended you when you were in detention, and she's leaning to pay the driver and through the dust and bloom of the glass I see you standing on the pavement next to the open taxi door and your back is turned towards me so all I can see are your shoulders hunched in a blue denim jacket. They're set in a line that speaks of concern, not for yourself, but for the woman who is paying the fare. I wave through the window and you turn and see me and smile hello.

This is a borrowed house that we're talking in. It's not my home.

We sit at the table and I don't know where to begin.

I don't know anything about you.

It is hard to ask questions.

You want me to ask questions, because you say it is easier to answer questions than tell your story. I don't want to ask you questions, because I think of all the questions you must have been asked before. But you want me to ask you questions, and so I begin with: when did you get here? And you write, in careful Persian numerals, *12, 2016*. December. And I ask more questions, and you answer them, and when the English words won't come, you translate using your phone, and this takes some time, and the sun slaps its flat gold light upon the table and the bowl of grapes and the teapot, all these quiet domestic things, as I wait to know what you might mean. Here are the words you look up while we talk: *Apostate. Bigoted. Depraved. Hide.*

You are a student of epidemiology. Epidemiologists study the mode of transmission of disease, the way it runs through populations from person to person. You tell me that back in your country you used to meet with your friends in your restaurant at night so you could talk of Christianity and read the Bible. There were Christian signs in your restaurant. You knew that you might be arrested for doing this. Secrecy is paramount, but faith is also faith.

This is what happens when you are denounced as an apostate. The authorities speak of you as if you were one of the agents of disease that you have studied. At prayers one Friday they denounce you, by name, in five regions, two cities and three villages. They said that a woman at your university had depraved you, by which they meant she had encouraged you to become a Christian. They said that you had changed your religion. And that now you possess this faith, you spread it to other men.

They see your belief as a contagious disease. They want to isolate it, contain it, and like all such malevolent metaphors that equate morality with health, the cure is always extinguishment. You know what happens to apostates, to those who have changed their religion, in your country. Even I know what happens. I am holding my breath just thinking of it.

When the intelligence services came looking for you at your grandmother's home she called you and told you that these men were your friends even though they spoke the wrong language for the region and they were wearing distinctive clothes that made it obvious, really, who they were, and why they were there, but she was old and you couldn't blame her for expecting friendship when what was offered was its scorched obverse. Your uncle knew better. He told you to flee. *Your life is in danger,* he said. Truth. So you fled. You left everything.

You drove from city to city and, in a city more distant, met two friends of your uncle. They told you they could take you to Europe with others by car. And once you were there, you wondered where you should go. Your uncle said, *The UK is good,* and he offered to pay the smuggling agents to get you here. The car unloaded you all in an unkempt garden and you had to hide there until the middle of the night when the truck came, and you got in.

Days in the darkness inside a lorry on its way north. A freezer truck. How many people were in there with you? I ask. And you laugh, and say, *Ten? I don't know. It was dark!* And I laugh too, a little ashamed, and wonder why I want to press you for these little details. None of us want to know what this is like. We don't want to know how it feels to not eat or drink or sleep for five days and nights, to be sustained in terror and darkness merely through the hope that there is light the other side. None of us wants to know what it feels like to be threatened with a knife, as you were threatened. To be held at gunpoint by people you have paid to bring you to safety.

You say, *It was the worst feeling.* Then you say it again. *The worst feeling.*

Several times, you tell me, *I see my death.* Then you say it again. *I see my death.*

The hardest things, I realise, you are saying them all twice.

And what I am thinking, as you say *sorry* into the silence while you wait to be able to once again speak, is this. I think of how scientists have only just found out how our brains make memories. They used to think that we record a short-term memory, then archive it later, move it to a different part of the brain to store it long term. But now they've discovered that the brain always records two tracks at once. That it is always taping two stories in parallel. Short-term memories, long-term memories, two tracks of running recollection, memory doubled. Always doubled.

Which makes everything that ever happens to us happen twice.

Which makes us always beings split in two.

You are an epidemiologist. You are a refugee.

You were one of the best epidemiology students in the whole country.

You are also an asylum seeker who has seen detention-centre inmates cut themselves with razors, lash out in violence,

86

numb themselves with Spice.

The government wants to send you back to the European country where you first arrived, but that would be dangerous because of people there who know who you are, who have threatened you, who have contacts with the authorities back home. So now you are in a hostel, with four hundred others. You have to sign in once in the morning and once again at night. You are a student, a brother, a son, who manages to speak to your family back home through Telegram, through WhatsApp, and you are also a man who asks the receptionist for help when violence or sickness breaks out in the hostel and watches the receptionist shrug dismissively and no help comes. All the things you see between refugees, you tell me, are *harmful for brain, for mind, for spirit*. You say, of the hostel, in the quietest, gentlest voice, that *there, nothing is good, really. Nothing is good. It is a very nasty place.* You tell me, twice, that *some people have not even any clothes.*

In December you'd called the police from the frozen dark inside the lorry. The police opened the doors and took you to a cell, questioned you, detained you for seventy-two hours. And when you requested asylum they moved you to an immigration detention centre. You were there for eighty days. I have heard a lot about the conditions there, this place that is known as a hellhole. So it is a mark of your kindly reticence that all you can say about it is, *The situation in detention was very bad.*

You are a refugee who sings in a talent competition in a detention centre where people are held indefinitely and you are also a man sitting at a sunny dining table laughing out loud at your mistake when you realise that you said your father is literature when what you meant to say was your father is illiterate. You are a man who can laugh at the ridiculousness of mistranslation, and you are also a man who has left a life behind, your father, your little brother, your ailing family members, and every corner of home, and that loss pours from you, silent through the laughter, like a cold current of air that sinks to the floor and fills the room beneath everything light that is spoken here.

You don't want to talk about yourself, except to give the facts. What you want to talk about are the problems facing the people around you. Your charity-worker friend tells me that after you saw an advert for WaterAid you asked her to donate what little funds you had to the children who were suffering, because the way the system works, you weren't allowed to do it yourself. She tells me, though she apologises for speaking because it is not her story, that you have been buying fruit and lentils for the children in the hostel because the food is so bad, it makes people sick, and you can see the children are malnourished.

You are a man whose eyes are bright with unspilled tears when you tell me of the horror of your journey here. But when you think of the people who have shown you kindness? That is when you break down and cry. You say, of the woman sitting with us, *I would maybe have suicide, without her.* When I ask you if the people in the city where you live are good to you, you say yes, because if you ask them an address, they will tell you where it is. They will tell you where it is.

I think about all the stories we tell about refugees and how they are always one story or another, never both at once. Tragic stories or threatening stories. Victims or aggressors. Never complicated, always simple, always with clean edges. Easy pigeonholes to fit people who have been forced to take wing.

But a hole is not just a pigeonhole. It's the space between two things. It's a hole that's the gap between a word in Urami, or in Farsi, or in English. It's the space between past and future, between old lives and new. Between years. When New Year came in March you went to the park in the city where the hostel is, and you sang songs welcoming the New Year by the water of the lake. What can a new year mean, when you are young and all you are able to do is wait?

I want to be useful, you say. *I don't want to spend my time in the hostel, waiting.* And then you rub your eyes with one hand and you say, *Please pray for me.* You say, *This issue is very distracted my brain, my mind. I want to quickly take a part in this society. And the culture. At the moment I haven't any certificate, because I am an asylum seeker. And I don't take a part in helping people because I don't have any money, I don't have any device for helping the people, and I think my living is very precious. Precious?* You try the word out as a question, as if the word is itself somehow wrong.

I don't like be spend it by the time, waiting, you say. *Because I am young.*

You are young. You are a student, an epidemiologist, a Christian, a refugee. You want to help people so much it hurts my heart. You are a man who I drive, after we have talked that afternoon, to the hospital so we can take a photograph of you standing outside the School for Clinical Medi-

90

cine, because bound up in a sense of your future is this brightness, that you might one day be able to help, to work in medicine here. And you are also a man who tips back his head and laughs when we discover that the School has been closed for rebuilding, and the windows are boarded up and the palings mean we can't see the building at all. We take pictures anyway. Us in front of the barriers. You alone, you with your charity-worker companion, you with me. We are all, all of us, waiting while the world is rebuilt.

ANTS

At first there's nothing notable about my drive back from the supermarket. I pass packs of schoolchildren on street corners, see a glossy SUV make a dickish manoeuvre at a roundabout, listen to someone complaining about something or other on the radio. Then my attention catches on something high and to the right of me. I tighten my hands on the wheel, pull into a roadside space a little further on, I lock the car and walk back, car keys loose in one hand, eyes turned up to the sky.

Some natural events track seasonal changes, and we treasure them for it. We wait expectantly for our spring swallows and swifts, the first summer butterflies; we listen for the mating calls of autumn foxes and deer. But in Britain we don't have many visibly spectacular, large-scale yearly events whose precise calendar timing is unpredictable, like the spring spawning of thousands and thousands of silver grunion fish on Californian beaches for a few nights after a high tide. Even so, everyone here knows one. It doesn't happen on the same day everywhere, but wherever you live, there'll be one still, humid, bright day that triggers it, and today it's happening right here.

Above me is a towering column of flying ants. I only know they are there because there's also a column of about a hundred herring gulls borne on lean grey black-tipped wings, some cruising at rooftop height, others circling hundreds of feet above. They aren't flying in the usual laconic manner, a lazy flap and glide from one place to another. They're feeding. I can't see the ants that they're eating. But I know exactly where individual ants are, because every few seconds a gull twitches itself to one side, beats its wings once, twice, and snaps at the air. And another, and another. Above me is as much a feeding frenzy as any bait ball in a tropical ocean, but featuring gulls and ants rather than anchovies and sharks.

What I'm witnessing is the nuptial flight of a species of ant called *Lasius niger,* the common black ant of our town streets and suburban gardens. For the last twenty-four hours worker ants all across town and county have been enlarging the entrance holes to their underground colonies to make them big enough for winged virgin queens to emerge. The male drones, also winged, are already massing on the ground, and as the queens take flight, trailing pheromones, the drones chase them aloft. The queens take their pursuers higher and higher, waiting for males strong enough to reach them. They'll mate, sometimes with a few different males from different colonies, in brief coincidences that herald the birth of tiny empires. On their return to earth, the drones die, while the queens rub off their wings and search for a place to start a new nest. Though these queens may live another thirty years, they will never mate again. Every fertilised egg they lay for the rest of their life will use sperm they store in their bodies from that one ascent on a summer afternoon.

I watch gulls from all points on the compass flying in to join the bonanza. The ants are caught up in a thermal of rising warm air, and as the incoming gulls meet its outside edge, the tip of one wing is tugged by the updraught; they straighten their wings, circle into it, and rise effortlessly. This tower of birds is an attraction visible for miles, an ephemeral landmark above a roadside church in a small country town.

And these flocks of predators are one of the reasons why ants from a whole district all emerge at the same time; the more ants in the air, the more likely it is that some survive the onslaught of beaks. A red kite joins the flock, drifting and tilting through it on paper-cut wings stamped black against the sky.

We so often think of science as somehow subtracting mystery and beauty from the world. But it's things I've learned from scientific books and papers that are making what I'm watching almost unbearably moving. The hitching curves of the gulls in a vault of sky crossed with thousands of different flightlines, warm airspace tense with predatory intent and the tiny hopes of each rising ant. It isn't merely the wheeling flock of birds that transfixes me, or the magic of how the ants have carved out a discrete piece of unremarkable air and given it drama and meaning. It is that the motive power behind this grand spectacle is entirely invisible. This vast stretch of sky, the gulls, the imperceptible ants, is a working revelation of the interrelation of different scales of existence, and it is at once exhilarating and humbling. Humbling because this contemplation on scale and purpose can't help but remind me that I'm little more than an ant in the wider workings of the world, no more or less important than any of the creatures here. Mesmerised, I watch a party of swifts pile in to take their turn at the harvest, wings scything, pink gullets open wide to scoop ants from the air. Craning my neck, I follow them up until the flock banks between me and the sun, and the fierceness of the light erases them from sight. My eyes water, and I look down to the ground I'd forgotten, to tarmac covered with the glittering wings of drones and queens all readying themselves for their first, and final, flight.

SYMPTOMATIC

Migraines: something like rain, something like a bullet that's only chambered one morning days after the threat of violence. A slug that ratchets through and slots into your spine before the slow shot begins with an umbrella-towering nimbus of empty pressure that makes you as dizzy as if there really were a storm-cloud of rising air growing, billowing up and outwards until its edges feather and coincide with your skull. Then come two thumbs pressing on your sinus and moving over your jaw, and strange strips of fast pain like summer lightning when you lift a cup, pick up a pen, burying themselves in your shoulder, deep into places which don't exist until they hurt. And when the pain comes it is one-sided, sometimes on the left of your skull and sometimes on the right, although it is so intense it can't be kept in either place, and it ripples like a flag cracking in strong wind, or thrums deep like a heartbeat, and sometimes one of your eyes waters, the one on the same side as the pain, and there's what doctors call a post-nasal drip, which makes the world taste of scalding metal and brine. A few times, in the midst of my own migraines, I've had a strong and sudden intuition I'm made out of cobalt: partly it's that taste in my mouth, partly how heavy I feel, but mostly because the interference in my brain runs sometimes along the lines of those delicate scrawls of blue-flowered decorations on ancient Chinese porcelain. Shipwrecks, bones, pearls. So yes, migraines put me in mind of metaphors, and then more metaphors, and more, for they are always *too much* in a way that makes them unbearable, all filters gone.

Thirty per cent of migraineurs experience visual disturbances with their headaches. I've had them only once, on a stormy night at a literary festival. I was busily signing books when a spray of sparks, an array of livid and prickling phosphenes like shorting fairy lights, spread downwards from the upper right-hand corner of my vision until I could barely see through them. In textbooks the phenomenon is called *scintillating scotoma.* It scintillated. I freaked out. I kept signing, kept smiling, gripped the inside of my shoes tight with all ten toes, and worried that I was going to die until the pain came.

Although they hurt, make bright light a brutal intruder and force me to take to bed and swallow as many painkillers as I am allowed to without harming myself, my migraines seem useful. Their utility isn't in the pain. The pain is terrible. I hate it. I hate the time it takes from my life, my helplessness in the face of it, the tears soaking the pillows I'm curled around. But migraines remind me we're not built with the solidity so many of us blithely assume. That the World Health Organization's 1948 definition of health – *a state of complete physical, mental and social well-being and not merely the absence of disease or infirmity* – refers to precisely no one, is a sweetly turned phrase more ableist than utopian. That perfection cannot be intrinsic to us, built as we are of chemicals and networks and causal molecular pathways and shifting storms of electricity; none of us are ever in perfect health.

Migraines are an incredibly common – more than a billion people suffer from them – but highly mysterious neurological condition. We're not exactly sure what they are, though it's likely they're a tendency for the brain to lose control of its inputs, a sensory processing disorder that is partly inherited.

We know that meningeal blood vessels around the brain dilate during the headache, and that migraines are associated with activity in the trigeminal ganglion, the base of the nerve network that governs the face and the muscles used in chewing. We know that migraines with auras involve waves of electrical activity across the brain called *spreading cortical depression.* In the midst of a migraine, not knowing is very much to the point. Pain wipes you free of knowledge, makes understanding utterly redundant. There's nothing to know or understand. Subjects, objects, fail. All you are is all that is and all of it hurts.

Some people get migraines most often around the time of their period (three times as many women as men are migraineurs; sex hormones appear to play a role) and the correlation is pertinent to me not only because I am one of those women, but because menstruation is migraine's closest cousin in my life. There's no mistaking their occurrence – I bleed, or I curl up in pain and weep – and both involve a suite of premonitory symptoms.

It took me nearly thirty years to understand the robustness of my premenstrual pattern, but these days I know the week before my period will always include a single day in which I fantasise about murdering strangers, most specifically slow drivers, and another in which everything can reduce me to sentimental tears: supermarket adverts, the polished corner of an oak table glowing in the sun, a pigeon taking off from a hawthorn branch into the wind. For much of that week the voice of my interior critic is as seductive and honeyed as warm baklava. It tells me I am a terrible person and the worst writer in the world, and I believe it. But after decades of bafflement, these states are now something like old friends, and I greet them with a deal of archness.

The premonitory symptoms of my migraines are exceedingly specific. Two or three days before my head begins to hurt, my fridge fills with bottles of banana milk. I yawn a lot, become unaccountably thirsty. My joints ache. I shop for dark chocolate and sweet pickled beetroot. There's dust-and-ashes tiredness, and a bad mood so remorseless that even the sweetest birdsong irritates. I can enumerate them now, yet when the headache arrives, it is always a surprise. I never see it coming. These symptoms are aspects of the migraine's earliest stages, occurring in its *prodrome,* that part of it which precedes the pain. It turns out that some of the most infamous

101

migraine triggers are not triggers at all – a desire to eat chocolate is just as much part of a migraine as the full-blown headache that follows.

After the pain subsides, the migraine's *postdrome* begins, and it is a peculiar muse of mine. Though it makes me feel weak, muffled, slow and stupid, it's inside it that writing comes easiest. Whatever is going on inside my brain makes the words flow, the world sharper; it tips me into days that seem newly forged and prone to surprising beauties. I'm writing at my kitchen table right now in the midst of a postdrome, a heat pack draped across my neck and shoulders to unknot muscles locked after two days of hurt. Just after sunrise this morning, I looked out over the back fence of my garden across a field of oats into the valleys and hills around my house, the sky nacreous and the lower-lying ground obscured by luminous mist. For a migraineur in fear of bright sunlight, the slow slide into autumn's softer days and earlier nights is an enormous relief.

But something was off. I shook my head. Then I shook it again, and wondered if I were sicker than I thought, because I could hear a loud drone, a low-frequency roaring like the sound of an airliner overhead, but an airliner held somehow motionless mid-flight, for there was no dopplering, no shifting in the sound; the tone was as unmoving as the mist. It seemed to have no discernible source, was emanating from the ground, from the air itself – perhaps, I thought with a start, from *inside* me. Maybe this was some previously unknown annexe to my migraines, a novel auditory hallucination. The anxiety caught like brushfire and prickled in sharp, glittering waves along my skin until a woodpigeon started to sing in the tree above me, a low cooing sent out into the air at the same frequency as the noise all around, and with a slide of amazement running straight down the nape of my neck and rising in goose-bumps along my arms I understood that the roar was pigeons, hundreds of them, gathered here to glean the spilled grains from harvest. They were calling from trees and hedges and fence-posts for miles around, all at once, and in such number that their individual songs dissolved into one. I was not imagining it. This was not a symptom. It was *out there.* And amid the roar of hundreds of other minds, I was overcome by delight. No matter how old I am, I thought, sometimes I'll encounter things that are new. And perhaps my wonky neurology was reading too much from this experience, but sometimes, I went on to think, when you berate yourself, it might be the case that you do so needlessly. Sometimes it is not you. Sometimes the world is to blame.

I once told a friend about my perennial inability to recognise I'm in the midst of a migraine prodrome. Other people understand what their symptoms mean while they're happening, I said. Most people. Not me. I said, 'It's weird. I wonder if I'm in denial on purpose, because I hate having migraines?' She fell quiet for a while. 'It *could* be that,' she said carefully. Then she said, 'There's another possibility. Have you ever considered that your failing to identify the symptoms of your migraines while you're having a migraine may itself be a symptom? Because some things are structured so that not seeing them, not comprehending them, is part of the experience of what they are.'

Migraineurs like me are experts in denial. We know how it feels, that fingertip pressure behind the eyes and heart, knowing it's there and at the same time believing it does not exist. Which is why I keep thinking of migraines whenever I hear the news, although we have a much clearer understanding of the science of climate change than we do the science of migraines. As I write, forest fires in Siberia are tearing through millions of acres of slow-growing pine. The Amazon is burning. Villages are falling into the sea. Methane craters blossom across melting permafrost. Dogs drag sleds through meltwater. The hottest summer. The hottest summer, again. And again. Hurricanes lining up across the Atlantic. One, two, three. And while it's easy to grieve over a photo of a starving polar bear, be terrified by the predictive pronouncements of scientists, feel the utmost grief and horror at the human cost of hurricanes or floods, it's even easier to disavow the knowledge of systemic breakdown. We can't connect the dots. We know we're in trouble, but we shift anxieties to conjure terrors that are palpable, thinkable. We fret about the existence of drifting drinking straws and shopping bags that mimic jellyfish and ctenophores in trash-polluted seas. Some of us anchor ourselves in an imagined notion of home while home burns or drowns around us. Others conjure enemies who threaten our homes and familiar ways. We cleave to narratives online that canalise our terror into notions of cabals and great replacements, conspiracies fluttering like millenarian pamphlets, old hand-printed broadsides newly rendered in digital ink. But we know we're in trouble.

One explanation for our incomprehension is something I've read so many times it's started to seem the kind of repetition born of desperation. We are unable to conceptualise the fact of climate emergency, the argument runs, simply because of the way our brains have evolved. It's our deep evolutionary past that makes us unable to respond. We're hard-wired to not be able to comprehend something so big and all-encompassing. And while it's a relief to be told that it's not our fault, that is not relieving. The reason I think of migraines when I read about the climate emergency is that I have come to suspect that our inaction might work the way my migraines do. What if it is not our evolutionary past that makes us unable to see? What if it has nothing to do with selective pressures in the lives of early humans? What if it's us, right now, experiencing a structural issue that makes it impossible to comprehend symptoms as premonitions? My migraine symptoms are a concatenation of unrelated things that seem to have nothing to do either with each other or with the pain that follows them: beetroot, banana milk, yawning, phonophobia, exhaustion. It's hard to imagine how those things relate, or how they could fit together into a whole. And it's just as hard for us to

106

comprehend that things we have been taught are unrelated to each other, that seem only incidentally connected to the workings of the world – things like agricultural production, food distribution, international trade agreements, global corporate culture, among a thousand others – it's hard for us to comprehend that such things might be causal symptoms of the climate emergency. We've been conditioned by our times not to process some types of problems and solutions because they do not fit with how we've been taught to think about society. We've been led to believe we can make decisions that change the world in the supermarket; that only our individual decisions matter; that to bring about large-scale change we should concern ourselves with the smallest actions: changing light bulbs, eschewing diesel cars and plastic straws. But sometimes it is not you. Sometimes the world is to blame. Defiance and change in process are collective acts, not individual ones. Massive, concerted cultural action is what we need, and that is what we should be hastening to organise.

For many years, a great fatalism would overtake me when I felt the first twinges of an oncoming migraine. I knew that it was too late – whether I took to a darkened room, drank pints of soda water, listened to tapes of whale song, nothing would make any difference at all. All I could do was hunker down and wait for the pain to come that would take away the world. Then, quite recently, I tried taking a migraine drug that works by mimicking the effect of the natural chemical serotonin to selectively constrict migraine-inflamed cranial blood vessels. It can be dangerous to postmenopausal women and people with heart problems, among others, so while it can be bought over the counter here in the UK, you have to fill out a comprehensive questionnaire and discuss your health at length with a pharmacist before you are allowed to buy it.

For so many years I had assumed that my only option was to ride the migraine out, lash myself to the mast and wait for the storm to pass. And that is still an option: some migraines are terrible, but not world-ending, and I'll suffer them because I know that frequent use of the drug will render it less effective. But if the pain ratchets up to breaking point – and I know when that is, when it happens, with absolute certainty – I will swallow a pill and in just over an hour the pain will be gone. The light of the sky will soften again, my eyes will cease watering, the agony will disperse like clouds after a passing weather front. I'll feel foggy and strange for days. But the pain will be gone. The most striking thing about this is that every time I take a dose of the drug I believe it won't work. It seems an absolute impossibility. Yet every time it does. Its action is as close to a miracle as anything I've experienced in my life.

Of course what is happening to our planet is not like what happens to a migraineur's brain. When it's only your own body, you are justified in making your own decisions about how to handle things that impinge upon it. But there are aspects that chime. My migraine mantra was always *that's just how it is* until I realised it need not be. We're already in the early stages of planetary ecological breakdown, the prodrome of catastrophe. Our eschatological traditions tend to envision the apocalypse as happening very fast, with the dawning of one final, single, dreadful day. But the systems of the wider world do not operate according to the temporalities of our human lives; we are already inside the apocalypse, and forest fires and category five hurricanes are as much signs of it as the rising of the beast from the pit.

Apocalyptic thinking is a powerful antagonist to action. It makes us give up agency, feel that all we can do is suffer and wait for the end. That is not what we must be thinking now. For an apocalypse is not always a cataclysmic ending, and not always a disaster. In its earlier senses the word meant a revelation, a vision, an insight, an unveiling of things previously unknown, and I pray that the revelation our current apocalypse can bring is the knowledge that we have the power to intervene. Just as the structures of the migraine-stricken brain can be altered, even if we don't believe it to be true until it happens, so might the structures of a world locked into what feels like an inevitable reliance on fossil fuels and endless economic growth. There are actions we can take that seem impossible and pointless and yet they are entirely, and precisely, and absolutely required. We can exert pressure, we can speak up, we can march and cry and mourn and sing and hope and fight for the world, standing with others, even if we don't believe it. Even if change seems an impossibility. For even if we don't believe in miracles, they are there, and they are waiting for us to find them.

SEX, DEATH, MUSHROOMS

It's raining hard and the forest air is sweet and winy with decay. I'm walking with Nick, an old friend and former Ph.D. advisor, emeritus professor of the history of science and amateur mycologist. For the last fifteen years I've accompanied him on autumn mushroom hunts; today we've come to Thetford Forest in Suffolk. We're carrying trugs, traditional English wooden baskets of willow and sweet chestnut, to hold our prizes, perhaps tiny fungi with hair-fine stalks, lumpy shelves broken from the trunks of rotting trees, masses like discarded round pillows, or splayed red starfish arms emerging from the ground.

Hunting for mushrooms can feel surprisingly like hunting animals, particularly if you're looking for edible species. Searching for chanterelles, I've found myself unconsciously walking on tiptoe across mossy stumps as if they might hear me coming. It doesn't work well if you walk around and try to spot them directly. They have an uncanny ability to hide from the searching eye. Instead, you have to alter the way you regard the ground around you, concern yourself with the strange phenomenology of leaf litter and try to give equal attention to all the colours, shapes and angles on the messy forest floor. Once you've achieved this relaxed and faintly predatory gaze, brilliant wax-yellow chanterelles often pop out from behind leaves and twigs and moss, and now they look quite unlike the false chanterelles growing beside them. Nick says that with enough experience, 'you can reliably tell, at least for the commoner species, what the thing is, even if they are enormously variable, and you could not begin to explain how'. He has been an enthusiastic mycologist since his teens and has the names of at least several hundred species committed to memory.

Mushrooms are the fruiting bodies of fungi that live as networks called mycelia, made up of tiny branching threads. Some are parasitic, others feed on decaying matter and many are mycorrhizal, growing in and around plant roots and sharing nutrients with their host. Picking a mushroom doesn't kill the fungus; in a sense, you're merely plucking a flower from a hidden, thready tangle which may be vast and extraordinarily ancient: one honey fungus in Oregon covers almost four square miles and is thought to be nearly two and a half thousand years old.

Soon Nick and I come across scores of mushrooms set in ragged half-circles, their broad tops like cooling milky coffees inexplicably placed among dead leaves. They're cloud caps, a common species here, and considered to be rather toxic. We leave them and walk on. A little while later, Nick spots a yellowish gleam in the long grass. This one is more interesting. He crouches beside it and, frowning, pushes a thumb and index finger underneath the specimen and gently pulls it free of moss and grass. '*Tricholoma*,' he says, with satisfaction. '*Tricholoma sulphureum*.' Mycologists generally use scientific names to describe fungi, as their common names vary widely. The mushroom he holds is sometimes called the sulphur knight or the gas agaric. He offers it to me, gesturing that I should smell it, and an unpleasantly sulphurous tang makes me wrinkle my nose. He stows it in the basket.

I am not very good at identifying fungi, but I am better than I used to be. Over the years I have not only learned to identify a few species by looking at them or smelling them, or seeing the colour their cut surfaces turn, but I've become more and more intrigued by the curious place they occupy in our imaginations. We've been foraging and eating mushrooms for millennia, and they still have the power to disturb us, to conjure the deepest human mysteries of sex and death. Nineteenth-century sensibilities were especially horrified by the common stinkhorn, a fetid fly-attracting species that bursts out of a membranous egg into a shape well described by its scientific name, *Phallus impudicus.* In her later years, Charles Darwin's daughter Henrietta went into the woods to collect stinkhorns for the express purpose of bringing them back to be 'burned in the deepest secrecy of the drawing-room fire, with the door locked; because of the morals of the maids', according to a memoir by her niece. Our continuing pieties about sex are reflected in the way some modern field guides describe the distinctive odour of mushrooms like Inocybes as 'unmentionable' or 'disgusting' rather than the more accurate 'spermatic'.

The unpredictable flowering of beautiful alien forms from rotting wood, dung or leaf litter in a forest moving towards winter is a strong and strange conjuration of life-in-death – in Baltic mythology, mushrooms were thought to be the fingers of the god of the dead bursting through the ground to feed the poor. But mushrooms have a more direct relationship to mortality. Many of them, of course, are deadly. You might survive after eating a destroying angel or death cap, but to do so you'll probably need a liver transplant. What's more, the particular toxicity of fungi is as mysterious as the forms they take. A mushroom can contain more than one kind of toxin, and the toxicity can change according to whether it has been cooked, how it has been cooked, whether it has been eaten with alcohol or fermented before ingestion. Mycologists talk about poisonous fungi the same way herpetologists talk of 'hot' snakes: with more than a modicum of transgressive relish.

If you're collecting fungi to eat, your expertise in identification is all that keeps you from death or serious illness. There's a daredevil side to the activity, a sense of repeatedly staking your life against terrifying possibilities. Today's vogue for wild foods, spurred in part by famous foraging chefs and a nostalgic desire to reconnect with the natural world, has resulted in some popular guides that feature a selection of

115

edible and poisonous species. Nick thinks many of these are irresponsible, even dangerous. 'They don't explain the full range of things you might be running into,' he warns. Many toxic fungi closely resemble edible ones, and differentiating each from each requires careful examination, dogged determination and often the inspection of spores stained and measured under a microscope slide.

Puzzling out tricky specimens is satisfying in itself: if you call on Nick the evening after a fungus expedition, you'll find him at a table spread with fungi, several frighteningly expensive volumes on mycological identification, a microscope and a magnifying lens, and he'll be wearing an expression of joyous, fierce concentration. 'For some species, the colours are unbelievably variable,' he enthuses about one group, the russulas, 'and they get washed out by rain, and then the exact distribution of the warts on their spores is an alternative. So you're doomed, as an ordinary citizen. Because the colours won't do it, and you haven't got a powerful enough microscope.' Fungi force us to consider the limits of our understanding: not everything fits easily into our systems of classification. The world might be, it turns out, too complicated for us to know.

After a couple of hours, the rain is beginning to ease. We're soaked but triumphant. Nick's trug is full of small, difficult and poisonous species. Mine is heaped with edibles, including several crab brittlegills whose shining caps are the colour of toffee apples. We start to make our way back to the car through a dense stand of pines. The air is damp and dark in here. Taut lines of spider silk are slung between their flaking trunks; I can feel them snapping across my chest. Fat garden spiders drop from my coat on to the thick carpet of pine needles below. I'm about to step back on to the path when something catches my eye under a tree a few yards away. I know instantly what it is, though I've only ever seen it in books. 'Cauliflower fungus!' I cry, and run up to it. It's a pale, translucent, fleshy protuberance the size of a soccer ball that seems to glow in the dripping shade, its complicated folds an unnerving cross between boiled tripe and a sea sponge. Looking at it, I remember its Latin name, *Sparassis crispa,* and that it is parasitic on conifers. And also that it is fragrant and delicious when torn and simmered in stock. I sit down on the wet ground to regard it more closely.

We are visual creatures. To us, forests are places made of trees and leaves and soil.

But all around me now, invisible and ubiquitous, is a network of fungal life, millions of tiny threads growing and stretching among trees, clustering around piles of rabbit droppings, stitching together bush and path, dead leaves and living roots. We hardly know it is there until we see the fruiting bodies it throws up when conditions are right. But without fungi's ceaseless cycling of water, nutrients and minerals, the forest wouldn't work the way it does, and perhaps the greatest mystery of mushrooms for me is in how they are the visible manifestations of an essential yet unregarded world. I reach forward, break off half the brittle, furled mushroom and place it in the basket, eager to taste this souvenir from a place full of life hidden from our own.

WINTER WOODS

I try to walk in woods for a few hours before nightfall on every New Year's Day. I've walked them in low sun, deep snow, rain, and in dank mist that clings to the skin and seems more water than air. I've walked blocks of scruffy adolescent pines, ancient lowland forests, beechwoods, farm copses; I've made my way down muddy paths through stands of alder and birch. Sometimes I'm with family or friends. Most often I'm on my own. I'm not sure exactly when my New Year walks began, but over the years they've become as familiar a winter tradition as overcooking the turkey or spending too much money on a Christmas tree.

There's a special phenomenology to walking in woods in winter. On windless days there's a deep, soft hush that makes the sound of a stick breaking underfoot resemble a pistol shot. It's a quietness that fosters an acute sensitivity to small sounds that earlier in the year would be buried under a riot of birdsong. The rustle of a vole in dead bracken at my feet, the dry scratches of a blackbird turning over dead leaves in search of spiders. Now the trees are leafless, wildlife is more visible, but so am I. I'm often met by the alarm calls of jays, nuthatches, robins, grey squirrels, harsh noises designed to inform me that they know I am there. Being sworn at by woodland creatures is disquieting, but comforting too. Modern cultures of nature appreciation so often assume the natural world is something to watch and observe merely, as if through thick plate glass. These alarm calls remind me that we have consequential presence, that the animals we like to watch are creatures with their own needs, desires, emotions, lives.

A winter wood reveals the bones of the landscape it grows upon, the geographical contours of slopes, gullies and hollows. Its trees become exercises in pattern recognition, each species possessing its own texture of bark, its own angles and arrangements of branches and twigs. After the leaves have fallen, winter lets light and weather into the wood, and trunks newly exposed to sunlight turn green with algae as winter days lengthen towards spring.

Because life is less obvious in a winter wood, where it does subsist, as bright stars of moss, or fungal fruiting bodies enduring winter frosts with antifreeze-packed cells, it demands attention. One year a cloud of winter flies in a patch of weak sun in the middle of a woodland ride held me spellbound for long moments, intensely aware of their fragility, their momentary purchase on this world. And the lack of obvious life in winter reminds me of the limits of my own human perception. Most of the life here is too small for me to see or exists underground. Beneath my feet, an intricate network of mycorrhizal fungal threads links plant roots to each other and the soil. They not only grant trees access to crucial nutrients, but give them a means of communication.

It's easy for us to think of trees as immutable, venerable presences against which we can measure the span of our own lives, our own small histories. But trees grow, leaves fall, winters grip the ground. That woods are places of process and constant change was something that took a long time for me to understand. As a child I assumed that the woods near my home would stay the same for ever. Today, many of the paths

I used to walk are blocked with thickets of birch trees, though my memories of those routes live on.

Summer forests give me little sense of time past, or times to come; they're rich with a buzzing, glittering, shifting profusion of life. Everything seems manifested; there's no obvious sense of potentiality. But forests in winter do the opposite: they evoke the passage of time. Winter days are always moving fast towards darkness, and when the wind is bitter it's not easy to walk without thinking of what it will be like to be back in the warmth of home. Above and around me are last year's birds' nests, built to hold broods long fledged, along with signs of life usually obscured by dense growths of summer vegetation: woodpecker nest-holes, deer-nibbled saplings, fox earths, tufts of badger hair on low thorns. And while my feet are treading on last year's leaves, those of next spring are already furled in buds on the tips of twigs around and above me.

After a light covering of snow, the prints of woodland mammals and birds can be read to rewind time. Pheasant tracks end with an imprint of wings, each indented primary feather furred with frost, recording the moment the bird took off from the ground the previous evening to fly to roost.

In a Wiltshire wood that seemed utterly devoid of animal life, I once followed the prints of a brown hare right across the snow to a pool of dark water, saw the place where it drank, and, from the spacing of the prints of each padded foot, saw how fast or slow it had travelled on its way.

So often we think of mindfulness, of existing purely in the present moment, as a spiritual goal. But winter woods teach me something else: the importance of thinking about history. They are able to show you the last five hours, the last five days, the last five centuries, all at once. They're wood and soil and rotting leaves, the crystal fur of hoarfrost and the melting of overnight snow, but they are also places of different interpolated timeframes. In them, potentiality crackles in the winter air.

ECLIPSE

Long ago, when I first decided I wanted to see a total solar eclipse, I planned to do so in romantic solitude. I was in my early twenties, was inclined to think myself the centre of the universe, and imagined the eclipse to be an event in which the sun and moon – and me – would line up to provoke some deep and abiding revelation. The presence of other people would detract from the meaningfulness of it all, I thought, convinced that the best way to experience the natural world was to seek private communion with it. It's embarrassing to recall this conviction now, because as soon as I saw my first solar eclipse I knew that the last thing I needed was to be alone as it happened.

Witnessing a total eclipse wreaks havoc on your sense of self, on rational individuality. Nineteenth-century scientists on eclipse-viewing expeditions saw them as a test of self-control. They were beset by anxiety that they might fail to maintain their objectivity in the face of the overwhelming emotions totality would bring. In the event, as the historian Alex Soojung-Kim Pang has described, their hands shook so much that many could barely record their data, and one observer was so overwhelmed by the 1871 eclipse in India he was forced to retreat to his room and plunge his head into water. Charles Piazzi Smyth, the Edinburgh Astronomer Royal, wrote in surprise that during the eclipse of 1851 it was not just the 'volatile Frenchman' who was 'carried away in the impulses of the moment' but also the 'staid Englishman' and the 'stolid German'. National stereotypes aside, his concerns point to the exquisite contradiction of solar eclipses. While their paths and timings can be predicted with astonishing mathematical accuracy, their action is always to instill the very opposite of empirical description and objective science: they provoke a flood of primal awe.

Before my first eclipse I'd always been nervous of crowds. It's not just because I'm an introvert. Growing up watching television in Britain in the 1970s and '80s was a primer in their dangers. Political demonstrations, rock festivals, riots: all were to be feared for the same reason nineteenth-century scientists feared eclipses. That is, they made you forget yourself. Dissolving all individual rationality and restraint, coursing with uncontrollable instinct and emotion, this conception of crowds as irrational and contagiously violent entities was the legacy of European theorists like Gustave Le Bon, whose own views had been shaped by the political turmoil of late-nineteenth-century France. To him, crowds were barbarous agents of destruction. All this social history fed into the nervousness I already felt about being in groups of people. I used to spend a lot of time out on my own in woods and fields mostly because I wanted to watch wild animals, which are hard to sneak up on if you're part of a crowd. But there were more troubling reasons behind my desire to be alone. It's reassuring to view the world on your own. You can gaze at a landscape and see it peopled by things – trees, clouds, hills and valleys – which have no voice except the ones you give them in your imagination; none can challenge who you are. So often we see solitary contemplation as simply the correct way to engage with nature. But it is always a political act, bringing freedom from the pressures of other minds, other interpretations, other consciousnesses competing with your own.

There's another way of escaping social conflict, of course, and that is to make yourself part of a crowd that sees the world the same way that you do, values the same things as you. We're familiar with the notion that America is a land of rugged individualists, but it turns out that it has a long tradition of sociability when it comes to seeking out the sublime. As the historian David Nye has argued, groups of tourists who travelled to natural sites like the Grand Canyon or to witness awe-inspiring events like space-program launches were engaged in a distinctly American kind of pilgrimage. Their experience of the sublime supported the idea of American exceptionalism, with marvelling crowds newly assured of the singular grandeur and importance of their nation. But the millions of tourists who flocked to the total eclipse of 2017 didn't see something time had fashioned from American rock and earth, nor something wrought of American ingenuity, but a passing shadow cast across the nation from celestial bodies above. Even so, it's fitting that this total eclipse was dubbed The Great American Eclipse, for the event chimed with the country's contemporary struggles between matters of reason and unreason, individuality and crowd consciousness, belonging and difference. Of all crowds the most troubling are those whose cohesion is built from fear of and outrage against otherness and difference; they're entities defining themselves by virtue only of what they are against. The simple fact about an eclipse crowd is that it cannot work in this way, for confronting something like the absolute, all our differences are moot. When you stand and watch the death of the sun and see it reborn there can be no them, only us.

In 1999 my father and I walked on to a packed beach in Cornwall to witness the first total eclipse to cross the UK in over seventy years. We found ourselves standing between milling tour guides, eclipse-chasers, schoolchildren, camera crews, teenagers waving glowsticks, New Age travellers and folks in fancy dress. It was my first-ever eclipse. I was nervous of the people around me and still clinging to that sophomoric intuition that a revelation would only come if none of them were there. Depressingly, the sky was thick with clouds, and as the hours passed it became obvious that none of us would see anything other than darkness when totality came. But when the light dimmed, the atmosphere grew electric, and

128

the crowd became a thing of overwhelming importance, a palpable presence in my mind. I felt a fleeting, urgent concern for the safety of everyone around me as the world rolled, and the moon too, and night slammed down on us. Though I could hardly see a hand held in front of my face, far out across the sea hung clouds tinted the eerie sunset shade of faded photographs of 1950s atomic tests, and beyond them clear blue day.

And then the revelation came. It wasn't what I'd expected. It wasn't focused up there in the sky, but down here with us all, as the crowds that lined the Atlantic shore raised cameras to commemorate totality, and as they flashed, a wave of particulate light crashed along the dark beach and flooded across to the other side of the bay, making the whole coast a glittering field of stars. Each fugitive point of light was a different person. I laughed out loud. I'd wanted a solitary revelation but had been given something else instead: an overwhelming sense of community, and of what it is made – a host of individual lights shining briefly against oncoming darkness.

The experience of viewing an eclipse in a cloudy sky is not anything like seeing one in the clear. Seven years after the Cornwall eclipse, that is what I witnessed, and it is an event that still lives in the part of me where everything is in the present tense, as if it is still happening, as if it will never stop happening.

I travel with friends to see it, to a ruined city called Side on the Turkish coast. On the allotted day we find a place to stand amid drifts of sand and bushes of flowering sweet bay, in the branches of which flit scores of plump warblers snatching leggy, winged insects from their leaves and sticky flowers. Spectacled bulbuls sing. There is life everywhere. And slowly, over the course of an hour, the moon will move in front of the sun and eventually cover its face.

There are four of us. Three men in sneakers and T-shirts who are experts in maths and coding, and a woman wearing a straw hat and carrying a pair of binoculars who can barely add up a list of simple figures without making an elementary error. That's me. As we pace about our small wilderness of wrecked stone and scrub I look left to where dunes have made inroads into the ruined city, heaped high upon half-buried walls. Behind them, the desert is running with sleek lizards and crested larks, pale sands crossed with myriad painted tortoise tracks. I watch the birds, idly, as we stand

130

and wait, our little pack of people on a dune-top. Similar groups of people are everywhere, some focusing telescopes on to flat white paper to show first contact, the moment where a tiniest scoop of darkness eats into one side of the sun. It takes a long while between first and second contact – that is, when the sun is completely covered by the moon; it's a long, steady diminution in the amount of light reaching the world. For a long while my brain tricks me. It has a vested interest in reassurance: *Nothing is wrong,* it says. It tells me I must be wearing reactive sunglasses, which is why I'm seeing the world changing through tinted glass. Why everything, the luggage-strap leaves of dune grass under my toes, the broken walls, bay trees, the sea in front, the mountains behind, everything's still darkly fine. Then I remember I'm not wearing sunglasses, which hits me with the bad-dream force of an arm brought down hard across a piano keyboard, the psychological equivalent of that discordant crash as I have a fraught little struggle with my brain. Then I shiver. Surely it was absurdly hot here an hour ago? There's a horrible old chestnut about boiling a frog to death. Put a frog in a pan of cold water and put it on the stove, and apparently the blithe amphibian will fail to

131

notice the incremental rise in temperature until it's dead. There's something of that story's creeping dread in what is now going on. I feel a strong need to warn people, to somehow jump out of the pan. Everything is changing, but our brains aren't equipped to notice things on this scale. My eyes dance over the landscape in an automatic, anxious search for familiarity. Lots of things are familiar. Groups of people. Bushes. Sea. Walls. But though their shapes are re-assuring, the content isn't. For everything is the wrong colour, the wrong hue.

Remember those day-for-night filters they used to use filming old westerns? Watching afternoon matinees on television as a child, I assumed that night-time in America was different to night-time in England. Much later I realised it was always day, stopped down and filmed through a blue filter. So: imagine you're watching a night scene in a Technicolor western. Maybe Gary Cooper is hiding behind a crag, rifle in hand. Doesn't that night look strange? Now imagine the same footage with an orange, rather than a blue cast. Everything around me is washed heavy, damp and alien. The sand is dark orange, as it might be at sundown, but the sun is high in the sky. We're all mesmerised by the refracted point-source glitter from the sea in front of us. I don't have any grasp on the physics, but the white brilliance playing on the dark Mediterranean feels somehow far too sharp. And on the ground, right by our feet, even stranger things are happening. Where I expect to see sun-dappled shadow cast on the sand through branches – as confidently as I expect any other unacknowledged constant of the world – I am confounded: amid the shade are a perfect host of tiny crescents, hundreds of them, all moving against the sand as a wind that has come out of nowhere pushes at branches.

The backs of the swallows tracing their sinuous hunting flights over the ruins are no longer iridescent blue in the sun, but a deep indigo. They're calling in alarm. A sparrowhawk is flying over, slipping down the sky, losing height, stymied in its search for thermals to soar upon. They're all disappearing in the rapidly cooling air. The hawk shrugs its way north-west, falling all the while. I check the sun, again, through my eclipse glasses. All that is left of it now is a bare, fingernail curve of light. The landscape is insistently alien: short, midday shadows in a saturated world. The land is orange. The sea is purple. Venus has appeared in the sky, quite high, up to the right. And then, with a chorus of cheers and whistles and applause, I stare at the sky as the sun slides away, and the day does too, and impossibly, impossibly, above us is a stretch of black, soft black sky and a hole in the middle of it. A round hole, darker than anything you've ever seen, fringed with an intensely soft ring of white fire. Applause crackles and ripples across the dunes. My throat is stopped. My eyes fill with tears. Goodbye, intellectual apprehension. Hello, something else entirely. Totality is so incomprehensible for your mental machinery that your physical response becomes hugely apparent. Your intellect cannot grasp any of this. Not the dark, nor the sunset clouds on every horizon, nor the stars, just that extraordinary wrongness, up there, that pulls the eyes towards it. The exhilaration is barely contained terror. I'm tiny and huge all at once, as lonely and singular as I've ever felt, and as merged and part of a crowd as it is possible to be. It is a shared, intensely private experience. But there are no human words fit to express all this. Opposites? Yes! Let's conjure big binary oppositions and grand narratives, break everything and mend it at the same moment. Sun and moon. Darkness and light. Sea and land, breath and no breath, life, death. A total

134

eclipse makes history laughable, makes you feel both precious and disposable, makes the inclinations of the world incomprehensible, like someone trying to engage a stone in discussions about the price of a celebrity magazine.

I'm dizzy. My skin crawls. Everything's fallen away. There's a hole in the sky where the sun should be. I sink to the ground and stare up at the hole in the sky and the dead world about me is a perfect vision – with its ruins and broken columns – of the underworld of my childhood imagination, straight out of *Tales of the Greek Heroes* by Roger Lancelyn Green. And then something else happens, a thing that still makes my heart rise in my chest and eyes blur, even in recollection. For it turns out there's something even more affecting than watching the sun disappear into a hole. Watching the sun climb out of it. Here I am, sitting on the beach in the underworld, with all of the standing dead. It is cold, and a loose wind blows through the darkness. But then, from the lower edge of the blank, black disc of the dead sun, bursts a perfect point of brilliance. It leaps and burns. It's unthinkably fierce, unbearably bright, something (I blush to say it, but here it comes) like a word. And thus begins the world again.

Instantly. Joy, relief, gratitude; an avalanche of emotion. Is all made to rights, now? Is all remade? From a bay tree, struck into existence a moment ago, a spectacled bulbul calls a greeting to the new dawn.

IN HER ORBIT

Nathalie Cabrol was five years old when she watched the first moon landing on television. She pointed at Neil Armstrong in a snowy haze of transmission and lunar dust and told her mother that this, *this*, was what she wanted to do. Even before then she used to stare up at the stars in the night sky from her home in the Paris suburbs and knew questions were up there waiting for her.

Cabrol is an explorer, an astrobiologist and a planetary geologist specialising in Mars. She is the director of the Carl Sagan Center at the SETI Institute, the nonprofit organisation based in Mountain View, California, that seeks to explore, understand and explain the origin of life in the universe. Its work has the glamour of science fiction, but it involves rigorous research and, as Cabrol told me, 'people who are passionate enough that they can put themselves into dire straits'. That is what she does, travelling to some of the world's most extreme and dangerous environments in search of organisms that live in conditions analogous to those on Mars. Cabrol was the chief scientist on a team testing an experimental rover in the Atacama Desert in 2002 and was instrumental in choosing the landing site on Mars for Spirit, the rover that explored the planet from 2004 to 2010; she has dived in volcanic lakes at high altitudes to study the creatures within, and designed and installed an autonomous floating robot on an Andean lake standing in for lakes on Titan, one of Saturn's moons.

I met Cabrol on an October morning in Antofagasta, a port city of oxide-coloured high-rises and copper sculptures that sprawls between dry hills and the dark waters of the Pacific. I'd travelled to Chile to join her team for an expedition to high-altitude desert to test methods of detecting life on Mars. I'd flown from London to Madrid, and then to São Paolo, and then on to Antofagasta. I had brought a sleeping bag, altitude-sickness pills and a considerable amount of anxiety about the conditions we'd meet ahead.

Petite and slight, with short-cropped silver hair and a striking, finely carved handsomeness, Cabrol, who is fifty-four, resembles

Isabella Rossellini with an otherworldly dash of David Bowie. Her eyes shine like grey-green polished granite, always emphatically outlined with eyeliner even when she is deep in the desert. She's charismatic, warm and extremely funny but possesses an indefinable, unpredictable wildness: talking to her sometimes disconcertingly reminded me of encounters I have had with forest animals uncertain whether to flee or defend themselves. That first bright morning in Antofagasta, watching her break into peals of smoky laughter as she held up a SETI Institute flag for the camera, I realised I liked her very much.

Over the past few decades the search for life beyond Earth has entered a new phase. Some models have suggested that perhaps a hundred million planets in the Milky Way might hold complex multicellular life. We have learned too that planets need not closely resemble Earth to potentially harbour life; subsurface oceans on distant moons like Saturn's Enceladus and Titan, for instance, could support microbial organisms. The universe, Cabrol told me, is probably full of such simple life, and the purpose of this expedition would be to refine methods of finding it – of detecting biosignatures. These are signs of life, or lives once lived:

organisms, or the structures they have made, even the chemical compounds they have produced.

Over the next few weeks, we would visit five sites at varying altitudes. The higher we climbed, the further we'd go back in time – not on Earth, but on Mars. The high-altitude sites are water-rich, with a thin atmosphere and high levels of UV radiation. They resemble Mars at the beginning of the transition it underwent three and a half billion years ago, when solar winds began to strip away its atmosphere, allowing cosmic rays to reach its surface, and the water that once flowed there vanished into space or was locked deep underground or at the planet's poles. During this period, any life on the surface would have died or taken refuge in the same kinds of places in which life exists in inhospitable regions like the Atacama. The surface of Mars is exposed to harmful radiation; no life can survive on it today, Cabrol told me, but it might still be hiding underground. The salty, arid sites we visited first were terrestrial analogues for present-day Mars.

For Cabrol, there is much more in the search for life on Mars than answering the old question, 'Are we alone?' Billions of years ago, rocks thrown off by comets and asteroids colliding with Earth reached Mars, and vice versa. Perhaps some carried early life. Finding evidence of the transition from prebiotic chemistry to life here on Earth is impossible, because any such records were long ago destroyed by the Earth's rapid geological activity, by erosion and plate tectonics. But ancient rocks from the time Mars's crust cooled down are still present on that planet's surface; if we share our ancestry with Mars, traces of our own life might still be found there. 'Mars may hold that secret for us,' Cabrol says. 'This is why Mars is so special to us.'

It's October 2016, and Cabrol is in her second year of leading the SETI Institute team on a biosignature-detection expedition to Chile. A stiff Pacific breeze blows dead mimosa blossoms across the pavement as I climb inside a minibus to join them on the long drive to our first field site, where the team had scheduled three days of sampling and working on the problems of how best to find signs of life. Through the blue-tinted windows, the soft yellows and buff oxides of weathered rock and sand are turned a dusty, livid red. Fredrik Rehnmark, a mechanical engineer from Honeybee Robotics, is fizzing with delight. 'If they built a road on Mars, it would look like this!' he exclaims.

We drive north, passing pale rocks arranged into the patterns of names and initials on hillsides. Almost nothing moves in this desert. There are places here that haven't much changed in five million years. Those names written in stone are a kind of biosignature that will outlive not just the people who set them there but all of us and all we know.

Salt begins to spread along the edges of the sandy road as we turn inland. Time drifts. Everything outside the windows is so featureless it seems like a theatrical backdrop. At the site, we set up tents on the shores of Salar Grande, a nine-mile-long salt flat that was a lake millions of years ago. There are flats similar to this on Mars.

The salty air makes my face twitch and burn; I blink constantly. The hyper-arid core of the Atacama is far to the east; here, fog rolls in from the Pacific and has shaped the landscape around us. Close up, the salt flat is composed of broad polygonal plates whose edges are heaped with something that looks like half-melted lemon sorbet, or the dirty, refrozen snow that collects along the roadside in winter. Other salt nodules are heaped in piles like dry and dirty bones, and the ground behind our tents is littered with the detritus of long-abandoned salt-mining operations: boots, open sardine cans, scraps of newsprint, corroded lumps of metal.

Drills echo in the morning air. The engineers from Honeybee are excavating salt cores to test prototype tools for future rovers. A team from the University of Tennessee deploys a drone to map the terrain, a tiny dark star that sounds like a distant nest of wasps. The SETI Institute research scientist Pablo Sobron is analysing salt samples with a laser spectrometer; one will be a feature on future rovers. And students from the Catholic University of the North in Antofagasta are out collecting salt nodules for microbiological lab analysis with the SETI Institute and NASA scientists Kim Warren-Rhodes and Alfonso Davila.

Cabrol picks up a chunk of salt and holds it to the light. 'Look,' she says. Inside the nodule are two bright bands of colour: pink on top, green below. These are communities of halophilic – salt-loving – microbes that can survive this extreme environment only by living inside translucent nodules. The green bacteria photosynthesise nutrients from the light filtering through the pink colony above. The pink pigment works as a sunscreen, protecting both colonies from UV radiation that would otherwise damage their DNA.

I'm humbled. I've been walking on these nodules all day, and I hadn't seen the life beneath my feet. 'Habitability is not something very obvious,' Cabrol says to me. 'It can be hidden.' I look at her slight figure, the salt dusting her gloved fingertips, the faintly mischievous smile on her face, and then stare out at the vastness of the landscape around us. It's dizzying to think of the scales her work spans: millions of miles of space, billions of years of planetary evolution, the vastness of the universe, the canyons and valleys of Mars, the expanse of salt here, our small forms standing upon it, and these exquisitely tough, tiny, almost invisible signs of life held between finger and thumb.

An only child, Cabrol spent a lot of time alone in her family's small apartment while her parents worked, and in her solitude she created an imaginative, hermetic world of her own to live in, filling her hours with words and symbols and numbers, writing stories and tracing lines upon atlases. She told me that as a child she had a talent for connecting things that were not obvious to

144

others. She believes that this is still one of her greatest strengths as a scientist. But even as she started to apprehend the vastness of space, her social world remained circumscribed. 'For a long time,' she said, 'I thought that I could do without interacting with others. I didn't have many friends at all, and I didn't look for them. I had enough. I was busy enough in my mind.' Her parents saved to buy her astronomy books and magazines. Her mother understood her passion. Her father was less certain. 'For him, that was a phase, you know?' she said wryly. 'That was a phase that lasted a long time!'

Cabrol's teenage years were troubled. Things were difficult at home, where her parents were fighting; she didn't fit in and was bullied at school. Some of her schoolteachers thought she lived in a fantasy world. Although she wanted to study planetary sciences, she studied the humanities, for until she taught it to herself later in her career, maths was not her forte.

Cabrol was taking earth sciences in her final year at Paris Nanterre University when her lab director suggested that she visit the historic Meudon Observatory south of Paris to meet Professor André Cailleux, a pioneer in planetary geology. Cailleux showed her maps of Mars and explained that his colleagues were working on the history of water on the planet. Would she be interested in joining them? 'All these years I thought I was going 180 degrees from where I needed to go, but the path was taking me exactly where I needed to be,' she told me. Stepping out from that first meeting, she gazed around at the observatory domes and felt them strangely familiar. 'All these domes I had been drawing as a little girl, always repeating the same landscape, the planetary landscape, of a planet that was completely desert. And with Saturn in the background, always a dark sky and domes.' At Meudon, she had finally found a way to get nearer to Mars.

During the day she worked on her master's degree on the evolution of water-carved valleys on Mars, but she spent her nights looking through Meudon's famous nineteenth-century telescope, the Grande Lunette, dragging a sleeping bag there to rest between hours of observing. Through the eyepiece, there was Mars. It was small, and at first she couldn't see much, but the more she looked, the more she saw on the dusky, changing face of the planet that would become a focus of her career, a planet whose gullies and dried lakes have become as familiar to her as the backs of her hands. And it was at Meudon too that she had a moment which left an indelible mark. Professor Audouin Dollfus, the eminent astronomer who had discovered Saturn's satellite Janus, asked her if she would like to see moon dust. 'Duh! Do I want to see lunar dust?!'

He produced a small container from a safe, and Cabrol looked at it and was disappointed. 'I had a feeling like: *So? That's it?*' she told me. Politely enthusiastic but secretly unmoved, she left the lab to go home, but when she looked up and saw the moon hanging bright over Paris, she was stricken with awe. 'All of a sudden this moon dust that looked like nothing looked like the most precious thing ever,' she said. 'Because it is not so much what it is but the journey it took to get here.' It was a revelation. 'I don't think that anything I saw through an eyepiece told me the same thing: the journey it took, the spirit of exploration, the danger of exploration, the things you have to accept, that there is a sacrifice, and the sacrifice might be your own life.'

Exploration lights her imagination. 'I breathe it, imagine it every day of my life, and I dream about it at night,' she wrote recently in a private manuscript. She told me of a childhood memory: her father carefully opening prickly sweet chestnut cases for her to uncover the glossy, marbled nuts inside. She was entranced. Early moments like this planted the desire for discovery inside her, an urge to find again the wonder of seeing hidden things brought to light.

While working on the question of how flowing water formed lakes on Mars for her Ph.D. at the Sorbonne, Cabrol met Edmond Grin, an eminent retired hydrogeologist who had gone back to earn a Ph.D. in astrophysics. 'This is his thing,' she told me. 'When he has nothing to do, he plays with Einstein's equations.' She was twenty-three and he was sixty-six when she first saw him talking to a professor before her class began. 'For some reason,' she said, 'I could not look in any other direction. I was stuck. I was looking at him, and at that time in my brain, that was like: *I know this man. I know this person. From where do I know him?*' He sat near her in the class, they looked at each other and: 'That was it – it took us, you know?' she said. 'I cannot explain, but I was waiting for him to show up.'

In the years that followed, Grin helped focus her work and her research methodology and was a transformative presence in deeper ways. 'He did a magical act on me,' she told me. 'From being an introvert writing those codes and symbols and novels and papers, it's like he took a glove and turned it inside out, and all of a sudden everything that was inside came out.'

When Cabrol travelled to NASA's Ames Research Center in Silicon Valley in 1994 to work on a landing-site study for a proposed mission to search for life on Mars, Grin went with her. All they took with them was one suitcase, and inside it was a map of the 100-mile-wide Gusev Crater on Mars, made of taped-together photocopied images from the Viking mission, the unmanned spacecraft that surveyed and landed on the planet in the 1970s. 'The two of us had to take a very big leap of faith,' she said. More than thirty years after their first meeting, they are still together, still inseparable, now married. In 2010, they edited *Lakes on Mars,* the first academic book on the subject. Cabrol calls him Merlin, after the magician. He has grown frail now, and this is the first time Cabrol has been to the Atacama without him. That he had to stay behind is a source of deepest sadness for her, something that I realise only later in the expedition, when she leaves the group at a lookout near San Pedro de Atacama to walk down an incline and gaze at the pyramidal, distant slopes of Licancabur, a volcano they once climbed together. She tilts her head to one side and doesn't move for a long time. She looks small and terribly alone.

We move south, up on to the Altiplano, the second-largest plateau on Earth, where the landscape has an astonishing luminosity; it glows like a scene painted on fine bone china. It's wetter, too; there are golden grasses on the hillsides. When Cabrol first came to this place and saw the snowcapped Andes, it was a shock. She felt, she told me, as if she were back somewhere she belonged. There was a connection, just as when she first saw the Atacama Desert through a live feed from an experimental rover, its arid landscape projected on to a screen in a science-operation room. Even with that distance, that robotic mediation, she said, 'the love story started', and 'there was something that I knew was drawing me to this place'.

She has a similar affinity with the Gusev Crater, into which water may once have poured from the immense canyon of Ma'adim Vallis. She and Grin studied it and chose it as a landing site for the Spirit rover. 'I had the same feeling when I first saw Gusev from the surface. I was the first person on the planet to see a new landscape. And you don't get over this. You cannot. I will die with these images. It's in me for ever.'

On one of our long expedition drives, Cabrol stares out of the window, shoulders tensed with what I realise is happy anticipation only when we crest a rise and see the first dark peaks of volcanoes before us. She turns to us all with a blazing smile and announces, 'I'm home.'

At first, Salar de Pajonales is a distant patch of white between dark volcanic slopes, but as we meet it and drive through its broad expanse of gypsum sands, sunlight flashes across thousands of crystalline flakes, ephemeral points of fierce white light. The salts here are chemically different from those at Salar Grande. Cabrol visited the site briefly five years ago and is thrilled to return and discover what it held. Underfoot, the ground crunches and tinkles; it's like treading on sugar mixed with broken glass. Huge bosses of gypsum are dotted around us, round structures like crumbling coral, the colour of milk chocolate. Fascinated, I pull out the sun-rotted blades closest to their surface with my hands, as if extracting teeth.

Life is less easy to locate here. Only when Bill Diamond, the SETI Institute's chief executive, kicks a rock do we find a broken chunk colonised by those familiar microbes in shades of pink and green. Her face half obscured by mirrored glasses and a scarf, Cabrol tenderly uncovers the fossilised imprints of ancient bacterial colonies called stromatolites. They look like pitted fragile cups, chalky fingerprint impressions. Samples are photographed, noted, bagged to be sent on to the lab. Overhead, the drone starts mapping this terrain, struggling in the wind.

That afternoon, I hop in a truck with a biologist and a biochemist from the Catholic University of the North who want to take bacterial samples from a nearby lake. Its turquoise waters are surrounded with pale gypsum blades like thickets of kitchen knives. It is too surreal; I return to the truck feeling unaccountably blinded, though I can see. It is as if a white light is shining behind my eyes. My nose runs; my sinuses ache. The things I write in my notebook have become increasingly bizarre. I scrawl *questions asked in glass* across a whole page, an uncanny aide-memoire for something I never remember. As we drive back to the main study site, I see Cabrol in the distance, a slight shadow moving slowly across the pale fire of sunbaked gypsum, something strangely like a mirage of a person.

That night we sleep in an abandoned mining camp. In the early hours, in the rat-dropping-dusted particleboard and corrugated-iron shack we are using in lieu of tents, I lie in increasingly irritated denial until I drag myself out of my sleeping bag to pee. It is minus 0.4 degrees outside. Above me, the Southern Hemisphere stars are all dust and terror and distance and slow fire in the night, and I stare up, frozen, and frozen in wonderment.

Then we climb higher still, to volcanic sites that resemble formations found on Mars, so high that there isn't enough oxygen for the engine of our minibus. It stalls halfway to our destination. We make a U-turn, return to Antofagasta and rent a new minibus. This also stalls. When we finally reach the geyser field of El Tatio, it is deserted. At about fourteen thousand feet, it is one of the highest active geothermal sites in the world. Tourists flock here at dawn, when the freezing air turns the locale into columns of roiling steam. Some geysers are low to the ground and hardly visible, just a faint shimmering of warm air above them; others look like tall berms of clay pouring out thick gouts of steam. This kind of volcanic, fumarolic environment would have been present four billion years ago on Mars, and old hydrothermal environments like it are one of the most likely habitats to hold life, or the remains of former life, on the planet.

Cabrol dons her red-and-black rucksack, black fleece hat and mirrored glasses, picks up a geologic hammer and starts hacking at an inactive geyser. The surface looks devoid of life, but soon she is delighted to discover bright emerald colonies of chasmoliths – microbes that live in cracks and fissures – thriving on the underside of lumps of geyserite. The hot springs here are full of algal mats and organisms which have evolved to live in water that is almost boiling; they glow purple and dark pink in the sun, their colours protection against UV rays.

Cabrol has always been drawn to both volcanoes and lakes, to fire and water. They're completely opposite, she says, 'but if they work synergistically together, they create steam, which is a source of energy. And then you can produce power. And you create things with that. But if the water goes on the fire, then you have destruction. And my entire life is just trying to find this balance between creation and destruction. For the things that I create and the things that

154

are eating me inside. And it's a very fine balance.' There is a pattern in her life, she tells me, where the highest of highs are swiftly followed by the lowest of lows. She speaks to me of the deaths of her mentors, friends and family members, of times she came close to death, of times when she struggled with inner darkness. 'What people see in me is the successful woman, the leader, but all of this is built on sweat and work and temper, you know? It's losses, tragedy, death and tears. I guess you cannot be strong if you never have been hurt and learn how to survive that.' As she tells me this, she looks bone-tired. It is the third week of our expedition, and she is sleeping badly, two or so hours a night, she says. And the altitude medicine she is taking is making her sick.

Cabrol's search for life in extreme conditions began in the Atacama but took a turn in 2000, after she watched a French television documentary that showed the crater lake atop Licancabur on the Bolivian Altiplano. There it was, onscreen, the perfect place to search for extremophile life adapted to the punishing conditions of high-altitude lakes. She wrote a research proposal and three years later donned a black wetsuit with a weighted belt and free-dived into the lake at an altitude of nearly twenty thousand feet, discovering zooplankton species new to science.

'Water is my thing,' Cabrol tells me. 'I feel comfortable. I feel at peace.' On a family vacation when she was two years old, she wore water wings to float on the surface of Lake Garda in Italy. She clambered onshore, took off the wings and went back to the water. 'I am thinking to myself that if I go underwater, I cannot sink,' she laughs. Submerged, she swam instinctively in a new world of shining pebbles and vivid colours. She learned to free-dive as a teenager in Cap d'Agde in the South of France. 'It was always beautiful and peaceful; there was no stress,' she says. 'There was this sense of being responsible for myself, of being in charge and seeing beautiful things, and exploration and discovery.' We are talking in her tent, and the silence between her words is filled with the crack and ripple of nylon stock, the sides of the tent inhaling and exhaling in the wind, the floor billowing up around our planted feet.

'When I entered that lake,' she went on, 'I was thinking I was entering the past, actually entering a time machine that was telling me what Mars was like four billion years ago. It's really a place where time and space get warped.' Diving in these high lakes provokes emotional states, she says, that are intensely beautiful and spiritual. There was one time, in 2006, when she was suspended in the middle of the volcanic lake, caught midway between earth and sky, the water arctic blue and each ray of sunlight diffracting around her, so that she felt surrounded by diamonds. 'And on top of that,' she says, 'copepods, little zooplankton, tiny shrimps, and they are so red. It's a symphony of colour. I'm suspended like that, and time stands still. And for one fraction of a second, everything is perfect. I don't need to have to explain anything. For that very moment, you understand everything. And there is nothing to understand.' Then she remembered she was on a not-so-dormant volcano. 'I thought, *I have a suit and forty-five minutes of oxygen,*' she says and shakes her head. 'My last thought would have been so serene and so peaceful.'

As we take the trucks in a convoy up to our final site, I look back on the Atacama and think of the Apollo astronauts. Far behind and below us is a haze-softened blue expanse streaked with clouds, making this climb feel like a journey away from Earth. We are among volcanoes now, vast blisters on the plateau. Cabrol points out Simba, which the group plans to climb to sample the bacteria in its crater lake. Cabrol has a history with Simba. She was climbing it with her team in 2007 when the Tocopilla earthquake hit. They avoided the avalanches, but when Lascar, the volcano sharing a slope with Simba, began to emit poisonous gases, Cabrol fell into what she called a 'surgically cold' mindset, concerned only with logic, practicality, survival. During their descent, a large tumbling rock just missed her. 'And this,' she said, 'was when I got mad.' She stood up in the middle of the gully and started yelling at the volcano. ' "Is it going to be all today?! Is there anything yet you can?!" I was shouting! I was outraged!' She got everyone down safely and then nearly passed out in the truck back to base camp – partly from an adrenalin crash, partly from the knowledge that everyone might have died.

We camp under an extinct volcano in an abandoned military barracks that the team calls Chilifornia. The cinder-block rectangle has no roof, but the walls shelter our tents from the wind. Cabrol gathers us together and warns us not to go wandering. In the 1970s, this territory was disputed with neighbouring Bolivia, and there are still landmines here. It's a worry. I grow even more anxious when I overhear Cabrol and Cristian Tambley, who is handling logistics for the expedition, talking about installing UV-monitoring systems in this region. Strong UV radiation damages DNA, and the World Health Organization warns against being outside when the UV index is over eleven. In 2003 and 2004, Cabrol observed unexplained UV storms here of extraordinary intensity, though they lasted only a few hours. On Licancabur, she detected UV spikes of over forty-three. That night I dream of wearing a spacesuit.

It takes an hour to drive to Laguna Lejía the next morning, a copper-coloured lake shivering in the hard light of the sun. Cabrol is visibly shocked as we arrive. 'It's substantially reduced in size compared with when I last saw it, in 2009,' she says. 'Our planet is actually changing in front of our eyes,' she tells me later, 'at a speed that is extremely scary.' We are heading along what was once a drove route for cattle from Argentina into Chile, and I can't look away from the bones littering this place. The skulls left behind are so old that the keratin layers of their horns have peeled apart to make them things like delicate pine cones or the brittle pages of old books left in the sun.

Cabrol has worked closely with robotics engineers for many years, and her 2011 Planetary Lake Lander project set an autonomous floating robot in Laguna Negra in the Andes. Ever since, Cabrol has made it her mission to push the two things together: climate change on Mars and climate change on Earth. The Planetary Lake Lander wasn't just preparation for future missions to lakes and seas beyond Earth, or simply an analogue for climate change on Mars, but a way of investigating climate change here and now. The region near Laguna Negra is suffering from rapid deglaciation, and we see that change too. We move to another lake, surrounded by creeks and frozen grass. The wind is brutal, the sky the darkest blue. Cabrol crouches at a site where she found freshwater springs seven years earlier. Fascinated and forlorn, she tells us that this is like Mars three billion years ago. The surface water has receded, but there is some water underneath. She is shocked by how fast the climate is changing here. 'Seven years ago, this was a beautiful spring, a pond with zooplankton, but now you can't tell the difference between this and the rest of the desert.' She scrapes gently at frozen mud with the point of her geologic hammer. Later, she points out that the Earth itself is in no danger whatsoever. 'It will survive whatever we throw at it. What is in danger is the environment that made us possible. We are pretty much cutting the branch we are sitting on. So either we understand that very quickly or life will go on – but a different one.' She thinks it will not be a slow disappearance. 'It's going to be sudden and frightening,' she says.

At night in my sleeping bag, I woozily speculate on the meaning of life and death, the fate of Earth, the end of things. I ask Mario, one of the expedition doctors, if déjà vu is a recognised symptom of altitude. 'Absolutely,' he says. I am relieved. It keeps happening. It is starting to scare me. The day before, a llama sheltering from the wind behind an outcrop stepped down with leisurely, measured grace across talc-dusted slabs of rock. I knew I'd seen it before. More than twice, certainly. Perhaps five times, six. I knew I hadn't, of course, but these miraged recollections were instantly telescoped and pleated together like a pack of cards all of the same suit flicked through with a thumb. There is a sense that reality is unreliable here, as if I could put a hand to the air and it could slip right through to another universe if I weren't paying sufficient attention, or paying a little too much. As if I could free another reality by rubbing corners of air together like trying to open a recalcitrant plastic bag. And the wind pours on us as we drive, making dust devils spin over the distances, everything outside seemingly inimical to breath.

These high places, Cabrol says, were sacred to the Inca people, who would climb the mountains to make ritual offerings to the gods. Crouching behind a rock to keep us out of the sharp mountain wind, she explains how up here the scientific search for life beyond Earth and the spiritual search for meaning cannot help but run in parallel. 'The Incas would come here to the mountains to ask questions of God – and so, in a way, are we,' she says. 'That's the same question. Who we are, where we are coming from, what's out there? We are trying to connect to our own origins. So we are doing this scientifically; they were doing it in a more intuitive way.'

Cabrol has a deep respect for the cultural histories of the landscapes she works in. Her Quechua guide Macario made offerings to Pachamama, an Incan goddess, before he and Cabrol's team climbed volcanoes, and Cabrol always makes offerings, usually crystal spheres, to the high crater lakes she dives in on mountains. She had planned to climb to Simba's crater lake at the expedition's end, but she hadn't brought an offering to give its blood-coloured waters. Tentatively, she asks me if I have anything that might work as a replacement. I hand her a piece of lapis lazuli polished into the shape of an egg that I bought in San Pedro de Atacama. The exchange seems an entirely rational act. Both halves of Cabrol, scientific and spiritual, are perfectly conjoined in her work, in her insistent, careful reaching for the deepest of questions: why are we here?

Cabrol has stopped working. She's staring at plumes of vapour rising from the volcano on the near horizon. Bright white at their bases, they soften rapidly into haze that climbs up and up, before losing coherence and resolution against the sky. The steam is ascending vertically, even in this vicious wind, so there is serious force behind it. The volcano is Lascar, the one that shares a slope with Simba. And the team has people on Simba right now, local guides preparing our ascent.

Cabrol calls everyone in. We stand in a line before her, waiting for orders. She pushes her mirrored glasses up on to her hat and speaks to us with terse authority. As soon as the guides are down from Simba, she says, we'll go back to camp. She'll get out the satellite phone and speak to Bill Diamond, who is now back at the SETI Institute, and call the United States Geological Survey and the University of Chile to find out more about the situation here. And then we will need to decide not only if the team should cancel the planned ascent of Simba but also whether any of us should stay in camp at all.

The phone call brings no immediate bad news, so we stay. Cabrol will keep an eye on Lascar's activity and let us know if it worsens. She instructs us to sleep in our clothes and keep our passports at hand, ready to leave in the middle of the night if need be. All of this gives me a strange kind of dread. It has a lazy, slow, opiated quality. It's been a long time since I've had none of the tools I need to judge a situation. We find out that very recently there'd been a 5.5-magnitude earthquake in Calama, only an hour and a half away. That isn't optimal: if water makes its way into the magma chamber beneath the volcano, the volcano might explode. This is not comforting. I withdraw to my little orange tent, sit on my cot and scroll through photos of home on my phone. Outside, the light is dying on the old volcano. I can hear people packing and the generator buzzing behind the cinder-block wall. Tambley is assembling a weather station and playing Pink Floyd's 'Shine On You Crazy Diamond', the saddest of songs, on his laptop. Zips, whispers, laughter, the sounds of Pelican cases being hauled over rough ground.

I stare at my hands. They look like ancient lizard skin, each crease outlined in pale dust. All my clothes are white with it. My hair feels like greased fur. There is a moth in my tent, but I am too numb to move it. Blankly, I watch this scrap of life bump about the orange walls. The tent flap is open; all it needs to do is turn around and fly the other way. It does not. I lose sight of it for long minutes, then jump at its touch. It has bumbled its way on to my hand and rests there, quivering. I put it outside. We leave the next day.

HARES

I'd left the snow behind for a work trip to California, for hot blue air and palm trees and bougainvillea and a mockingbird that serenaded my first sleepless night with an exquisite repertoire of stolen phrases. Numbing cold at home, searing heat in Santa Barbara brought a confusion that was more than jetlag; I'd lost any sense of the season I was in. Driving back from Heathrow a week later the snow had gone but my seasonal disorientation was worse than ever, disquiet lying dully inside. But as I passed a field of winter wheat beside the A505, somewhere between Royston and Newmarket, I glimpsed something that made everything right itself, slam me back into what I knew must be spring. Brown hares, five of them, circling, running, hopping, turning to stand on their hind legs to box at each other, kicking mud around under wide and wet silver skies.

I first saw boxing hares out on a misty field near Winchester when I was a teenager, convinced that what I was witnessing were buck hares competing with each other for does. So perfectly did this reading of their behaviour correspond with our societal mores, it had the force of absolute truth. The hares circling the fights, I thought, were does, carefully assessing the pugilists' prowess, and I assumed the victor would take all. I was wrong. Most boxing hares are does unwilling to mate with bucks making sexual advances on them. They rise up and fight them off, an animal analogue to a form of violence just as much a feature of our society, though only in recent years have we begun openly to speak of it.

Talk to people of hares and you'll hear the word 'magical' again and again. Books about hares are rich with lore and legend. Of the hare Boudicca kept under her cloak to release before a battle, the direction of its flight a prediction of the outcome. Of shape-shifting hares. Of hares with an affinity to the moon. Hares as a sign of Easter, of resurrection, of renewal, of spring. Most of us think of hares as magical and mysterious because lore and legend tells us they are so. But these old stories were based on the behaviour of real hares, which are indeed mysterious. They might not be able to change sex at will, as early modern writers assumed, but female hares can become pregnant again before they give birth to their young – leverets that enter the world fully furred with open eyes and rapid independence. Hares eat their own droppings, can run at forty miles an hour – they're our fastest land animal – and they feed mainly at dusk and dawn, dim presences in the gloom. Solitary animals, they'll gather in numbers to feed when pickings are rich. Two years ago I was standing in a Norfolk field of beet at sundown when down the tractor lines loped a crowd of hares, astonishingly slow and eerie, their ears glowing red in the dying light and their fur sabled by shadow.

Humans brought hares from the Continent and released them into our landscape around the time of the Romans, or perhaps earlier, and these creatures from elsewhere quickly turned to natives with a talent for invisibility. Hares don't burrow. They live always under the sky, making a series of depressions called forms across their territories. These are body-shaped spaces into which they'll crouch, close to the ground, turning themselves into a low curve of russet you are sure must be a rock sunk in winter cereal before you notice two black-tipped ears laid to its back. A form is the space a hare makes to see everything and be invisible. Tread too close to one and the hare will spring up at your feet, tearing herbage with its hind claws, white tail flashing, and your heart thumping in surprise as it races into the distance. Hares are things of eyes and speed and fear; they have an astonishing capacity to outrun, jump and dodge things that pursue them – foxes, dogs, eagles.

Predators aren't the reason hares are declining in Britain; it's agricultural intensification that has hit them hard. Leverets crouching in silage fields are mown down by harvesters and modern monocultures leave adults short of food. I don't see hares often these days. I encounter them mostly in photos, in paintings, or in shop windows displaying boxing hare figurines – stylised, long-eared forms wrought into shapes of graceful confrontation. But you don't need to have ever seen a real hare to know what it is supposed to mean. They're magical harbingers of spring.

Spring has of late become thin to me. It's starting to mean supermarket daffodil bunches and Easter promotions, rather than its richly textured changes, the scent of new herbage, algae greening on the trunks of oaks, the echoing drum of woodpeckers, rising skies and the return of that indefinable light to hollow out winter. All these are things I've missed after a few years of mostly working inside. And just as the meanings we have given hares are nowhere near as rich and complex as the living, breathing creatures hares are, so our firm ideas about spring belie what is happening to it. Climate change has made our seasons creep; now catkins appear in winter, cuckoos are rarely heard, and rather than a slow progression, springs are increasingly a short flash of sudden warmth before summer, hardly a season at all. Those boxing hares were a glorious sight, but behind their sparring forms flickered a shadow of disquiet, a glimpse of how the meanings we have given things like hares and seasons persist so strongly once their models have gone that it's hard to see, sometimes, the precipitous alteration in things we've long assumed eternal.

LOST, BUT CATCHING UP

Fate saw fit to make me allergic to horses, dogs and foxes. I discovered my dog allergy early: we had a dog. I discovered my horse allergy during riding lessons, and my fox allergy while skinning a road-killed fox to turn into a rug. Which, I realised, I couldn't have in my house.

Allergies never fail to make life new. A few days ago I discovered I was allergic to reindeer. Indeed, the longer life goes on, the more I realise that most quadrupeds make me ill. Though I can ride, I can't ride for long. Twenty minutes on a horse, and my eyes are closed, my hands mottled with nettle rash and I've lost the ability to concentrate on anything other than fighting for breath.

So – quite apart from my moral qualms – it's unsurprising that I've never ridden to hounds. And I've never really understood foxhunting. I've never been part of that particular rural crowd, and even though the Hunt met often outside my parents' house, by the grain dryer at the top of the hill, ready to take in miles of good country, I never really understood what it was all about. I only ever saw the pink coats and the horses and the hounds clustering and the fence-menders and the police and the saboteurs. That didn't seem very interesting to me. And I also felt very sorry for the fox.

It was a Saturday, and I was at my mother's house. It was a day of heavy rain and wind, and I was tired, and sad, and distracted, for it had been a year that week since my father died. And while lots of times, talking to Mum or my brother helped share the pain, sometimes the words wouldn't come, and the loneliness stoppered me up, and I couldn't talk at all. So much pressure was building up inside me that day that by mid-afternoon I had to hide. I left the house to have a cigarette out on the porch. And standing in the murky light by the drive, I heard the music of hounds.

Even with my sporting ignorance, it seemed clear that the Hunt was drawing the covert at Ham Farm, a thick copse of coppiced hazel, sweet chestnut and bluebells just across the road and away. I pulled up the collar of my coat and walked out into the near-sleet. Sure enough, a succession of muddied, battered 4x4s passed where I stood at the edge of the drive, windows steamed on the inside. They all turned left down the track to Wadgett's Copse.

After they'd gone, a long silence but for the hounds in the distance. A giddy, wet, rainy echo of a cry. My hair was soaked and my cigarette damped to extinction. The asphalt at my toes was running with water, and shallow pools were slowly being born in the waterlogged paddock across the road.

And I heard a light pattering of footfalls growing louder; a pattering of nails and pads through water to tarmac. Coming along the road towards me on his way to the covert, his head high, his body smeared all breast-deep in clay that stained the lower half of him copper-ochre, came a foxhound. A pale hound. He was alone, which was wrong. But being alone made him the type of all hounds that ever existed. He was running as if he'd been running all day, and he was running as if he would never stop, tongue out and eyes fixed. He was running to be with the rest of the hounds, and the sound was drawing him along the rainy roads as if he were underwater and swimming up to the light to breathe. I was transfixed. I'd never seen a hound be a hound before. He was doing exactly what he needed to be doing, and he was tired but joyful. He was late, but getting there. Lost, but catching up.

SWAN UPPING

In the days after the Brexit vote, I became obsessed with an oil painting called *Swan Upping at Cookham,* which portrays a scene from an ancient and colourful English tradition. Swan upping refers to the annual summer voyage of a flotilla of wooden skiffs that sets off from the town of Sunbury-on-Thames on a five-day journey to catch all the swans on the upper reaches of the River Thames. The crews check the parentage of young birds and place a mark on them to claim their ownership: some belong to the Queen, others to the Worshipful Company of Vintners and the Worshipful Company of Dyers, two ancient trade guilds based in the City of London. The painting depicts a traditional stop on the uppers' trip. Here is the river and the Ferry Inn, wooden punts, moody clouds, women carrying cushions, a fretted iron bridge and a swan bound and hoisted in coils of rope and canvas, white neck craning from a man's shoulder.

Swan Upping at Cookham was painted by the mystical, eccentric English artist Stanley Spencer, who left it half-finished in his bedroom in Cookham when he went off to war in 1915, and the knowledge that it was there sustained him over the next three years. He longed to explain to his military superiors that he couldn't take part in attacks because he had a painting to finish at home. On his return, he picked it up. 'Well there we were looking at each other,' he wrote in his diary. 'It seemed unbelievable but it was a fact. Then I wondered if what I had just come from was fact & caught sight of the yellow of the Lyddite or whatever the Bulgars used in their shells on my fingers & finger nails.'

He finished his painting. But the war is caught up in it. Years before he had laid complex, sunlit ripples on the river below the bridge, but the lower post-war parts of the picture are lifeless, muddy and dark. Boats are painted odd colours and have the wrong shapes, his familiar childhood landscape coursing with new and ominous strangeness. And in the days after the referendum, as the purple 'Take Back Control' pro-Brexit posters on telephone poles near my house faded to violet in the sun, and as I read of a 42 per cent upturn in hate crimes since the result came in, I realised two things: first, that Spencer's painting had unwittingly recorded a schism in national history, and second, that it was haunting me because I felt I no longer recognised my country, that everything around me had become ominous – muddy and dark.

The past was always conjured in Brexiteers' dreams of the future, as it was in Donald Trump's stump speeches across the Atlantic. The winning power of the Brexit campaign slogan used by the UKIP leader Nigel Farage, 'We want our country back', lay partly in its vagueness, which let it appeal to all manner of disaffected constituencies, but also in its double meaning. 'Take it back' in the sense of saving the nation from things perceived to threaten it – seen variously as immigrants, faceless European Union bureaucrats, globalisation, the 'Westminster elite' of Britain's political establishment – and 'take it back' also in the sense of back in time, to some ill-defined golden age. Preserving a continuous national heritage and tradition was an explicit part of the 'Leave' campaign. For years I had read in tabloid articles that the EU was destroying much-loved English traditions – baseless claims that its bureaucrats were going to ban everything from English breakfasts for truck drivers to the Queen's favourite dog breed, even barristers' wigs. The quaintness of these conjured shibboleths was no accident: Brexit rhetoric was all about a battle to save English values and an English way of life beleaguered by waves of immigration and European interference. It had weaponised history and tradition.

In its antiquity, its pageantry and its evocation of deep English history, the subject of Spencer's painting exemplified these themes, and I wondered if seeing swan upping firsthand could help me understand a little more about the state I was in. In a few weeks, the uppers would set out on their journey. I decided to go with them for part of the way. I could have chosen to witness any number of English customs, from Morris dancing to village cricket matches, but swan upping drew me, partly because of the painting but also because I'm fascinated by the relationship between natural history and national history. Symbolically, swans have long been entwined with nationhood and identity. Politics is bound up with them.

The swans on the Thames are mute swans, a native species with a curious history in Britain. In past centuries, when they were commonly served roasted at feasts, fewer free-flying wild ones existed here, and even today they seem to me more like feathered livestock than birds: huge, faintly menacing inhabitants of local parks and rivers, neither fully wild nor fully tame. Swans' royal ownership dates at least to the twelfth century, and certain flocks – known traditionally as games of swans – were granted by royal charter to hundreds of favoured dignitaries and institutions. All the young swans in the country were once upped each summer, the last joint of one wing cut away to render them flightless, and patterns incised in their bills or webbed feet to establish ownership. Exquisitely inked manuscript records of these marks still exist: lines and crosses scribed across diagrammatic beaks. As geese and turkeys became popular eating – less territorial than swans, they were much easier to keep – ownership of swan flocks reverted to the Crown in all but a few locations, like the Thames.

In Britain, killing a swan still generates unexamined outrage: it is wounding the body politic, a thing akin to treason. The symbolism of swans is so commonly understood in Britain – emblems of the monarchy, and by extension the nation – that these birds have long been counters in the game

179

of what is us and what is not. Perceived threats to swans closely track the imagined enemies of British society. All the swans on the Thames, or so one story goes, were killed by Cromwell's soldiers during the Civil War, and the river was restocked only with the restoration of the monarchy. Mournful Victorian obituaries for Old Jack, the swan who lived at the seat of the monarch at Old Buckingham House, relate how his decades-long reign over his pond was brought to an untimely end by a gang of warlike Polish geese. A nineteenth-century magazine article claimed that swans in the royal parks were killed and skinned and their remains tied to trees by Jewish feather traders.

It's easy to read these fables of nationhood as curios from another age. But they are not. In the early 2000s, the *Sun* tabloid accused asylum seekers of stealing the Queen's birds for barbecues. Later it transpired that the basis of the story was a telephone call to a swan sanctuary to report that someone had been seen pushing a swan in a shopping trolley.

'Undoubtedly people do eat swans,' Chris Perrins, a swan expert and retired Oxford ornithology professor, told me. Perrins accompanies the uppers every year as the

Queen's swan warden. He thinks the culprits are as likely to be British as they are to be immigrants. Many swans are killed by young men with air rifles, bricks and bottles, but these crimes receive far less attention from the news media.

On 19 July, nearly a month after the Brexit vote, I stood expectantly inside the view that Spencer had painted. It was the hottest day of the year, the air heavy and luminous. Moored in slack green water in the shade of a sycamore was a collection of skiffs flying flags embroidered with swans and crowns. Waiting for the uppers to emerge from the Ferry Inn, I chatted with an older woman named Siân Rider sitting alone at a table. She wore a straw hat festooned with daisies and a gold-starred blue tabard that she had sewn herself from an EU flag. She loathed the engineers of Brexit and was dismayed by the number of people who had revealed their racist colours to her since the vote. She was following the swan uppers partly because walking the river was good exercise, but also because it offered a reassuring continuity to set against political upset. 'It would be a shame to lose our old customs,' Rider said. 'Especially what's been happening this past year all over the world, where we all seem to be going to hell in a hand-basket. It is just nice to have something that . . . What's the word? Sustains?' She shook her head at the tide of recent history and offered me a mint.

'It's just a slice of English tradition and pageantry,' Casey Fleming told me. Fleming is a trim, cheerful man with silver hair who works as a sustainability manager in Qatar. Friends with one of the Queen's uppers, he had come with his young son, Reilly, to watch from the press boat in which I, too, had been granted a seat. Fleming was careful to stress that upping is a quintessentially English, rather than British, phenomenon. 'By nature,' he mused, 'I think the English are traditionalists. Conservative. And we like to hang an anchor to the past. And this sort of event gives us that. It's culture. Lineage. And without that, without celebrating past events or keeping traditions alive, what defines you as a country or as a race?' People in Britain have been too ready to sneer at events like this, he told me, but they are beginning to realise that they should be celebrated. 'To be proud of being English, ten years ago, was to be thought of as being small-minded, racist – you know, had nega-tive connotations. But I think now it's dif-ferent. And I think Brexit has helped that.'

182

The meanings of traditions can change over time, their social functions can shift. Swan-upping data is now used to monitor the health of the Thames' swan population, and before they set out each morning the uppers meet with local schoolchildren to teach them about swans and river conservation.

David Barber, the Queen's swan marker, who oversees the upping, emerged from the Ferry Inn, resplendent in a red jacket detailed with gold braid, a swan feather tucked into his captain's hat. He was followed by Perrins and the crews of the Queen's boats and the boats of the Vintners and Dyers, skilled watermen from the lower reaches of the Thames clad in white cotton caps and coloured shirts. Here, too, was Wendy Hermon from Swan Support, a charity that rehabilitates sick and injured wild swans. I clambered into the press boat, an elegant wooden umpire launch, and we set off upstream searching for swans.

It didn't take long. Two feathered white bergs and a lone cygnet drifted serenely past the riverside mansions of Bourne End. *'Allll up!'* cried the crews, manoeuvring their skiffs to box the swans into a shrinking patch of water. Confusion. Raised oars, shoulders, shouts. The male swan raised his wings heraldically, defensively, and was

183

grabbed by the neck. 'There's a catch!' Then things went awry: the female and the cygnet ducked under a gangplank and escaped downstream. The boats raced after them, heading them off, and tried again. 'That worked well,' Barber shouted across the water. 'That's how it should be done.'

Soon the female and the cygnet were in the bottom of a skiff, their black webbed feet tied above their tails with strings of the soft braided cotton the uppers kept looped into the belts of their white cotton trousers, and the adult bird's wings tied, too. I couldn't see the swans clearly from the press boat – just one distant curved white neck like the spout of an elegant porcelain coffee pot. As we drew closer, I noticed the uppers' strangely courteous conduct now that there were swans on the boat, quite at odds with the decisive force it had taken to grab them. 'My swan hook's broke,' a waterman said to me, sadly holding a long pole like a shepherd's crook. He thought it might have been a hundred, maybe a hundred and fifty, years old. He pulled a wry face. 'You just can't get good swan hooks these days.'

Hauled up from the skiffs, the swans were set down reverently upon the lawn of a riverside house. Close up, the adult swan had a snaky neck, glittering black eyes and a waxy orange bill that opened to make nasal, squeaking grunts like an unoiled gate. The bird was a strange coincidence of solidity and air. Sleek contour feathers over thick down, pearls of water running over white feathers thick and curled as paper sculpture. The 18-week-old cygnet resembled a huge, skinny plush toy. Hermon knelt next to it and opened her box of rings. Swan uppers haven't clipped swans' wings for decades; these days the birds are marked with stainless-steel leg rings, not knives.

After the ownership of the cygnet's mother was ascertained – she was one of the Queen's birds – and the correct ring was selected and fitted to the cygnet, Barber, his face tanned dark, the feather in his cap glowing with steely light, explained to Reilly what they were doing. 'You have to check them over to make sure everything is OK,' he said, gently picking up the cygnet. 'Here.' Reilly took a deep breath and extended both hands in front of him, and the swan was deposited into his outstretched palms, his shoulders bowing slightly to take its weight. I asked him later what it was like.

'Like it had a silk wrapping on it,' he said, and the smile he gave me then was shy and full of astonishment. 'How did it make you feel?' I asked. He told me it would stick in his mind for the rest of his life. 'Hopefully it will come back to me and inspire me,' he said. 'Hopefully it will inspire me to be somebody.'

The sun dipping westward, we set off once more upriver. Pulled by motorised tugs for this section of the Thames, the watermen lay back in the skiffs checking their phones. We were passing by some of the most expensive real estate in Britain, architecture inspired by feverish dreams of lost golden ages: vast mock-Tudor mansions, fake castles with crenellated concrete battlements. There were willow trees, summerhouses, immaculate sun-drenched lawns, water-meadows where cattle stood hock-deep in the river, dazed by the heat. A crowd of teenagers smoking weed by a disposable barbecue. A woman sitting with her shopping bags on a wooden bench by a car park, tossing fragments of supermarket sandwiches to ducks on the water below. She waved at us. So did the teenagers. Everyone did. They waved and smiled, and I waved and smiled back.

I had expected to be cynical about this voyage. But as we progressed upstream, I began to feel a luxuriant, drunken joy. Under the boat, constellations of tiny fry darted through sunlit weeds. The river surface was thick with craft following us: large passenger boats with bars serving beer and decks crammed with sightseers, a near-naked man sunk so deeply in a tiny rubber dinghy that it crowded into his shoulders as he paddled, grinning, along the middle of the river. We passed rowing boats, catamarans, sleek pleasure craft resembling 1920s Daimlers. A common tern clipped overhead, translucent supple wing beats over a river crowded with traffic, and something about its flight made me think that it was flying under clouds, but there were no clouds, there were no clouds anywhere and had not been all day, and the sky was the stretched, varnished perfection of linseed-thinned oils.

I had got lost inside a hallucinatory English dreamscape. And no wonder. So many of the books I had read as a child were written about this place, like *The Wind in the Willows* and *Three Men in a Boat.* This was where Noël Coward had set his elegant comedies of manners, where Enid Blyton and Edgar Wallace had lived. It was where the stories were written that taught me what it was to be English. And so I listened agog when the affable press coordinator, Paul Wilmott, pointed out one of the Little Ships, part of a seven-hundred-strong fleet of private boats that rescued British and French servicemen from Dunkirk during the Second World War. And I laughed out loud at his story of the Spitfire pilot flying under the bridge at Marlow to impress his girlfriend, only to be hauled over the coals by an air commodore who witnessed the feat. These were stories designed to foster a reassuring sense of national pride, one in which the war is stripped of horror and political complexity and turned into a patriotic tale of plucky English derring-do.

Swan upping is a progress in the old-fashioned sense, a journey upriver that claims the right not only to own swans but to own their meanings, the meanings of the river, the meanings of Englishness. You move through a landscape thick with narratives handed to you by others, and what you read from the banks as you pass is part of what you choose to believe about your nation and who you are. You might see only Dunkirk boats and lines in the air carved by ghostly Spitfires. You might see leisurely eighteenth-century landscapes in the loose herd of cattle standing in the river. But you might see there, too, the ghosts of forgotten farmworkers, or feel fellowship with a woman eating sandwiches from a plastic packet on a bench or with a gaggle of youngsters smoking pot around a barbecue. Lying in the boat as we hastened towards a new group of swans, I thought of how we choose to see only the things that speak to us of the way we are told the world should be, and then felt a small burst of shame and the breaking of my fever-dream.

Staggering off the boat at Marlow at the end of the day, I thought of Reilly's rapt face as he held the swan, the genial conviviality of the uppers, the sun-splashed slipway at Cookham and then Stanley Spencer again. Not the painting this time, but the story of a trip he made to Beijing in 1954 as part of a cultural delegation. Towards the end of the tour, Zhou Enlai, the Chinese premier, gave a long speech about how much Chinese people loved China and then asked for a response. It was a politically perilous moment. No one knew what to say. 'There was a silence,' the cultural historian Patrick Wright, who wrote a book on the subject, *Passport to Peking,* told me. 'And then Spencer got up, much to everyone's absolute horror, and said: "The Chinese are a home-loving people, well, so are the English. Have you heard about, have you ever heard of Cookham? Have you ever been to Cookham?" '

It was a stunningly successful gambit and

189

sparked an animated conversation with Zhou. Spencer told him that the people of Cookham are the same as people everywhere: they want to get on with their lives, get on with their neighbours and, as Wright put it, not be bombed. 'I feel at home in China,' Spencer said, 'because I feel that Cookham is somewhere near.' He is often mocked for his parochialism, his attendance to small things, but, as Wright maintains, his vision was ultimately one in which 'through the small, through the located, you enter a more universal domain of human experience'.

Heritage traditions like swan upping have clear conceptual value for nationalists; they promote a sense of seamless historical continuity that works to erase differences between past and present, burnishing an illusion of unchanging Englishness. But remembering the story of Spencer in China made me wonder if swan upping could offer us something other than these exclusionist dreams of a sacrosanct Englishness deep-rooted in an imagined past. For besides the pageantry, what I had watched that day was a beautiful display of expert animal handling and river knowledge. Skiffs crewed by men who know how to row, how to navigate complicated waters, how to catch swans, how to corral them, how to deal with a bird the size of a dog with a flexible neck and wings that can break ribs.

These are craft knowledges, ones learned by apprenticeship, not from books, and universal in the very nature of their specificity. Like Spencer's Cookham villagers in China, they are global by virtue of being local and cannot easily be fitted to simple stories of race and nationality, of us and them. Later that evening, watching a full moon rise through air thick with the scent of lime blossom, I thought of how there are always counter-narratives, hidden voices, lost lives, other ways of being, and how it is possible to see a different, more inclusive England in the most recondite of traditions. And I cherished the thought that grand historical and political narratives might falter, just slightly, in the face of skilful interactions with things that are not us. Small things. Swans, rivers, boats, currents, knotted loops of braided cotton string.

NESTBOXES

I ordered them on the internet; they arrived in two cardboard boxes packed with brown paper. Four rough brown bowls with truncated backs and tops fitted tight against right-angled plywood boards. Made from a mixture of concrete and wood fibre, each has a scoop cut out of the front. When they're fitted under the eaves of my new house, I'm hoping those scoops will be the point of entry for pairs of house martins, those delicate, orca-coloured migrant birds whose arrival is one of the milestones of north Palaearctic springs. They can build their own nests, of course, made of a thousand or so beakfuls of mud collected from local puddles and pond-edges and carefully pushed together, one by one, to dry. Last year's drought made their nest building difficult, and with catastrophic declines in their flying-insect food, their populations have been nosediving year on year. I bought these nestboxes to help birds in trouble. But only partly.

In India a few years ago I stayed in a hotel room that also held a pair of nesting laughing doves. The hotel was fine about it: the housekeeper put fresh newspaper on the floor each morning to catch the mess. They'd squeeze inside through a gap above the AC unit and fly to their nest with pattering wingbeats, and at night I'd watch their eyes blink closed as they fell asleep. It would have been less delightful if I'd been fearful or allergic to birds, but there seemed a grace and generosity to that quiet sharing of space which swelled my heart out of all proportion to the presence of birds in the room. It brought home to me how fiercely in Britain we are ridding our human spaces of everything that isn't us. None of us wants rats and cockroaches, but what of swifts? They need holes in eaves and under roof tiles to nest, and we're increasingly blocking them up. Sparrows like ivy-covered walls and thickets of bushes, but they're messy and no longer fashionable in gardens. And while it's illegal to destroy active birds' nests, developers have started netting trees and hedges to stop them from nesting at all. The recent furore about netted trees is testament that for now, at least, we still balk

193

at extending our zone of control outside of our gardens to things so obviously not ours.

On the web, you'll find martin nestboxes in the category of 'specialist' boxes, along with those for treecreepers, owls, swifts, dippers, grey wagtails and ducks. The kinds you can buy in any garden centre or hardware shop are far simpler: boxes with a round hole in the front for great tits and blue tits, and those with a half-open front for robins. These were the kind we put up in my childhood garden. We did it for the pleasure of having familiar birds raise a family in a home we'd supplied. I remember the curious thrill of seeing a prospecting great tit drop into the darkness of the box hung on the side of my house. It was a little flush of pride dangerously near possession. One spring my father built a backless nestbox and mounted it against the single glass window of our garden shed. Inside, a blackout curtain kept the nest dark. After school, my brother and I would creep inside, shut the door, lift the curtain and press our noses to the glass. What we saw was all secret: three inches of moss and feathers and, pressed deep into it, the back of an incubating blue tit, so close we could see the rising and falling of its breathing, the tiny feathers around its beak lit with the light falling through the hole above. The nest fledged successfully and later that spring we'd sit on the lawn hearing the begging calls of blue tit fledglings and think, *They're ours.* These days, nestboxes in gardens faintly remind me of the provision of workers' cottages on landed estates. Indeed, one nestbox pioneer was the eccentric nineteenth-century naturalist Charles Waterton, who installed sand martin nest pipes and other avian households at Walton Hall, his Yorkshire estate now famed as being perhaps Britain's first nature reserve.

In Britain, the class system inflects nestboxes as it does everything else. You can buy boxes that resemble scale models of pubs or churches, ones with poems or flowers painted on the front, or with tiny glued-on gates and picket fences. These are frowned upon by the gatekeepers of British nature appreciation, who recommend plain wooden ones. The Royal Society for the Protection of Birds explicitly warn against using decorative boxes in case their bright colours attract predators, even though they've admitted there's no real evidence for this. Yes, metal boxes are a bad idea because they can overheat nestlings, but a handwritten 'Home Sweet Home' isn't much of an issue when robins can and will nest happily in discarded teapots.

Like garden gnomes, decorative nestboxes fail to conform to the aesthetics of middle-class garden design. Making them cute and homely raises the spectre of anthropomorphism, something still anathema to bird protection organisations who in their earliest days battled for cultural capital by denying accusations of sentimentality and cleaving instead to hard ornithological science. Nestboxes are supposed to be for the birds, not us, in this view. There's a kind of performative largesse about the utilitarian ugliness of plain nestboxes in gardens, whereas decorative ones bespeak delight for people too. The birds don't care, of course. They really don't. And while my house martin nests aren't colourful, I am all about the personal enjoyment I hope they will bring me. I bought them because I want those birds here. I want their submarine chirrups to fall through the open windows while the late-spring evenings lengthen, want to watch their hawking flights to scoop flies from the burnished air. I want the mess, the drifting feathers, the small faces of youngsters peering down at me as I walk up to our own front door.

DEER IN THE HEADLIGHTS

The deer drift in and out of the trees like breathing. They appear unexpectedly delicate and cold, as if chill air is pouring from them to the ground to pool into the mist that half obscures their legs and turning flanks. They aren't tame: I can't get closer than a hundred yards before they slip into the gloom. I've been told these particular beasts are fallow deer of the menil variety, which means their usual darker tones have been leached by genetics to soft cuttlefish and ivory, and they're the descendants of a herd brought here in the sixteenth century as beasts of venery, creatures to be pursued and caught and cooked. The look of the estate hasn't changed much since then. It's still an extensive patchwork of pasture and forest – except now the M25 runs through it, six lanes of fast-moving traffic behind chain-link fence threaded with stripling trees. The mist thickens, the light falls, the deer appear and disappear, and the deep roar of the motorway burns inside my chest as I walk on to the bridge that spans it. This bridge is grassed along its length, and at dusk and dawn, I've been told, the deer use it as a thoroughfare from one side of the estate to the other. I know my presence will dissuade them from crossing so I don't want to stay too long, but I linger a little while to watch the torrent of lights beneath me. For a while the road doesn't seem real. Then it does, almost violently so, and at that moment the bridge and the woods behind me do not. I can't hold both in the same world at once. Deer and forest, mist, speed, a drift of wet leaves, white noise, scrap-metal trucks, a convoy of eighteen-wheelers, beads of water on the toes of my boots and the scald of my hands on the cold metal rail.

Deer occupy a unique place in my personal pantheon of animals. There are many creatures I know very little about, but the difference with deer is that I've never had any desire to find out more. They're like a distant country I've never wanted to visit. I know the names of different deer species, and can identify the commonest ones by sight, but I've always resisted the almost negligible effort it would take to discover when they give birth, how they grow and shed their antlers, what they eat, where and how they live. Standing on the bridge I'm wondering why that is.

Perhaps my feelings about deer might partly be down to their place in British culture. About five years ago, their images started appearing on soft furnishings and home-ware. Deer candles, deer drinking glasses, stag's-head wallpaper, prints of antlers on curtains and cushions, mock trophy heads stitched out of patchwork tartan. I was used to reindeer motifs all over Christmas, but this cervine proliferation was new. At the time, one design spokesman ascribed it to the British public's love of cosy country hotels and log fires in winter. But I suspect there was more to it than a yen for seasonal hotel atmospherics. The years following the financial crash of 2008 were marked by a growing glorification of myths of Englishness, ranging from a flourishing of books on the countryside and rural life to 'Keep Calm and Carry On' Second World War posters and chintz-printed aprons – and a strong shift towards political populism. When a country is hurting it so often grasps for ideas of itself in a longed-for past, and a simple motif like a stag's head can function like an upholstery button to pleat together a whole slew of useful meanings.

Deer tend to signify a conservative view of the world. I learned that in my twenties, at a time when I was spending a lot of time with hunters, mostly men, many of whom expressed a sneaking admiration for the antics of powerful stags who battled each other to take possession of harems of docile hinds. And it was around that time that I spent a rainy afternoon wandering around an exhibition of paintings by Edwin Landseer in a London gallery. The walls were hung with sad dogs, gleaming horses, various British game animals being torn to pieces, and numerous portraits of red deer stags that seemed the very type of elite Victorian manhood. These stags were grand and harried and very good at striking poses, Monarchs of the Glen whose fragile rule was perpetually threatened by upstarts, whose crowned heads were always lit perfectly by mountain sunlight, paragons of strength bound entire into unshakeable courses of action by virtue of being what they were.

The wash of traffic noise subsides as I leave the bridge to regain the path. It's too dark now to see the deer but I can hear the hollow thump of hooves trotting on sward and when I look behind me the motorway casts the palest, faintest glow behind the trees. Something about this place, I think, will solve the puzzle of my attitude to deer, and I'm beginning to understand that this puzzle isn't just about a type of mammal. It's about animals more generally, and what it might mean to not want to know more about them: a much bigger why.

I trudge back to the car, wondering whether motorists passing this place sometimes glance up and see a procession of antlers against the sky, a slow parade of ancient beasts walking across modern infrastructure. The thought brings to mind much older notions of deer, like the white stags that were Celtic emissaries from the underworld, or creatures in medieval romances whose appearances portended the beginning of a quest or great adventure. In this tradition they're slippery, spooky beings in possession of the deepest spiritual significance and their visitations are always a surprise. I think of one quiet, cold afternoon nearly twenty years ago when I was glumly traipsing through a small wood near my parents' house musing on the shape of my life and finding it sorely wanting. As I approached a tangle of briars growing over a fallen tree I saw a small, slow curl of smoke rising from behind it, glowing palely on its ascent through rays of winter sunlight. It was exceptionally unsettling. I moved closer and was treated to more incomprehensibility; a sweeping arc of something like upraised bone, something skeletal behind the leaves, and then the resting fallow buck whose rising breath I had been watching leapt up and crashed away into the trees. My heart kicked and raced and for a long while afterwards the wood seemed made anew, fretted with rich possibility, and for a long while after that my life also.

Not knowing very much about deer has made my encounters with them less like encounters with real animals and more like tableaux of happenstance, symbolism and emotion. My ignorance, I think, has been purposive. It has been me saying: *I wish there was more magic in the world.* And then the deer have appeared to say, *Here it is.* This is what deer are for me. They stand for the natural world's capacity to surprise and derail my expectations. And I have wanted them to do that more than I have wanted them to be anything else.

Driving home in the dark I know I've reached this understanding because of the geography of the place I've just visited, its conjunction of asphalt and trucks and deer.

For the capacity of deer to surprise, to hijack the quotidian, is not merely a matter of legend or of remote and ethereal speculation. It is a blunt fact, bloody and frequently deadly, and it happens so often there's an acronym for it: DVC, which stands for deer–vehicle collision. Thankfully, it has only ever been an almost, for me.

A few years ago, driving a downhill curve at night, I saw a deer in the road in front of me, stark and tense with shock, and then the deer lofted itself into the air, bright and somehow motionless, like the etiolated horses with outstretched legs in eighteenth-century hunting prints. A blooming scald spread under my skin and the car felt as light as if it were sliding on water, even before I braked. What I remember most about that endless moment apart from the blind heat of it was the angular neatness of hind hocks and ankles, and the deer's hard landing against the hedge, the way it shoved itself into that cross-hatched, thorny difficulty before disappearing. And all the rest of that journey I saw nothing but deer crossing the road where there were no deer at all.

Deer are dangerous animals. In America around two hundred people die every year after their vehicles collide with them, and while official figures put the number of DVCs at about one and a half million, it's likely much higher, for many go unrecorded. The correct advice for drivers encountering a deer in the road is never to swerve, for most human deaths occur when people wrench the wheel away, hit trees, rocks, fences, other cars. But how can you not? There it is, right in front of you, cut out of black and surrounded by a suffused halo of reflected light, a beating heart the size of a fist in a hundred, a hundred and fifty pounds of pearl and terror. It's coming towards you at fifty, sixty miles an hour. How can you do anything else?

If you live in places prone to DVCs you can buy deer alerts: small whistles for the exterior of your vehicle that are supposed to warn deer of your impending arrival. Some drivers swear by them, but it might just be that knowing the alert is there makes you drive differently, perhaps a little more slowly, a little more defensively, a little readier to expect a deer to appear in your path, because I've read that there's no statistical proof that they have any effect and deer may not be able to hear them at all. They're tech solutions that work like nazar, those dangling blue and white glass charms against the curse of the evil eye.

It happened to my friend Isabella. She is an artist, and a truly excellent one. When I first met her she was gilding pieces of fresh fruit to make art of their slow collapse over the coming months into corrugated, shining nuggets. I asked her, 'You hit a deer. What was that like?' She drew her eyebrows together, just a little. 'It was like a collision with the divine,' she said. 'You've read Euripides, right?' I said, 'Yes. I have.' She said, again, 'Well. It was a collision with the divine.' Turning on to a fast road at night, lights shone in her eyes from a car in the wrong place. That car had already hit a red deer she couldn't see. It was lying right across the carriageway. 'I drove over it,' she said, shivering with the recollection of the rise and sink of the car's traverse, feeling the give of flesh and the cracking architecture of ribs. The deer may already have been dead, or perhaps was only stunned, but it was opened up by the weight of her car, which sent a wave of blood across the wet road. Her headlights shone on it. "There was so much blood,' she said. She leaned forward when she told me this, her eyes on mine. 'So. Much. Blood.' She told me she could smell the terror of her daughter sitting in the seat next to her. The air around the car that night was foggy, yellow with sodium street-lamps, and there was, there was this sheet of blood running in front of the car for what seemed for ever.

'Was it like *The Shining*?' I asked.

She looked at me levelly, as if I'd not heard a word she'd told me.

'It was much worse.'

Roads belong to us. We don't expect things that aren't us to interact with them, to cross from their territory into our own, and with such brute physicality. Even if you escape unscathed, the effect of a DVC can be life-changing. You can see something of that in the way they are handled in the movies, where they're scripted narrative shocks, horror-movie jumps, choice *dei ex machina* that derail narratives as they total cars. Sometimes the deer breaks through the windscreen. There'll be blood, antlers that fill the car like candelabras, and the dying stag will have its eyes fixed on the character to whom this event has the deepest significance. Sometimes, in movies, the deer lies on the road in the aftermath of the DVC. If the deer is on the road, and the deer is not dead – and it is not very often dead in Hollywood – there's the matter of how to deal with this. Often it will be making noises that dying deer don't make. It will be an animatronic deer, for there are companies in Hollywood who will take a dead deer, skin it, flense it of fat, cure it, lay it over a form that contains a mechanism that, once covered with skin, will mimic the slow in and out of breath. DVCs on screen cast a fierce, traumatic light on the innermost hearts of the characters with the bad luck to experience them. And that is often what they do in reality, too.

All of us know at heart that driving is always challenging fate. We are just very good at pretending it isn't. A deer in the road is part of the wager we all make and do our best to forget when we drive, as we make our way through life. DVC survivors often maintain that everything changed after the accident, that their life felt recast into something more precious and precarious than before. The deepest ramifications of the DVC are tied intimately to their sense of who they are; they speak of the collision as an event that does not admit the secular, the random, the rational. Often they will not speak of it at all. 'The car was destroyed,' they'll say, or, 'The windscreen was smashed', as if mentioning the other participant in the collision was taboo. And that one line, over and over again: 'It came out of nowhere.' Fate comes up out of nowhere in the headlights glowing like a goddamned unicorn, and whatever meaning drivers choose to take from the collision falls upon them as inescapably as any medieval allegory. *Look at yourself,* says the DVC, cutting through all that is quotidian, cutting it all away. *Look at yourself. Here you really are.* The old dramatists called that moment of self-understanding anagnorisis.

Most DVCs occur between nightfall and midnight, and again in the small hours before dawn. That's when deer are moving, but also when we are most prone to oneiric states of mind. Driving in dusk and darkness is a perfect dream of solipsism. Headlights unspool into rises and curves and bulks of fences and passing houses; you call these things into momentary existence, smear them with light and mass before they are gone. And because everything you see is ceaselessly pulled towards and under you, it's easy to fall prey to the illusion that you are stationary and the world is flowing into you. The fractional somatic forces the terrain exerts, the ghostly burr of the road surface, the small forces of corners and hills are things you feel in your physical frame and the liquids of your ears. And this all means that if a deer appears in front of you, it can feel more than a surprise; it can seem as if some part of you called it into existence, as if it were fashioned by your subconscious mind.

Since returning from the deer forest, my own subconscious mind is full of DVCs. I have tightened my hands on the wheel in anxious anticipation of disaster as I drive through rural woods. At night I've dreamed of roads, of mist, of slicks of oil printed with hoofmarks, windscreens crazed by impacts, herds of running deer. I mention this strange new preoccupation to a friend in an email. 'Are you OK?' they reply. 'Is something bad happening in your life?' I write back and say, 'I'm fine; I think I want to write about deer collisions, is all.' They have a suggestion: 'Have you checked YouTube? You know there are *actual supercuts*?' Of course there are. I don't want to watch them, just as I don't want to watch videos of other traumatic events that are clickable currency on the internet, things far worse than the accidental coincidence of a deer with an offside fender. But I sit down, find one of the videos and press play.

The video is made of dashcam footage from many different vehicles edited into a long montage of DVCs. The first thing it makes me think of is first-person shooter video gameplay, with deer bursting into view so unexpectedly they seem ghostly artefacts on the screen – until they hit metal. It happens again. Another hit. Another cut. Now dusk, the lights of a gas station, the murmur of talk radio. A roe deer colliding with the car, turning over and over in the air before it lands deadweight on the grassy verge. The car slows and halts. A woman gets out. She wears a blue fringed top and a woollen shrug pulled over her shoulders. She walks to where the deer lies, looks down, looks back at the driver, raises both hands, palms up, in a gesture of helplessness. The driver gets out, shoulders set, ignores the deer and leans down to examine the front of his car. Another vehicle, another overheard conversation, another collision, another dashcam dislodged from the dashboard to point upwards at stricken faces. I pause the video, get up, pace about the kitchen. I sit back down, watch some more, stop again. It's getting harder to continue. Sometimes the deer leaps high over the hood of the car and escapes all harm; most often it does not, and it will fall lengthways onto the bonnet and slide down, or smash the windscreen, or spin balletically away in parabolae of antlers and flesh and bone. I see the puff of fur as a fender makes contact, hear the click of hooves hitting steel. What most surprises me as I watch this repeated, terrible carnage is how high the deer are thrown in the air. Ten, twelve, twenty feet, tumbling end over end, limp and pathetic. Towards the end of the video I start reading the comments beneath it. I expect them to be grim and they are. 'Cool ragdoll physics,' says one. Another suggests that deer have very low IQs. Another thinks deer are suicidal. 'Am I the only one who thinks it's funny when they B O U N C E off of the cars?' The answer is no. 'Oh man,' writes another, 'I haven't laughed this hard at a compilation in a long time, great job seriously.'

I don't laugh. I sit very still. It takes me a long while to work out how upset I am. My pet parrot understands what I'm feeling faster than I do; he jumps from his perch on the back of a chair, runs along the tabletop and snuggles against my forearm, extending his soft feathery neck to nibble gently at the back of my hand.

I've witnessed a series of extremely violent deaths, and the bodies of deer are sufficiently large that they can't help but remind us of our own. But I don't think that's the reason for my upset, not entirely. The tone of the comments is perturbing,

211

but pretty much par for the course on the internet. Besides, inappropriate laughter is not an unusual response to emotional difficulty. No, my upset is more about how the commentators view the deer as obstacles to progress like the random antagonists in videogames; things that have consequential presence but no meaningful existence in and of themselves. And that's when I realise that most of my upset is directed at myself.

I've valued deer for their capacity to surprise and delight me, which is why I've resisted learning more about them. The more you know about something, the less it can surprise you. But it's hard to feel sympathy with a thing whose reality you have chosen to ignore, which makes my attitude not so very different from those who would write approvingly of the physics of a dying deer, or how the best thing about a deer collision is how funny it can be. Deer–vehicle collisions have gripped me so tightly because they are my own attitude to deer writ large and covered in blood and tattered fur and broken glass: everything about them is made of deer being surprising, deer derailing our expectations of the world. I sit at the table and think of deer that die because they have no conception of the nature of roads. Deer that die because they are creatures with their own lives, their own haunts and paths and thoughts and needs. I don't think I could ever laugh at the sight of a deer being hit by a car. But I have not been innocent. I close the You-Tube window, go to a website that sells second-hand natural history books. I buy a book called *Understanding Deer.*

The Falcon and the Tower

I'm standing on cracked asphalt by a high-security fence at the eastern edge of Ireland. The sky is cold pewter, the salt wind bitter. Though I've come all the way here to watch wildlife I've just turned my back on the only birds I can see. The miles of sand behind me have been washed by the Irish Sea into a perfect blankness, pearled with gulls and flocks of migrant waders. It's beautiful. But my friends Hilary and Eamonn have told me to look instead at Dublin's Poolbeg Power Station, a giant's playset of brutal turbine halls facing the shining sands. Set amid sewage works, derelict redbrick buildings, wharves, cranes and shipping containers, this is a bizarre spot for a wildlife pilgrimage. Two decommissioned cooling chimneys tower above us, marked with vertical washes of rust and horizontal bands of red and white. Rising from the horizon, they are your first sight of Ireland if you arrive from the east by sea and the last when you leave. Visible throughout the city, they have come to mean home for a whole generation of Dubliners – and for the peregrine falcons that have nested on them for years.

For a while, not much happens. We watch flocks of pigeons clattering about the roofline in shadowless winter light. My face grows numb with cold. Then, below the chimneys, a pigeon cartwheels like a thrown firework through a broken window into the darkness beyond. There is something horrible about its descent. Had it been shot? Had some kind of fit? It takes me a little while to work out that the pigeon was trying to get inside as fast as possible, and it's then I know that the falcons have come.

A narrow black anchor appears, falling fast towards the west chimney as if on an invisible zip wire. Seeing something alive descending to earth at such speed brings a hitch to my throat. A faint, echoing call drifts towards us, the unlikely *ee-chip, ee-chip* of a swinging, unoiled door. It is the male, the tiercel. He swerves, spreads his wings wide to brake and alights upon the rail by a nestbox that has been fixed to a metal walkway a hundred feet above. He shakes his feathers into place and sits looking towards the estuary, flat-headed, an inverted bullet shape black against the sky.

'Do you want to see?' Eamonn says, gesturing to his telescope. Through the device, the falcon is oddly two-dimensional, rippling in the bright circle as if seen through water, and my eyes ache as I try to focus on small points of sharpness: the barred feathers of his chest, his black hood, a faint chromatic fringe ghosting him with suggestions of dust and rainbows. He's exquisite, the colour of smoke, paper and wet ash. He starts preening his feathers, puffs out his belly, half closes his eyes, angles his head back to zip single scapulars through his neat, curved beak. Gusts of wind rising up the chimney face blow his feathers the wrong way. His talons are curled around rusting steel. The wind has ice in it. He looks utterly at home.

This perch gives him vantage on miles of hunting territory: estuary, docks, city streets, parks and golf courses. The divisions between those things are of little consequence to him. But they are to us. What we are watching is a small, feathered rebuke to our commonplace notion that nature exists only in places other than our own, an assumption that seems always one step towards turning our back on the natural world,

216

abandoning it as something disappearing or already lost.

For much of the twentieth century, falcons were celebrated as romantic icons of threatened wilderness. The mountains and waterfall gorges where they chose to nest were sublime sites where visitors could contemplate nature and meditate on the brevity of human existence. But there's a romanticism to industrial ruins too. The rusting chimneys and broken windows of the Poolbeg site have their own troubling beauty, that of things that have outlasted their use. Falcons haunt landscapes that speak to us of mortality: mountains, by virtue of their eternity; industrial ruins, by virtue of their reminding us that this, too, in time will be gone, and that we should protect what is here and now.

Perhaps the peregrine is becoming the imagined essence of landscapes like these. When Eamonn was a child, he went with his father to search for peregrines in the Wicklow Mountains because books told him they nested on cliffs and crags. He saw none at all. His first wild peregrine was sitting high on a Dublin gasometer. Falcons have nested on tall buildings for centuries, but the rise of urban peregrines is a relatively recent phenomenon. In the 1950s and '60s, the pesticide DDT sent peregrine populations into free fall across Europe and North America, before it was gradually banned. As their numbers recovered, peregrines moved into cities, lured by flocks of feral pigeons. In the eastern United States, no wild falcons remained, so Cornell University's Peregrine Fund released captive-bred birds from artificial nests on towers and tall buildings to repopulate their former range. Traditional nest sites on cliffs were deemed too dangerous: lacking parents to protect them, inexperienced youngsters fell prey to great horned owls. When grown, these falcons gravitated to buildings and bridges, searching for nest sites that resembled their own. Additional release programmes followed.

Today peregrines have become a familiar sight in cities. New York has about twenty breeding pairs, London around twenty-five. Nesting on high-rises, coursing pigeons through city streets, they have developed novel behaviours in response to their surroundings. Some have learned to hunt at night, ascending into darkness to grab birds lit from beneath by streetlights. Urban environments are not without risk: the sheer sides, reflective glass and unexpected gusts of wind around tall buildings can result in crash-landings when young birds take their first flights, and dedicated locals who follow the lives of particular pairs through binoculars, telescopes or webcams sometimes intervene to rescue grounded birds from traffic. Even so, peregrine populations are growing in cities. Perched high on corporate headquarters, scanning the sky and streets below, the falcons can readily be viewed as reflections of our own fascination with vision, surveillance and power. But falcons are not merely handy symbols for human anxieties. Their greatest magic is that they're not human at all.

Eamonn comes to this site in Dublin nearly every day and has been doing so for years. He started watching the Poolbeg peregrines after a personal bereavement because it 'was . . . *away*', he told me. I understood what he meant. At times of difficulty, watching birds ushers you into a different world, where no words need be spoken. And if you're watching urban falcons, this is not a distant world, but one alongside you, a place of transient and graceful refuge. These days, working in Dublin, Eamonn keeps one eye on the sky, scanning churches and city towers. Up there, he sees falcons looking down on the streets below. 'Bits of eternity,' he calls them. Sometimes he sees one speeding overhead, a black silhouette over Temple Bar or the Olympia Theatre. In an instant, his city is transformed. Buildings become cliffs, streets canyons.

Time passes. The tiercel has gone. Now the female appears on the edge of the nest-box. She is larger and paler than her mate. For a minute or two, she sits undecided, looking about. Then she opens her wings, wheels and glides down towards the other chimney. I raise my binoculars, wincing at the difficulty of focusing them with frozen hands. I see her wings flex and her primaries flare. She turns slowly in mid-air. There is a change in the quality of her flight. I'm not sure what it is. Then with a skip of the heart, I see an incautious pigeon flying low towards her, flapping in a leisurely manner. It can't have seen her. But she has seen it. The world shrinks to the space between the two birds. I hear an intake of breath from my companions as she sideslips and falls towards it with the finality of a rock flung from a bridge. The stricken pigeon dodges, closes its wings and drops to last-minute safety in the buildings below. The falcon circles, climbs and disappears inland.

We take the binoculars from our eyes and look at one another. We have all been reminded that a day can be cut in two by three seconds of a hunting peregrine and leave you stilled into silence and the memory of each curve of its flight. I'd swear, if I were of a more mystical persuasion, that a hunting peregrine changes the quality of the atmosphere it flies through, makes it heavier. Like thunder. Like slowed-down film in which the grain shows through. The Poolbeg site is about as far as you can get from a thriving natural ecosystem, but the act of watching a falcon chase its prey above the scarred and broken ground below feels like quiet resistance against despair. Matters of life and death and a sense of our place in the world tied fast together in a shiver of wings across a scrap of winter sky.

Vesper Flights

I found a dead swift once, a husk of a bird under a bridge over the River Thames, where sunlight from the water cast bright scribbles on the arches above. I picked it up, held it in my palm, saw the dust in its feathers, its wings crossed like dull blades, its eyes tight closed, and realised that I didn't know what to do. This was a surprise. Encouraged by books, I'd always been the type of Gothic amateur naturalist who preserved interesting bits of the dead. I cleaned and polished fox skulls; disarticulated, dried and kept the wings of road-killed birds. But I knew, looking at the swift, that I could not do anything like that to it. The bird was suffused with a kind of seriousness very akin to holiness. I didn't want to leave it there, so I took it home, swaddled it in a towel and tucked it in the freezer. It was in early May the following year, as soon as I saw the first returning swifts flowing down from the clouds, that I knew what I had to do. I went to the freezer, took out the swift, and buried it in the garden one hand's-width deep in earth newly warmed by the sun.

Swifts are magical in the manner of all things that exist just a little beyond understanding. Once they were called 'devil birds', perhaps because those screaming flocks of black crosses around churches seemed pulled from darkness, not light. But to me they are creatures of the upper air, and of their nature unintelligible, which makes them more akin to angels. Unlike all other birds they never descend to the ground. As a bird-obsessed child, I was frustrated that there was no way for me to know them better. They were so fast it was impossible to focus on their facial expressions or watch them preen through binoculars. They were only ever flickering silhouettes at twenty, thirty, forty miles an hour, a shoal of birds, a pouring sheaf of identical black grains against bright clouds. There was no way to tell one bird from another, nor to watch them do anything other than move from place to place, although sometimes, if the swifts were flying low over rooftops, I'd see one open its mouth, and that was truly uncanny, because the gape was huge, turning the bird into something uncomfortably like a miniature basking shark. Even so, watching them with the naked eye was rewarding in how it revealed the dynamism of what before was merely blankness. Swifts weigh about forty grams, and their surfing and tacking against the pressures of oncoming air make visible the movings of the atmosphere.

They still seem to me the closest things to aliens on Earth. I've seen them up close now, held a live grounded adult in my hands before letting it fall back into the sky. You know those deep-sea fish dragged by nets from fathoms of blackness, how obvious it is that they aren't supposed to exist where we are? The adult swift was like that in reverse. Its frame was tough and spare and its feathers bleached by the sun. Its eyes seemed unable to focus on me, as if it were an entity from an alternate universe whose senses couldn't quite map on to our phenomenal world. Time ran differently for this creature. If you record swifts' high-pitched, insistent screaming and slow it down to human speed you can hear what their voices sound like as they speak to one another: a wild, bubbling, rising and falling call, something like the song of northern loons.

■ ■ ■ ■

Often, during stressful times when I was small – while changing schools, when bullied, or after my parents had argued – I'd lie in bed before I fell asleep and count in my head all the different layers between me and the centre of the Earth: crust, upper mantle, lower mantle, outer core, inner core. Then I'd think upwards in expanding rings of thinning air: troposphere, stratosphere, mesosphere, thermosphere, exosphere. A few miles beneath me was molten rock, a few miles above limitless dust and vacancy, and there I'd lie with the warm blanket of the troposphere over me and a red cotton duvet cover too, and the smell of tonight's dinner lingering upstairs, and downstairs the sound of my mother busy at her typewriter.

This evening ritual wasn't a test of how much I could keep in my mind at once, or of how far I could send my imagination. It had something of the power of incantation, but it did not seem a compulsion, and it was not a prayer. No matter how tightly the day's bad things had gripped me, there was so much up there above me, so much below, so many places and states that were implacable, unreachable, entirely uninterested in human affairs. Listing them one by one built imaginative sanctuary between walls of unknowing knowns. It helped in other ways, too. Sleeping was like losing time, somehow like not being alive, and drifting into it at night there sometimes came a panic that I might not find my way back from wherever I had gone. My own private vespers felt a little like counting the steps up a flight of steep stairs. I needed to know where I was. It was a way of bringing me home.

Swifts nest in obscure places, in dark and cramped spaces: hollows beneath roof tiles, behind the intakes for ventilation shafts, in the towers of churches. To reach them they fly straight at the entrance holes and enter at full tilt. Their nests are made of things snatched from the air: strands of dried grass pulled aloft by thermals; moulted pigeon-breast feathers; flower petals, leaves, scraps of paper, even butterflies. During the war, swifts in Denmark and Italy grabbed chaff, reflective scraps of tinfoil dropped from aircraft to confuse enemy radar, flashing and twirling as it fell. They mate on the wing. And while young martins and swallows return to their nests after their first flights, young swifts do not. As soon as they tip themselves free of the nest hole, they start flying, and they will not stop flying for two or three years, bathing in rain, feeding on airborne insects, winnowing fast and low to scoop fat mouthfuls of water from lakes and rivers. European swifts spend only a few months on their breeding grounds, another few months in winter over the forests and fields of the Congo, and the rest of the time they're moving, making a mockery of borders. To avoid heavy rain, which makes it impossible for them to feed, swifts with nests in English roofs will fly clockwise around low-pressure systems, travelling across Europe and back again. They love to assemble in the complicated, unstable air behind weather depressions to feast upon the abundance of insects there. They depart us quietly. In the second week of August the skies around my home are suddenly empty, after which I'll see the occasional single straggler and think, *That's it. That's the last one,* and hungrily watch it rise and glide through turbulent summer air.

On warm summer evenings swifts that aren't sitting on eggs or tending their chicks fly low and fast, screaming in speeding packs around rooftops and spires. Later, they gather higher in the sky, their calls now so attenuated by air and distance that to the ear they corrode into something that seems less than sound, to suspicions of dust and glass. And then, all at once, as if summoned by a call or a bell, they rise higher and higher until they disappear from view. These ascents are called vespers flights, or vesper flights, after the Latin *vesper* for evening. Vespers are evening devotional prayers, the last and most solemn of the day, and I have always thought 'vesper flights' the most beautiful phrase, an ever-falling blue. For years I've tried to see them do it. But always the dark got too deep, or the birds skated too wide and far across the sky for me to follow.

For years we thought vesper flights were simply swifts flying higher up to sleep on the wind. Like other birds, they can close one eye and put half of their brain to sleep, with the other half awake and the other eye open for flight. But it's likely that swifts properly sleep up there too, drift into REM states where both eyes are closed and flying is automatic, at least for short periods. During the First World War, a French aviator on special night operations cut his engine at ten thousand feet and glided down in silent, close circles over enemy lines, a light wind against him, the full moon overhead. 'We suddenly found ourselves,' he wrote, 'among a strange flight of birds which seemed to be motionless, or at least showed no noticeable reaction. They were widely scattered and only a few yards below the aircraft, showing up against a white sea of cloud underneath.'

He had flown into a small party of swifts in deep sleep, miniature black stars illuminated by the reflected light of the moon. He managed to catch two – I know this is impossible, but I like to imagine that he or his navigator simply stretched out a hand and picked them gently from the air – and one swift was pulled dead from the engine after the flight returned to earth. The remote air, the coldness, the stillness, and the high birds over white cloud suspended in sleep. It's an image that drifts in and out of my dreams.

No longer do I conjure the stratifications of earth and air as I go to sleep. Instead, I play an audiobook on my phone, set it on my bedside table and let the whisper and catch of the narrator's voice turn to white noise as I drift away. Hearing the same words spoken by the same voices over and over again is a habit that began after my father died, when letting my attention wander as I dozed took me to places I didn't want to go, towards matters of whys and wheres and hows and what-ifs. Listening to mystery novels was a perfect distraction, and to begin with I'd be caught up in their plots. But after a few weeks of repeats, what I learned to love most of all was the soft predictability of each oncoming line, the comfort of knowing the words about to be spoken. I started this night-time ritual over a decade ago, and I'm finding it hard to shake the habit.

In the summer of 1979 an aviator, ecologist and expert in the science of aircraft bird-strikes called Luit Buurma began making radar observations in the Netherlands for flight safety purposes. His plots showed vast flocks of birds over the wide waters of the IJsselmeer that turned out to be swifts from Amsterdam and the surrounding region. Every evening in June and July they flew towards the lake, and between nine and ten o'clock they hawked low over the water to feed upon swarms of freshwater midges. Just after ten they began to rise, until fifteen minutes later all were more than six hundred feet high, gathered together in dense, wheeling flocks. Then the ascent began: five minutes later they were out of sight, and their vesper flights took them to heights of up to eight thousand feet. Using a special data processor linked to a large military air-defence radar in the north of Friesland to more closely study their movements, Buurma discovered that swifts weren't staying up there to sleep. In the hours after midnight they came down once again to feed over the water. It turns out that swifts, beloved *genii locorum* of bright summer streets, are just as much nocturnal creatures of thick summer darkness.

But he made another discovery: swifts weren't just making vesper flights in the evenings. They made them again just before dawn. Twice a day, when light levels exactly mirror each other, swifts rise and reach the apex of their flights at nautical twilight.

Since Buurma's observations, other scientists have studied these ascents and speculated on their purpose. Adriaan Dokter, an ecologist with a background in physics, has used Doppler weather radar to find out more about this phenomenon. He and his co-workers have written that swifts might be profiling the air as they rise through it, gathering information on air temperature and the speed and direction of the wind. Their vesper flights take them to the top of what is called the *convective boundary layer*. The CBL is the humid, hazy part of the atmosphere where the ground's heating by the sun produces rising and falling convective currents, blossoming thermals of hot air; it's the zone of fair-weather cumulus clouds and everyday life for swifts. Once swifts crest the top of this layer, they are exposed to a flow of wind that's unaffected by the landscape below but is determined instead by the movements of large-scale weather systems. By flying to these heights, swifts cannot only see the distant clouds of oncoming frontal systems on the twilit horizon, but use the wind itself to assess the possible future courses of these systems. What they are doing is forecasting the weather.

And they are doing more. As Dokter writes, migratory birds orient themselves through a complex of interacting compass mechanisms. During vesper flights, swifts have access to them all. At this panoptic height they can see the scattered patterns of the stars overhead, and at the same time they can calibrate their magnetic compasses, getting their bearings according to the light polarisation patterns that are strongest and clearest in twilit skies. Stars, wind, polarised light, magnetic cues, the distant rubble of clouds a hundred miles out, clear cold air, and below them the hush of a world tilting towards sleep or waking towards dawn.

What they are doing is flying so high they can work out exactly where they are, to know what they should do next. They're quietly, perfectly, orienting themselves.

Cecilia Nilsson of the Cornell Laboratory of Ornithology and her team have discovered that swifts don't make these flights alone. They ascend as flocks every evening before singly drifting down, while in the morning they fly up alone and return to earth together. To orient themselves correctly, to make the right decisions, they need to pay attention not only to the cues of the world around them, but also to each other. Nilsson writes that it's likely that swifts on their vesper flights are working according to what is called the *many-wrongs principle*. That is, they're averaging all their individual assessments in order to reach the best navigational decision. If you're in a flock, decisions about what to do next are improved if you exchange information with those around you. We can speak to each other. Swifts have no voices, but what they can do is pay attention to what other swifts are doing. And in the end it can be as simple as this: they follow each other.

The realm of my own life is the quotidian, the everyday. It's where I sleep and eat and work and think. It's a space of rising and falling hopes and worries, costs and benefits, plans and distractions, and it can batter and divert me, just as high winds and rainfall send swifts off course. Sometimes it's a hard place to be, but it's home.

Thinking about swifts has made me think more carefully about the ways in which I've dealt with difficulty. When I was small I comforted myself with thoughts of layers of rising air; later I hid myself among the whispers of recorded works of fiction. We all have our defences. Some of them are self-defeating, but others are occasions for joy: the absorption of a hobby, the writing of a poem, speeding on a Harley, the slow assembly of a collection of records or seaside shells. 'The best thing for being sad,' said T. H. White's Merlin, 'is to learn something.' All of us have to live our lives most of the time inside the protective structures that we have built; none of us can bear too much reality. We need our books, our craft projects, our dogs and knitting, our movies, gardens and gigs. It's who we are. We're held together by our lives, our interests, and all our chosen comforts. But we can't have *only* those things, because then we can't work out where we should be headed.

Swifts aren't always cresting the atmospheric boundary layer at dizzying heights; most of the time they are living below it in thick and complicated air. That's where they feed and mate and bathe and drink and *are*. But to find out about the important things that will affect their lives, they must go higher to survey the wider scene, and there communicate with others about the larger forces impinging on their realm. So I'm starting to think of swifts differently now, not as angels or aliens, but as perfectly instructive creatures. Not all of us need to make that climb, just as many swifts eschew their vesper flights because they are occupied with eggs and young – but as a community, surely some of us are required, by dint of flourishing life and the well-being of us all, to look clearly at the things that are so easily obscured by the everyday. The things we need to set our courses towards or against. The things we need to think about to know what we should do next. Swifts are my fable of community, teaching us about how to make right decisions in the face of oncoming bad weather, in the face of clouds that sit like dark rubble on our own horizon.

IN SPIGHT OF PRISONS

There's a species of summer magic I chase every year. It's small, fierce and insistently beautiful, and my best chance of seeing it is on hot nights in June and July. Tonight I'm searching for it in a disused chalk quarry on the outskirts of my university town, an eerie, lunar landscape of towering white cliffs and patches of bare ground resembling snow-fields strewn with bones. This is a nature reserve – one of only three UK sites where moon carrots grow – and it is crowded with life. Green longhorn moths the colour of stained gold velvet decorate pale scabious flowers; rabbits graze in drifts of trefoil, kidney vetch and thyme. The evening air is full of huge wood-coloured beetles with handlebar antennae, hooked feet and wildly erratic flights: cockchafers. I feel small, insistent tugs as they get entangled in my hair and impatiently comb them free with my fingers. I've not come here for them;

I'm waiting for something else, and it's nearly time. With a little thrill of anticipation I see that light is fading fast. By ten o'clock the last snowy glow has faded from the cliffs, replaced by thin starlight and a soft, mothy blackness. And then the magic begins.

Twenty feet away a point of intense light winks into existence. Over there, another. And another: tiny motes of cold fire mapping a sparse starfield over the ground. I walk up to one, kneel and peer carefully at the otherworldly brilliance. It comes from the tail end of a small, elongated, wingless beetle, clutching hold of a stem of grass and waving its abdomen in the air. It, and the lights around me, are glow-worms, *Lampyris noctiluca,* things both sublime and ridiculous: half intimations of remote stellar distance and half waggling beetle bums.

Only female glow-worms shine like this. They can't eat, drink or fly, but spend their days burrowed deep in stems and under debris, emerging after twilight, when the light drops to around 0.1 lux, to clamber up plant stems and glow to attract the smaller, winged males. Once mated, the females extinguish their light, lay fifty to a hundred and fifty small, spherical, faintly luminous eggs, and die. Their adult lives are short and made of light – but in their two years as larvae they are creatures of macabre darkness, using their proboscises to inject snails with paralysing, dissolving neurotoxins before sucking them up like soup.

Kneeling by this glow-worm and transfixed by its light, this encounter in the summer night feels more like the workings of magic than chemistry, though I know that the light is the result of a reaction when the enzyme luciferase acts upon a compound called luciferin in the presence of oxygen, ATP and magnesium. The precise mechanism of their cold luminescence long puzzled natural philosophers. In the seventeenth century Robert Boyle found that the glow was extinguished if they were kept in a vacuum – and went on to muse that the light of his experimental glow-worms, trapped behind glass, was akin to 'certain truths' that shine freely 'in spight of prisons'. In the early nineteenth century, John Murray conducted laborious experiments on Shropshire glow-worms, placing their luminous parts in water heated to various temperatures, or in acid, naphtha, oil or spirits. His accounts of these faintly gruesome experiments are almost as magical as his subjects. One specimen glowed for several nights when suspended in olive oil. 'Viewed at a distance of about 10 feet, it twinkled like a fixed star,' he recounted, while 'the eye steadily and tranquilly observed the beautiful phenomenon'. It is hard to write about glow-worms without recourse to metaphors of stars and lamps; their singular light populates myriad works of literature. These are the creatures of an 'ineffectual fire' in *Hamlet* and the 'living lamps' of Marvell's *Mower to the Glow-Worms,* courteous beasts who guide wanderers home to safety.

Glow-worms prefer chalky, limestone habitats and you can find them on old railway lines and embankments, in cemeteries, hedgerows and gardens. But no one knows how many there are in Britain; they often go unnoticed because their light is easily obscured by headlights and torches. Certainly they are threatened by habitat degradation and urban development – males are attracted to streetlights and brightly lit windows, and this particular colony survives partly because the sodium glow of the surrounding town is blocked by quarry walls. Because the females do not fly, colonies are often venerable in age and easily rendered extinct: it is hard for them to move. But where they are known, colonies are often guarded passionately, and glow-worm tours and walks have become a

239

much-loved summer's-night tradition in many parts of the country: local experts guiding visitors around the natural light show, often with drinks and snacks laid on.

We live in a world of distracting, endless glowing screens, but even so these shining, tiny beacons retain an allure that draws people out in droves to stand and wonder. It is hard in these days of ecological ruination to find ways to reconnect people to a natural world more commonly encountered on television and video than in its living reality. The greatest magic of these shining beacons that draw people out in hordes to stand and wonder is that it cannot be meaningfully captured on film. Glow-worms are part of our hidden countryside; like Marvell's living lamps, they are still able to guide distracted wanderers.

SUN BIRDS AND CASHMERE SPHERES

I only saw them once. I didn't know I'd never see them again. I assumed they'd be eternal, like Pan Am, and the Soviet Union, and so many other things in the world that existed when I was born. I went out early that morning, sun glowing faintly through stratus, and drove north-west until shapes rose syrup-slow on the far horizon. They looked like buildings, like aircraft hangars or warehouses, but they were stands of poplars planted in the 1950s by Bryant & May, the safety match manufacturers. Disposable plastic lighters and cheaper wood imports turned the trees into economic relics. But these plantations were beloved of birders because they were the only place in the country you could see breeding golden orioles. They were legendary birds. I'd read about them for years. They're dazzlingly pretty – the males buttercup yellow with shiny black wings and a strawberry-red beak, the females soft olive green – but much of their glamour came from their rarity. If you live somewhere other than Britain, you might see orioles all the time. There are many in the Americas, and golden orioles are common garden birds in countries across the Palaearctic. But in Britain we only had this one tiny outpost.

I'd arranged to meet my guide by the entry gate. I'd never met him before, but there wasn't much doubt that he was the man in a woollen hat waving at me with a pair of binoculars. Peter was a friend of a friend, an expert on these orioles, and he had, it turned out, been sleeping in his car all night on site waiting for daylight. He told me I'd missed the bitterns booming in the reed beds at dawn, that it was the strangest of sounds, like someone blowing across the top of a deep and wide-necked bottle. But, he continued, the orioles were still singing. And as we walked down the dew-soaked track towards the wood, I heard them, fluting, rich, melodic phrases that cut across distance and the rattle of leaves and the loud chatter of singing reed warblers as if they were drifting in from an impossibly remote place. That place, I realised, might be the past, the birds speaking of history.

Chaucer wrote of a bird called *Wodewale,* which has been variously identified by experts as a woodpecker, a woodlark or an oriole. I'm convinced it's the latter, for the word is such a beautiful phonetic approximation of an oriole's song: *Wo-de-wal-e, wo-de-wal-e,* a phrase like the curl of the cut ends of a gilded banner furling over the page of an illuminated manuscript.

It was easy to hear orioles. Seeing them was a different matter. The poplar plantation resembled, somehow, a scaled-up tabletop cardboard theatre set, and peering into it pulled me into all manner of perspectival tricks and traps. Rows of equally sized grey, columnar trunks marched back to vanishing points in the dim distance, and because poplar branches begin high up, the arches where the leaves met between the rows of trees seemed part proscenium, part cathedral buttress. It was *noisy,* too, with a near-continuous rattle and clatter. Poplar's heart-shaped leaves are arranged in little fists of long, flexible petioles that make them twist and flap, flag-like, in the least breath of wind. The whole forest looked as if it were made of torn paper, and somewhere in its leaves were orioles. They called, moved. Sang, then called again, moved unseen to a distant tree, called again, made a different call, a sharp cat-call *hzzzt!*, moved, called, sang, and then moved once more. They stuck to the very tops of the tree canopy, and after a while I began to wonder if they could throw their voices. We stood there for a very long while, binoculars raised, necks getting cricked, and we saw no orioles at all. Driving home, I held the memory of their song with me like a pebble in the palm of one hand. I hadn't been disappointed by my morning in the poplars. Even so, I knew I needed to come back and try again.

This was thirteen years ago, in 2006, and our little population was about to blink into nonexistence. At that point the outpost was only about forty years old: its first colonisers had come here from the Netherlands in the 1960s, where they nested in trees in the Polders just like these. They must have crossed the North Sea and found themselves somewhere that felt like home. They quietly thrived. By the 1980s there were about thirty pairs, but there was already concern for their future, for many of the most expansive poplar stands in the area were scheduled to be felled. People clubbed together to form a group to study, survey and help protect the birds, and some new poplar belts were planted in hope of future colonisation. But the largest block of trees was hewn down all the same, and their numbers plummeted. This coincided with the beginning of a wider decline in oriole populations across their northern range in the Netherlands, Denmark, Finland. It might have been the effect of environmental changes in the Congo, where orioles spend their winters, or perhaps because increasingly early springs in Europe have led to a mismatch in timing between the emergence of the insects that orioles feed upon and when they are most needed to feed their young. In Britain the end came fast. Three years after my visit, only one nest remained, after which there were no more British-bred orioles. They had been a visitation, living in a little snippet of economic history, settling gold on the papery branches, making the fens obliquely glorious with their song. We never thought of these birds as immigrants; this was no Lost Colony. We thought of them as returning natives, and cherished their foothold in our time.

I returned a week later in hot, thundery darkness just before sunrise. The site had been turned into a bird reserve a few years previously, and the carrot fields around the poplar plantations had been flooded and planted with *phragmites* reeds. My walk to meet Peter ran through these reeds, passing patches of unreflective water, flat pools with surfaces matte with milky pollen-dust, tiny froglets scrambling away from my feet, the grass running with scores of miniature, urgent amphibians. Though beautiful, reed beds are unsettling places. Unlike deserts and open water, they're not inimical to supporting human life except in a very literal sense. You can walk across deserts, foot by foot. You can't walk on water at all. With reed beds, who knows? Their stalks are spiky and soft at once, and reed beds do, in some places, become islands, as in the Danube delta, and sail off in matted arks of rot and life. They're delicate, different and faintly dangerous places. Let no one underestimate the strange effect on human psychology of not knowing whether the ground underfoot is ground at all. Unless you have special, local knowledge, reed beds can be as forbidding and as lethal as mountains.

As I looked over the reeds I heard a pinging sound, then four or five small, long-tailed birds flew in little musical slurs across the water and landed to catch like little spherical burrs in the reeds right in front of me. They were bearded reedlings, birds utterly reliant on stands of *phragmites* like these. The adults raise a couple of families a year, and this was a brood of adolescents let loose upon the reeds. Adult male bearded reedlings are legendarily glamorous, possessing grey cowls and long black moustaches. But these youngsters weren't in grown-up dress; they were sleek and fawn-coloured, as if they were made of very expensive cashmere, and somehow wearing long, black velvet evening gloves. Their tiny waxen beaks resembled the heads of all-weather matches, and set in a thumb-smear of sooty kohl were strange, pale eyes that caught the light oddly as they clambered among the reeds. Their movements were bewitching. They're birds built for a world of verticals. Their legs are long, black and glint like obsidian, and they have huge, cartoon bird feet. Orioles forgotten, I stood and watched these little cashmere balls bouncing up and down in the reeds, and was delighted to see that quite often a bird hopped from one reed stem on to two, grabbing one stalk in each foot before sitting there happily doing the splits to pick reed seeds from the nearest overhanging frond.

This time Peter had brought the technology; he had set up a telescope on the bank and already trained it on the nest. The nest adhered to the tree the way that papery burnet moth cocoons adhere to stems of grass.

It was shaped something like a half coconut woven carefully from a hammock of thin grass and slung between two whippy branches sixty feet up in the air, and it was like no nest I'd seen before, although for a long while I couldn't see it at all. Through the telescope there was barely enough ambient light for depth and modelling to appear, but as the sun rose higher, what I saw became something like looking into a Magic Eye picture. Here was a circle, and in it a thousand angles of stalk and leaf and scraps of shade at various distances, and every straight stalk or branch was alternately obscured and revealed as the wind blew. I began to feel a little seasick watching this chaos, but then, as magically as a stereogram suddenly reveals a not-very-accurate 3D dinosaur, the muddy patch just off centre resolved itself into the nest.

As soon as it happened I tensed with the effort of not losing it again. The telescope's focus was slightly out for my shortsighted eyes, so it required physical effort to keep what I saw from derealising back into nonsense. I wanted so much to see an adult oriole leaping on to the nest to make it real, the gaping mouths of begging chicks emerging from inside it, the flapping of newly grown feathers. But nothing happened.

If there were birds inside that nest, at this time of year they'd be close to fledging and leaving it, I thought, so why couldn't I see anything in it move? They'd be restless, surely, at this hour? I surrendered the telescope to Peter along with my misgivings, spread my coat on the grass and sat down. Our mood grew sombre as we came to suspect, then believe, then finally know that there was nothing in this nest at all. It had been exceptionally windy the previous day, so we wondered if the young had fallen from the nest. After thinking this, there was no question but that we needed to go into the wood and look for the chicks that might be underneath the tree.

I shrugged my coat back on. The wood was at least five feet deep in stinging nettles. I'd done a lot of birding, and walking, and hawking, in nettles, and knew that the correct way to treat banks of big nettles is to wear reasonably thick clothes and not give a cuss for them. Wade through and be damned. It's like the Red Sea miracle – with faith, they'll part harmlessly in front of you. But what I wasn't used to dealing with was nettles emerging from a swamp. We stepped through rushes growing etiolated through wet black mud, and across places where the ground was so saturated there was no vegetation at all but something akin to quickpeat. Mostly we walked in nettles, their stems so densely packed that neither of us had much idea of what was beneath them as we struggled through. The poplar branches here were low, permitting us only a tiny tunnel of clearance between the top of the stinging nettles and the thatch of twigs and leaves. It felt like river caving, tilting our chins upward to the foot and a half of air between water and rock. It was claustrophobic, intense, the greens rich and dark, and it felt very far away from England. Like Louisiana, perhaps. Mosquitoes descended on us, swarms of big *Anopheles* whose delicate stripes and long noses drifted purposively towards our faces. We halted at the nest tree, kicked carefully about. There was nothing beneath it but nettles. I slapped away one mosquito after another, noticed there was blood all over my hands.

Then we heard an oriole. It wasn't the oriole's otherworldly song, but a series of short, rasping calls. Then, very softly from the foggy, papery green, a soft *hoot hoot hoot* was sent back to it – the contact call of a chick. Then came the glorious swirling flute of one of the parents as he swept in from nowhere to feed. And that's when I saw him. Finally, I saw my oriole. A bright, golden male. It was a complex joy, because I saw him only in stamped-out sections, small jigsaw pieces of a bird, but moving ones, animated mutoscope views. A flick of wings, a scrap of tail, then another glimpse – this time, just his head alone – through a screen of leaves. I was transfixed. I had not expected the joyous, extravagant way this oriole leapt into the air between feeds, the enormously decisive movements, always, and the little dots like stars that flared along the edge of his spread-wide tail. It's hard to comprehend that in all these views through my binoculars, he was never more than the size of a fingernail at arm's length. But then a fingernail at arm's length is, I guess, exactly the size of the visible sun.

THE OBSERVATORY

I never cared much for swans until the day a swan told me I was wrong. It was a cloudy winter morning and I was suffering from a recently broken heart. I sat myself down on a concrete step by Jesus Lock and was staring at the river, feeling the world was just as cold and grey, when a female mute swan hoist herself out from the water and stumped towards me on leathery, in-turned webbed feet and sturdy black legs. I assumed she wanted food. *Swans can break an arm with one blow of their wing,* I remembered, one of those warnings from childhood that get annealed into adult fight-or-flight responses. Part of me wanted to get up and move further away, but most of me was just too tired.

I watched her, her snaky neck, black eye, her blank hauteur. I expected her to stop, but she did not. She walked right up to where I sat on the step, her head towering over mine. Then she turned around to face the river, shifted left, and plonked herself down, her body parallel with my own, so close her wing-feathers were pressed against my thighs. Let no one ever speak of swans as being airy, insubstantial things. I was sitting with something the size of a large dog. And now I was too astonished to be nervous. I didn't know what to do: I grasped, bewildered, for the correct interspecies social etiquette. She looked at me incuriously, then tucked her head sideways and backwards into her raised coverts, neck curved, and fell fast asleep.

We sat there together for ten minutes, until a family came past and a toddler made a beeline for her. She slipped back into the water and ploughed upstream. As I watched her leave something shifted inside me and I began to weep with an emotion I recognised as gratitude. That day was when swans turned into real creatures for me, and it has spurred me since to seek out others.

My favourite place to see swans in winter is the Welney Wildfowl and Wetlands Trust reserve. It's on the Ouse Washes, part of the highly engineered wetland landscape of the East Anglian Fens. The observatory here is far from the usual ramshackle wooden hide. It's heated and carpeted and even has a glass case of taxidermied swans inside. Age has rendered them nicotine-yellow so they resemble the live birds outside the way smoked kippers resemble live herring.

Just as unusual are the crowds sharing the observatory with me. There are a few wolfish-looking men with spectacular telescopes of a species common to nature reserves. But there are also impressively bouffanted ladies of a certain age peering through binoculars so elderly they resemble opera glasses. There's a woman in a wheelchair who sings joyously all the way down the bumpy slope to the door. There are teen Goths and toddlers and couples in their twenties and sixties and eighties and a baby in pink tights and a glittery top. All of us – apart from the baby, who is transfixed by the Goths – are looking out of the panoramic plate-glass windows across a mile of water broken by tiny islands and dotted lines that are the stalks of drowned grasses and huddles of sleeping black-tailed godwits. There are no shadows anywhere out there except in the moving lines between ripples that chase themselves across miles of shallow water. As the light diminishes, distant structures become unmoored and float on the horizon: trees, pylons, wind turbines. Closer, willows are frozen like ice on glass. The lake is mercury-bright and patterned with thousands of birds as far as the eye can see: moving dots of mallard, wigeon, pochard – and miniature bergs that are swans.

A lake the size of Loch Lomond appears here every winter and drains to wet pasture in spring. Famed for wildfowling and winter skating, it's become a traditional wintering site for thousands of swans that come to feast on potatoes left in the ground after harvest, on sugar beet, on winter wheat. These aren't the familiar mute swans of town parks and lakes, not the species that came up to me and made its presence known. They're whooper swans and Bewick's swans, birds that breed in arctic Iceland and Siberia, and they are very different beasts.

Whoopers cross the North Atlantic non-stop to get here, flying for twelve hours at around twenty thousand feet through icy and oxygen-poor air. They're huge and impressive creatures. But it's the smaller species here, Bewick's swans, that are the favourite of WWT warden Shaun, who has come into the observatory to talk with us before the evening feed. Shaun is a stockman, of sorts. In summer he looks after cattle that graze on the Washes. When it is flooded, he looks after the swans. 'The yellow from their beaks continues up and around their eyes,' he says reverently of his Bewick's. 'Like yellow eyeliner. They're such pretty little birds.'

Near the case of swans in this observatory there's a bronze bust of the WWT's founder, Sir Peter Scott. He loved them too. Fifty years ago he noticed that every swan had a different pattern of yellow and black on its bill. Fascinated, he started to name them and paint tiny swan reference mug-shots of each bird. This developed into a 'face book', a visual catalogue of individual swans that is continued today. Even now, WWT researchers memorise birds by sight, and Scott's initial tracing of swans and their family trees has become one of the longest-running wildlife studies in the world. In conjunction with radio-tracking and ringing studies, the data it produces is crucial for conservation. While whooper populations are healthy, Bewick's are not: climate and habitat change seem likely factors in their rapid decline.

When I was small, Bewick's swans were strange and glamorous because they migrated here from the Soviet Union, crossing the Iron Curtain with absolute unconcern. I've often wondered what lay behind Peter Scott's fascination with them. To an ex-naval officer, explorer's son and champion glider pilot, the heroic North Sea flights of whoopers would certainly appeal. But it's tempting to imagine that a particular strand of English conservatism influenced his desire to individuate Bewick's swans, to turn them into families rather than flocks, trace their family trees and give them names like Casino, Croupier, Lancelot, Jane Eyre and Victoria, before they returned to the Soviet Union each spring. Politics are so easily caught up in science, the Cold War unwittingly pleated into swans' rushing, beating wings.

Now the floodlights are switched on and the water shivers. There's a hush of anticipation as Shaun leaves the observatory and reappears pushing a wheelbarrow along the shoreline, casting great scoopfuls of corn into the lake. We crowd to the window. A raft of winter wildfowl is feeding busily beneath us: conker-headed pochards, mallards, scores of whoopers and Bewick's with cloudy pinions and snowy necks. These birds are entirely wild, yet here they are, tame as farmyard ducks, feeding on a wet stage lit up like a West End theatre. The experience is joyous, but messes with your everyday notions of what a wild animal is, what wildness is at all.

But something is missing. I'm chasing something like the feeling the Cambridge swan had given me, and it isn't here, though I have an intimation of where I might find it. Leaving the observatory I head for the old wooden hides next door, raise a narrow window and let in the soundscape outside. What do thousands of arctic swans sound like? A vast amateur brass band tuning up in an aircraft hangar. My heart soars. Every few seconds comes a carillon of new voices. The swans are coming home to roost in little family groups, silhouettes that rise over the observatory and plane down to the black water. They are calling to each other in the night, these beautiful migrants, some of their faces stained yellow, some dark with potato-mud, their broad webbed feet splayed to brake as they descend. They land, call, flap their wings, squabble, dip their heads under the water, preen, drink thirstily. This is why I came. It's impossible to regard the natural world without seeing something of our own caught up in it. Back on that wintry riverside, a swan had come towards me and offered me strange companionship at a time when I thought loneliness was all I could feel. And what comforts me now, watching these arctic swans in our era of rising political nativism, is how clearly they are at home.

WICKEN

On a foggy morning a long while ago, I took my brother and very young niece for a walk around one of Britain's oldest nature reserves. Wicken Fen is a tiny fragment of the lost marshland ecosystem that once covered around two and a half thousand square miles of eastern England. We spent a couple of hours in its mosaic of grassland and sedge, strolling in wet fields cut with scrub-shadow and water. It was spring, and everywhere was bursting with life: singing nightingales, snipe winnowing and bleating through the upper air, cuckoos tilting from the tips of willows and water rails squealing and grunting in reeds. As we crossed one of the fen's ancient waterways, a barn owl floated past us, mothy wings shining through particulate mist; at our feet a drinker moth caterpillar inched furrily across the path like a cautiously mobile moustache. We knelt to watch its progress.

Then my niece turned to me and asked, curiously: 'Auntie Helen, when they made this place, where did they bring the animals from?'

I didn't understand at first.

'What do you mean?'

'There are so many animals here. Did they come from a zoo?'

That was when I realised her intuition was a perfectly rational one, for the countryside that my niece knew was mostly green desert.

'They always lived here,' I said gently. 'All the countryside used to be like this. Little bits like this are all that is left.' And her frown made my heart break.

I have been coming to Wicken for many years, bewitched by its strangeness and beauty. And today I'm back again, walking its paths under drifts of pallid cloud, still haunted by my niece's reasonable inability to understand that the life that is here was once everywhere. But that was, after all, why we had come. Nature reserves are places in which we can experience the past – the British environmentalist Max Nicholson once described them as outdoor living museums. Fen landscapes are unstable places where familiar categories of water and land are disconcertingly confused, and they feel temporally unstable, too, rich with a sense of their layered ages. Walking in them is an act of virtual time travel.

I think of the natural wealth of the eleventh-century fens, where fish and wild-fowl existed in such astonishing plenitude that local debts were settled with payments of eels – known as fish-silver – and Saxon warlords hid in the swamps from Norman invaders. I think of seventeenth-century villagers who were at home here, who cut sedge and reed for thatching and dug peat for domestic fuel. In the nineteenth century naturalists flocked to Wicken in search of insects. So many people brought lamps to attract moths at night that there were complaints that the fen looked lit by street-lights. Charles Darwin collected rare beetles from Wicken-cut reeds sent to Cambridge in boats to light university fires, and sugar-smeared poles stuck in the ground by amateur entomologists specifically to draw moths to their sweetness took root and grew into today's vast willows. I pass one of these trees at the corner of the path, lately fallen, its split trunk spilling with old bee honey-comb. It had been planted by a visitor to the fen whose relationship to nature was very different from that of my niece. To him it was something to collect, fix and cata-logue. To her, it is a thing separate from us, something to revere and observe from a remove.

It is pleasurable to imagine that you can commune with the past in a place like this. But there are consequences to feeling that kind of pleasure. If you start to see ecologically rich habitats as temporally separated from us, then the lack of wildlife in modern landscapes seems unremarkable. Why bother reducing pesticide use on farms, or preventing housing development at the edge of a city, when a reserve exists a few miles away? Living museums may be comforting to visit, but the problem is that they cannot ever be really insulated from the present. Dam construction outside the McCloud River Preserve in California, for example, rendered the river's native bull trout extinct. In the Charcoal Tank Nature Reserve in New South Wales, Australia, many species have been lost through habitat degradation and predation by foxes and cats. Once they are gone, these species cannot recolonise, because the small reserve is now an isolated island in a sea of impoverished habitat.

The wildlife and vegetation around me here are not frozen remnants of another time but things with their own histories, moving and shifting ceaselessly in response to local conditions, and able to return to places where we thought them gone. Humans have shaped this fen for centuries, halted its natural processes of ecological succession and maintained its delicate and complicated life. During the past two decades, the custodians of Wicken Fen have undertaken an ambitious century-long rewilding project to enlarge the reserve by slowly returning about thirteen thousand acres to its former wetland state. The project is already winding time backwards: in the years I've come here I've seen farm fields turn back into wetlands and meadows. But it's also turning time forward. Herds of Highland cattle and Polish konik ponies now live on the fen, their grazing shaping its vegetation as part of a management regime designed to let the land develop over time. It is impossible to predict in detail how the course of this rewilding will run, but our separation from it is intrinsic to the plan. There will be no return of the intensive local human interventions that once shaped the fen. This rewilded landscape will be a place for humans to visit, not to live and work.

At Sedge Fen, the path narrows between walls of high reeds, its surface steeped in tea-coloured water that reflects the sky piecemeal from my feet, and the ground rocks with every step. When one boot sinks calf-deep in black mud, I'm forced to turn back. Places like this resist modern assumptions that everything is visible and accessible. When I first came here years ago, I found it frustrating and sometimes even boring. The reed beds were flat expanses of impenetrable vegetation, undulating in the breeze like the sea. Like the sea, I couldn't see into them. I couldn't walk in them. And like the sea they teemed with invisible life: warblers, bitterns, spotted crakes, otters, water voles and marshland insects like reed leopard moths.

At first I used to watch the ditches and droves that cut through the reeds like streets between skyscrapers, waiting for animals to appear. Then I saw my mistake. I learned to stop needing to see. I learned to listen, to tune in to noises and let them guide my eyes. I'd hear the faintest creak or splash or call, and fix on that spot. I might sit there for minutes and see nothing. But sometimes things would appear. Most often I caught only the briefest glimpses. A brown flash in the stems that could have been a reed warbler, a sedge warbler, a Cetti's warbler. That tiny squelching noise that might be a teal feeding in a pool obscured by reeds. An almost imperceptible disturbance moving slowly across the reed bed that could be an otter, a bittern or a snake.

Wicken Fen has taught me not only that I won't always see the animals that I know live there, but that sometimes knowing where an animal is but not knowing *what* it is can be better than seeing it. I've learned how to identify birds in pieces, through scraps of colour and shape glimpsed through undergrowth: an eyebrow stripe, a wing-bar, an up-cocked tail. I've come to know the inhabitants of this place through a long series of brief, partial encounters in which the animal in question becomes more and more distinctive over time, and never once resembles the flat portraits in field guides.

Wicken does let me visit the past, but it's not the past of a Saxon warlord, a Victorian naturalist or an imagined unsullied wilderness. It is an older way of observing animals, distinct from the way they are usually viewed today, through binoculars, from behind hides and blinds, or in close-up footage on television screens. It's nothing like visiting a living museum or a zoo. This way of watching wildlife is full of difficulty and mystery, and it makes the landscape seem intrinsic to what its creatures are: things in the present moment – bewitching, complicated and always new.

STORM

Driving on the M25 on a summer evening I found myself headed for a wide column of storm-lit rainbow above Heathrow. The sky was congested and bruised, and even at seventy miles an hour, the pull of wind towards the storm tugged at my car, rushing across the elevated motorway section to fill the vacancy left by air pulled up thousands of feet to the cloud's blossoming apex. I couldn't see its white top stroked windward, but I could see the small crosses that were transatlantic jets steering their courses around the storm's perimeter. Half-feared for them. There were clips of lightning through this atmospheric carnage, and small turquoise pools of clear sky. And across one of these I saw a flock of parakeets flying straight and fast, with clipped wing-beats and streaming tails straight out behind them. It was a moment cut from a few seconds of moving history that will hang bright in my mind forever.

Most summer weather seems to me merely a backdrop to half-remembered scenes: a sun-baked lawn, misty mornings by the sea, city streets in the rain. All my clearest summer memories are of storms. The afternoon in the early 1980s on the Kennet and Avon Canal when I heard my first nightingale singing into charged grey air, accompanied by distant thunder that swung closer and seemed a voice answering the bird. Or that hot week in Gloucestershire in the 1990s when thunderstorms came every evening so the air turned sepia at six and before the first drops of storm rain sent pollen-dust up in puffs from the skylight I'd open the windows and wait for thunder while little owls called through the thick air, and in the morning tiny white dots of storm-blown blossom covered the house with wet French lace. I've measured all my summers by their storms.

There are people in America who climb into cars to chase thunderclouds across the Great Plains. But part of the thrill of British summer storms is not that one seeks them out, but that when the conditions are right, they come to you. For all the anxiety that spreads within you as you hear the crackling static of lightning breaking through voices on the radio, or smell the petrichor of newly soaked ground borne in on a rising wind, the predictability of the life-cycle of a thunderstorm is strangely reassuring. Stand far enough away and you can watch a summer cumulus, a thing born of sun-warmed air and water, grow into an entity the size of a mountain, unleash hail and brilliant hell, then disappear. A thundercloud takes perhaps an hour or so to cycle through its life, first stretching and pushing upwards until its top hits the troposphere and is pushed sideways and brushed into ice. As water droplets are pulled up into the cloud they freeze, eventually growing too heavy to ascend further, and so they fall, bumping into smaller fragments on their way up. Each collision transfers electrons, so that the lower parts of the cloud collect a negative charge while the upper parts collect a positive charge. Eventually lightning leaps across these differentials between the cloud's top, its base and the ground, casting out shockwaves of superheated air that make the sound of thunder. The destructive power of storms forces you to recall the vulnerabilities of your human frame, and all the limits, safeties and certainties of your everyday world. *Unplug your television and telephone. Get out of the bath. Do not shower.*

Stand away from windows.

But storms are made of more than stuff. They're also things of metaphors and memory. Storms distressed my grandmother; to her, thunder recalled the terror of the Blitz. But to me thunder still carries that glowing moment as my father explained to small me how storms are born from sunlight and hot earth, moving air and water, and how you can count the seconds it takes between lightning and thunder – *one Mississippi, two Mississippi* – to work out how far away the storm is. Five seconds is a mile. You can calculate its progress towards you. And even now when I count those seconds, I feel a slow wonder that is as much connected to the passage of years as it is to that of a cloud over rain-soaked ground.

Summer storms conjure distance and time but conjure, too, all the things that come towards us over which we have no control. Such storms have their place in literature; the heavy air and mood of suppressed emotion as the storm brews so often standing for an inevitable catastrophe. A murder in Agatha Christie's *The Mysterious Affair at Styles* or Leo's revelation in Hartley's *The Go-Between.* No weather so perfectly conjures a sense of foreboding, of anticipation and waiting, as the eerie stillness that often

270

occurs before the first fat drops of rain, when storm light makes luminous all roofs and fields and strands black silhouettes of trees on the horizon. This is the storm as expectation. As solution about to be offered. Or all hell about to break loose. And as the weeks of this summer draw on, I can't help but think that this is the weather we are all now made of. All of us waiting. Waiting for news. Waiting for Brexit to hit us. Waiting for the next revelation about the Trump administration. Waiting for hope, stranded in that strange light that stills our hearts before the storm of history.

MURMURATIONS

Words to accompany Sarah Wood's 2015 film
Murmuration x 10

I lost my passport. Blind panic. I needed
one fast. So one morning I drove up the
A14 north past the sex shops and service
stations half-buried in fog and the convoys
of container trucks *Maersk Sealand Hanjin*
with an envelope containing two photographs of myself, one signed by an ac-
countant, and my details in capitals in black
biro on three pages of orange paper. And at
9.15 a.m. somewhere near Wisbech a flock
of plovers flew low in front of the windscreen and hung there before vanishing into
nowhere. Seamless fog. No visible land or
sky. And I thought of the blank air-age
globes they sold in the 1930s that had no
geography on them at all, that were perfectly
white except for the printed names of
airports because we were all to look skyward

back then, for history had brought us wings and borders would fade into obsolescence. Hope was a thing with feathers.

At the passport office thirty tight-lipped people file singly through X-rays. We turn off our phones and computers. Our bags are searched for sharp objects and compressed gas canisters. And we sit waiting to be processed, feet on grey carpet. Soft murmurs. Flatscreens. We watch BBC news in spooling text and clips, riots and far wars and a seaside political party conference.

That party conference was in Brighton. I was there one winter. I stood on the pier at dusk and watched the starlings coming in to roost, blobs of running oil over the ocean rising in packs to settle in the ironwork under the planked wooden floor, and as they settled in the dark beneath the arcade lights they began to sing and their songs mimicked the fairground music from the sideshows above, the same notes in new avian order, tapes spliced and doubled and whistling, a thousand shortwave radios tuning between circus stations out east, across the Baltic from whence they came. And I stood there hearing mimicked human music under the floor and the sea beneath us was slick and pointed with tiny lights and

> Nay,
> I'll have a starling shall be taught to
>   speak
> Nothing but 'Mortimer,' and give it him
> To keep his anger still in motion.

I look at the security guards at the passport office and they look at me and I remember a British officer called Peter Conder who spent the Second World War in prison camps in Germany. He survived by watching birds. Goldfinches. Wrynecks. Migrating crows picking through the waste spread on the frozen fields. Hours and days and years on end. When he came home he didn't talk. He stayed with his sister and stared out of the window at London starlings roosting in long lines on ledges of Portland stone. With war-worn eyes he perceived that they spaced themselves equally, just far enough apart to reach the next bird, so they could deliver a blow or a rebuke. Bunks and camps spooled out again in post-war ornithology. He christened it the *principle of pecking distance*.

And before that, after the First World War had made caustic maps of Flanders fields and woods, built no man's land, built fields of mines and wire and ingraved trenches of men and filthy water, a man called Henry Eliot Howard decided that birds held territories too. He told us that they did not sing for love. Told us that males sang to other males, and there was warning in every note. Each curl of song was staking a bird's small claim to a patch of English ground. And the birds' bright colours weren't to attract a mate. The plumages they wore were badges of threat: little warring uniforms.

I think of Julian Huxley on the wireless back in 1942, explaining that if you don't know your birds you can't fully know your country. He said the yellowhammer's song was the essence of hot country roads in July. The crooning of the turtle dove of English midsummer afternoons. Birds were 'the heritage we are fighting for'. When war broke out and the Navy sent Peter Scott to sea he looked back from the deck of his destroyer and knew he was fighting to protect the mallards and teal that reared their ducklings in the reed beds of Slapton Ley. Somehow they were England.

I clutch my numbered ticket and wait to be processed. I think of the new nature writing. Of *Springwatch,* migrant watch, leaflets through our doors. It has happened before, when things collapse, when ideas fail, when economies slide, when newsprint is crisp with fears of invasion and the loss of who we are. We mark ourselves on our maps to consider our territory. We police. We turn inward. Seek ourselves in the mirror of the countryside. See nature as refuge. As ours. As us. In the winter of 1934 Norfolk farmers learned the skylarks in their fields were migrants from the Continent. They shot them for raiding their spring wheat. 'No protection for the Skylark' ran the headlines in the local press: 'Skylarks that sing to Nazis will get no mercy here'.

A woman in a blue coat is sitting three chairs away, her eyes closed, her knuckles white against the envelope of application forms. Is she asleep? Can you sleep and hold something so very tightly? I close my eyes too. Perfect forms, held steady. Forms of sympathy.

When I was a child I had a book called *Garden Bird Study* that told me to draw a map of the land around my house. To mark upon it the singing positions of its resident birds. If you watched very carefully you could work out where one territory ended and another began. I did what the book told me to do. I drew lines on my map. I marked nests. I kept lists of birds, resident, summering, wintering, overflying. Every smudge of pencil tied myself closer to the birds and

276

the garden. But it untied me too. It unfolded layers of other eyes, other lives, other visions of what the world might be. When we left that house, years later, I mourned the memory of all my childhood rooms. But I mourned, too, the lines, the lists, the little crosses for the pigeon's nest, the blackbird's nest, the robins outside the door. They had become part of the nature of home.

1933 saw the formation of the British Trust for Ornithology. This new organisation didn't protect birds. It studied them, and it recruited the British public for its large-scale investigations. Birds were no longer to be watched. They were to be *observed* by a volunteer army made of sharp-eyed citizen-scientists. Trained observers on bicycles who followed the movements of swifts. They filled in cards and reports and questionnaires. They had their orders: to buy 'a 1-inch ordnance map of the whole district, a 6-inch map of local surroundings, and a 25-inch map of the immediate neighbourhood' upon which they could mark the distribution of birds. 'Use these,' they were told, 'and do not be afraid to mark them.' Thousands of new observers, tied to the idea of a nation through acts of looking, acts of walking, acts of counting, tallying, recording what was there. What they were doing was war work.

Auguries, perhaps. No one knew. Strange phenomena in the days of fear of invasion. Birds entering houses. Sparrows stripping wallpaper. Blue tits stealing cream from cardboard-topped milk bottles. Have you read Daphne du Maurier's *The Birds*? Not the film, the story. An English story, a fable of some great change that turned birds into foes, massing on the fields and sea before flying inland to attack humanity. *What he thought were the white caps of the waves, were gulls. Hundreds, thousands, tens of thousands . . . They rose and fell in the trough of the seas, heads to the wind, like a mighty fleet at anchor, waiting on the tide. Someone should know of this. Someone should be told.*

But there could be no signs and wonders for Britain's mid-century birdwatchers. Irrationalism and superstition were things of the past. Sentimentality was to be replaced by science; poetic vagueness by conscious control, by constructive, critical thought. Even so, something more than science made itself out of little England and all its delicate cliffs. White chalk. Coastal early-warning radar stations called Chain Home. Everyone was observing. Everything watched. The

Royal Observer Corps sent reports of aircraft movements while other observers sent reports of birds. James Fisher grew ever more obsessed with fulmars, ghostly onyx-eyed seabirds that were spreading their range along British shores. *From Lundy to Land's End and Tintagel; from Land's End to Scilly and Lizard; from Lizard to Start Point; from Start Point to Swanage; from Swanage to the Seven Sisters; from the Seven Sisters to Hastings . . . fulmars have been seen, recently, flying by the cliffs of Broadstairs and Margate,* he wrote. *I do not know where it will stop.* He recruited Coastal Command stations to watch for fulmars as well as enemy aircraft. He arranged RAF reconnaissance flights to photograph fulmar breeding sites. Confusions of wings and eyes. All the world at war.

There are bird observatories at prime migration points all around the British coast. Bardsey. The Calf of Man. Cape Clear. Dungeness. Flamborough. Gibraltar Point. Portland Bill. The Isle of May. Their great flowering came after the war. Imagine: you are a prisoner in Germany. You have an Army number, you have a POW number. When you are freed you come home. But you are not entirely free because you have to do it again, and again, and again. Some part of you is fixed in the past courses of troop movements and maps and borders and escape and hope and home. If you are George Waterston, you start a bird observatory. You establish it in ex-military buildings on the far-flung edge of Britain, on remote Fair Isle. And there you and your colleagues trap lost and migrating birds in nets and cages and give them numbered rings before you release them again. You hope that someone will find them, so you can draw maps that show the invisible movements of birds across the globe. You let them go, but part of you goes with them. Your birds are feathered proxies, transcending human borders. You envy them.

In the booth the passport officer holds my photograph up to the screen and narrows his eyes. There is no shadow anywhere in the booth; there is an entirely even distribution of light. *Yes, it is you,* he says. I am relieved. He turns to my forms on his desk and scribbles a string of figures on them. In the bright and glassy calm I think, *What do they mean?* Doubts wheel and swarm. Facts insubstantial.

There was a man called David Lack. He

worked during the war on the early-warning chain of coast-watching radar stations. When the wavelength of their transmitted radar waves shortened to ten centimetres the operators started reporting echoes out at sea. They were not ships or aircraft. They were ghosts. They moved at thirty knots. Air-raid warnings resulted. Planes were scrambled. Nothing was ever there. Lack and his colleagues established that they were the radar reflections of seabirds. But there was more. When higher-power radar was invented, more ghosts appeared. Operators called them angels. They were commonest in spring and autumn. They didn't drift with the wind. They disturbed those who saw them. In Marconi's research laboratory, scientists wrote of lines of angels moving along the coast. *Scintillating discrete angels broke away from the line during its strongest period,* they said. *And a well-marked stream of persistent angel echoes could be seen moving up the Thames estuary.* The angels were starlings rising from their roosts in pulsing circles, lapwings moving north along weather fronts, pushed by heavy snow. The whole sky etched livid with aircraft and the reflections of moving wings. This was a new thing. Science turned to romanticism. The particulate beauty of unimagined hordes of lives that aren't our own, tracked minute by minute across the sky and rising out of mystery. This is a music made comprehensible by war, but the songs the birds sing are hymns of slowly moving light.

I leave the building with the promise of a passport and so does the woman in the blue coat and the man with the shopping bag and the elderly couple off to meet their grandson in Australia for the first time and the teenage boy going to Ibiza with his mates and I'm walking to my car thinking of when a bird-bander told me what happens if you mist-net long-tailed tits. Because they forage in family flocks, these mouse-sized birds get trapped in mist-nets all at once. Freed one by one from the mesh they're hung in individual bags from hooks in the ringing shed, ready to be weighed and measured and ringed. And in that awful solitude they call to one another, ceaselessly, urgently, reassuring each other that they are still together, all one thing. And once the rings are closed about their legs, they're released, all together, to resume their lives, carrying their tiny numbers with them as they fly.

A Cuckoo in the House

It's a strange, sharp-winged grey bird with button-yellow eyes, a down-curved beak and an expression of perpetual surprise, and its song is one of the best-known and best-loved in Britain. But most people have never seen a cuckoo, and it is getting harder for anyone to do so. Over the past quarter of a century, England has lost more than 60 per cent of its cuckoos and no one knows exactly why. Habitat loss, the effects of climate change, or the myriad perils cuckoos encounter on migration are the likeliest culprits, and of all those the latter is the hardest to research.

We've only ever had the vaguest idea of where British cuckoos spend the winter, and no idea of the routes they take there and back. But we are starting to understand. Since 2011, the British Trust for Ornithology has fitted satellite tags to British-trapped cuckoos and tracked their migration routes to Africa and back. The project's 'band of feathered brothers', as the national press has christened them, have attracted huge media attention. And they are uncovering all manner of ornithological secrets.

The BTO project is important. But it carries with it more than science. When I read that BTO cuckoos are 'missing in action', I think of wars overseas. When I look at the project's migration route maps, I wonder how satellite-tagged 'sentinel animals' such as these cuckoos fit into our surveillance-hungry world, and into the digitised dreams of network-centric war. I remember, too, several international incidents in the past few years in which tagged and banded birds have been taken as spies – as feathered, living drones. And I start to wonder how notions of nationhood, defence, secrecy and surveillance are caught up in how we think about cuckoos.

When I was small, I read a book by a man called Maxwell Knight. It was the story of how he had reared a baby cuckoo. Back then I thought *A Cuckoo in the House* was just another animal book from the 1950s, and that Knight was just an ordinary man. But the BTO project spurred me to read it again, this time knowing more about Knight. On rereading, I found it a very dif-

284

ferent book – a troubling fable about the meanings we give to animals, and a book that unwittingly revealed all sorts of strange collisions and collusions between natural history and national history in post-war Britain.

This, then, is the story of Maxwell Knight – the man called M – and a cuckoo called Goo. Knight was a tall, patrician British intelligence officer in charge of MI5 departments dealing with counter-subversion on home ground. And yes, as 'M' he was the inspiration for James Bond's controller. From the 1930s to the end of the Second World War, Knight placed agents in organisations such as the British Union of Fascists and the Communist Party of Great Britain. He was an extraordinary character: secretly gay, a writer of appalling thrillers, a keen jazz trumpeter, a disciple of the dark magic of Aleister Crowley, and an inveterate keeper of animals – crows, parrots, foxes and finches all shared space with agents in Knight's safe house in the Home Counties.

After the war ended, Knight began a second career as a BBC radio naturalist. This new and much-loved Knight was an avuncular, tweed-clad expert, a regular fixture on programmes such as *Country Questions, The Naturalist* and *Nature Parlia-*

ment. On air he described the habits of British wildlife, and told young naturalists how to rear tadpoles and how to hone their observational skills by playing 'Kim's Game', tellingly named after the hero of Rudyard Kipling's novel about a boy training to be a spy. From a clandestine career to an audience of millions, agent-runner to family naturalist, Knight appeared to have had a spectacular change of identity. But that Kim's Game reference is a giveaway: the worlds of naturalist and spy were closer than one might think.

There are many similarities between the observational practices of field naturalists and spies. 'Birdwatcher' is old British intelligence slang for a spy, and if you read Robert Baden-Powell's *Scouting for Boys,* you'll see how long natural-history fieldcraft has been seen as a preparation game for war. In his MI5 communications, Knight had once recommended that agents should be taught 'when, where and how to take notes, memory training and accurate description'. And on the radio he gave exactly the same advice to young naturalists.

But it is Knight's animals, and their relation to his secret life, that are most relevant to this story. He shared his London flat with a bear cub, a baboon, vipers, lizards, monkeys, exotic birds and rats. And they were not confined to his home. 'He always had something live in his pocket,' recalled John Bingham, an MI5 colleague best known as inspiring John le Carré's character George Smiley. Writers on Knight are fascinated by his animal-keeping, but the animals themselves are always treated as ciphers: we are never given an inkling of his motives for keeping them, apart from the animals being, perhaps, a kind of camouflage or misdirection. In the words of the literary critic Patricia Craig, they 'helped to gain him a reputation for eccentricity, certainly an asset in the devious world of MI5, where a lot depends on your ability to keep things dark, to impress your associates, and to spring surprises'. But Knight's animals were no simple camouflage.

Despite his own exotic pets, Knight championed the keeping of British wildlife. In his 1959 book *Taming and Handling Animals,* he described them as 'infinitely more instructive than creatures from far-away climes'. This sentiment is much in keeping with the sensibilities of the period, for during the war, British wildlife had become firmly embedded in myths of national identity. As invasion anxiety and spy-fever swept the nation, concerns about allegiance and patriotic identity rapidly colonised both popular and scientific understandings of wildlife. National and natural histories blurred. In a series of wartime radio talks, the evolutionary biologist Julian Huxley, brother of the writer Aldous, explained that birds had special importance because they were the means through which you oriented yourself to your country.

Knight's radio persona was built on such patriotic understandings: his *Letters to a Young Naturalist* from 1955 – a fictional correspondence between a nature-minded boy and his naturalist uncle – opens with the following: 'My Dear Peter. So you want to be a naturalist! You could not have chosen a better hobby, nor a better way of getting round me to help you. Apart from you becoming an England cricketer in the future I can't think of anything I could have wished you to do more.'

Ordinary pets held little interest for Knight. He was interested in wild animals: the ones you had to tame. In his books, he defined the term with care. First, he explained, animals might pass as tame, but not be; they might turn. And domesticated animals might appear to be tame, but they are liable to turn spiteful and difficult. Starving animals could also appear to be

tame, but aren't; hunger has merely dead-
ened their fear. These animals are not trust-
worthy. To trust an animal, he wrote in *Taming and Handling Animals,* one must tame it
oneself, make it 'gentle and tractable':

> The accent is on the word 'make' because
> to tame a wild creature means that we
> have to gain its confidence, remove its
> natural fears, and in many cases even
> inspire affection, so that the animal con-
> cerned will feed readily and regularly; will
> look well; will refrain from biting and other
> forms of attack and will accept us as well
> disposed towards it – or possibly as one
> of its own kind.

One of its own kind. There's a world of
counter-subversion right there, a ghosting
of the topologies of his secret life. In his
books, Knight wrote of the correct relationship between animal and handler in almost
exactly the same terms he'd used to describe
the correct relationship between agent-
runner and agents – one in which the officer must 'at all costs make a friend of his
agents' and the 'agents must trust the
officer'. Most important of all, in both
animal-taming and agent-recruiting, 'a basis
of firm confidence must be built up'.

Our model of animal-keeping today commonly rests on an empathetic understanding between handler and wild creature. Knight's does not. For him, the lines between animal and human were sharply drawn. His animals were mirrors only so far as they reflected their keeper's expertise, and their tameness and trust were to be valued as evidence of the character and abilities of their owner. 'A fool of a person,' he said, 'will never own an intelligent pet; a nervous person will never succeed in winning the confidence of any wild creature.' And apart from demonstrating how skilful you were at gaining trust, animals had other uses: they were epistemological puzzles to solve. They allowed you to 'observe such things as the comparative intelligence of different species', or 'their readiness to adapt themselves to conditions of captivity'.

The boundaries between Knight and his animals were firmly policed, just as they were with his agents. In both cases, the aim was a familiar, expert, yet distanced, knowledge. Joan Miller, one of Knight's agents and his long-term companion, acerbically commented that 'M was always curious about animals, not fond of them; though ours, of course, were always loved sincerely by me'.

Knight's distanced model of animal-keeping ran into trouble when he decided to raise a cuckoo. It was a species for which Knight had a special regard. It's not difficult to see why. Cuckoos doubled as symbols not only of deep and abiding Englishness (their spring arrivals noted each year in the letters page of *The Times*), but also of suspicion, mystery and deceit. They laid their eggs in other birds' nests and their newly hatched chicks, after ejecting the eggs and chicks of their hosts, were raised by foster-parents that seemed quite unaware of the deception played upon them.

Parasitic, scientifically baffling, the cuckoo's ambiguous moral status revolved around concepts of cuckoldry, duplicity, sexual confusion and even species boundaries themselves: in books and in heated correspondence in the *Spectator,* the redoubtable Bernard Acworth, doyen of the Creation Science Movement, repeatedly claimed that cuckoos were, in fact, hybrids between male cuckoos and the female birds of host species.

The cuckoo also starred in a spectacular piece of popular science of the period. Using new techniques of flash photography, Eric Hosking and Stuart Smith's *Birds Fighting* (1955) made overt the place of the cuckoo in fables of nationalism, aggression and defence. Smith begins by quoting Pliny's description of the cuckoo as a 'common object of hostility among all birds' because 'it practises deception'. The book is a sort of ornithological death-match, a series of staged fights, photographed in blow-by-blow detail, of well-known, well-loved British songbirds tearing apart stuffed cuckoos in a frenzy of defensive aggression and 'extreme fury'. This was total war in the ecological realm: birds defending their families against an infiltrating enemy. The cuckoo – standing in for an invasion of the body politic – incited extreme violence in birds that were icons of rural Englishness.

Hosking and Smith wanted to find out what triggered this furious response. How does a bird recognise the enemy? What signifies 'cuckoo' to a wrathful nightingale? They made sectional cuckoo models, painted cardboard cutouts, and stuck stuffed cuckoo heads on sticks, then conducted a series of experiments born of cultural anxieties reflected on to a post-war nationalised avifauna. What they discovered was that British birds were reassuringly adept at uncovering dissimulation: a nightingale will still recognise and attack a stuffed cuckoo even if it has been draped in a spotted handkerchief.

This was the post-war cuckoo: a clandestine bird of deception and quiet murder. The enemy within. Knight, naturalist and counter-subversion specialist, was, of course, desperate to own one.

In *A Cuckoo in the House* (1955), Knight tells the story of how this came to pass. His networks of secret watchers and agents had been replaced by a vast team of natural-history informants recruited through the radio. When one wrote to him of a cuckoo chick in a back garden, Knight jumped at the chance to 'rescue it' from cats. He'd wanted to hand-rear a cuckoo for years. Why? Because they are interesting, he explained, and because they are familiar, but not well known. Though everyone knows the cuckoo's call, he continued, the bird itself was 'not thoroughly understood'. It is 'mysterious', he explained, with evident relish.

And indeed, the cuckoo's life beautifully mirrored the concerns of Knight's own. First, its sex life was mysterious and secretive. So was Knight's: for years, according to Joan Miller, he'd maintained a hearty heterosexual façade while picking up rough trade in local cinemas and employing motorcycle mechanics for reasons other than repairing motorcycles. Second, cuckoos were the avian equivalents of the officer-controller of penetration agents; they 'insinuated' their 'chameleon eggs' into the nests of their 'dupes'. A single cuckoo might lay eggs in as many as twelve nests, Knight explained, finding them by perching on a 'convenient lookout post from which she spies out the land with a sharp and particular eye'. Cuckoos were also 'competent and ruthless', and their secret identity was never compromised. Knight didn't share Smith and Hosking's conclusion that birds had an 'innate concept of "cuckoo"'. Far from it. He maintained that birds never knew they were cuckoos at all. Cuckoos lived their cover. Knight's view was that other birds attacked them because they resembled, or 'passed', as hawks.

As Knight reared Goo, his cuckoo, the careful boundaries he'd drawn between the worlds of animals and man, between agent and handler, began to crumble. He was delighted to observe the fledgling's initial aggression turning to absolute tameness and trust. Goo also had a 'very remarkable' discriminatory ability, and was easily able 'to sort out its regular friends from newcomers'. The words Knight used to describe Goo's behaviour were highly charged: friends, newcomers, handlers – all categories from his secret life. And not just his career in the intelligence services, but his love life, too: Knight's 'friendly advances' to the cuckoo were 'reciprocated in full'. 'Plumage, voice, and soft peckings showed quite plainly that he was pleased and satisfied, and strokings and murmured soft words were much appreciated too.' Reading Knight's book you sense his delight that this mysterious cuckoo has been turned, but also his disconcerted half-knowledge that what it has turned into is a strange, feathered proxy for Knight himself. For the first time, Knight admits, troubled, he is not sure that the 'gulf which exists between humans and other animals . . . is quite as wide as some people think'.

A Cuckoo in the House ends, of course, with the defection of Knight's avian agent. Young cuckoos migrate to Africa. Flying free in Knight's garden, Goo returned to his handler less and less frequently. Knight attached a numbered ring to the bird's leg to identify it, should it return the following spring, and when Goo left to fly south, Knight mourned his loss. The cuckoo, he said, was 'the most fascinating bird pet' he had ever owned. Of course it was: he identified with it hugely, saw it mostly as himself.

The story of the cuckoo and the spymaster tells us that our understanding of animals is deeply influenced by the cultures in which we live. But it shows, too, that we can – and do – use animals as our proxies; we use them to speak for us, to say things that we cannot otherwise articulate. It also reveals that the meanings we give animals can be strangely robust. Just as Knight's cuckoo was never just a bird, the cuckoos trapped and tagged as part of the British Trust for Ornithology's current project are never solely data points on a map. No matter how precisely they are tracked on their long migrations, they are still birds of mystery, things much greater than small bundles of bones and muscle and grey feathers. They tell us things about ourselves, about the way we see our world; and they carry their strange human histories with them on their way.

THE ARROW-STORK

Displayed on a small plinth in a university museum in the German city of Rostock is a famously gruesome exhibit: a stuffed white stork whose sinuous neck is pierced by an iron-tipped wooden spear from Central Africa. This unlucky bird survived the attack and flew back to Germany, only to be shot by a hunter in the spring of 1822. Newspaper reports revealed the spear's distant origin, and the newly christened *pfeilstorch,* or arrow-stork, became celebrated for solving the puzzle of where German storks spent their winters.

In the eighteenth century, many experts still held Aristotle's view that birds hibernated during the cold months and believed fishermen's claims that clumps of live swallows could be pulled from beneath the ice of winter ponds. It wasn't until later in the nineteenth century that European naturalists began sustained research into bird migration, fitting the legs of birds with numbered metal bands and carefully plotting the locations where they were later recovered. The Rostock *pfeilstorch* is an early, macabre example of the workings of wildlife-migration science. From unintentionally carried spears to GPS and satellite tags, tracing animal movements requires augmenting the animals with human technology.

Many thousands of animals and birds carry tags today. They're attached to sea-turtle shells with marine epoxy glue and fired from boats into the blubber of passing whales. Swans and bears wear tags on collars, and smaller birds are fitted with harnesses that mount solar-powered transmitters high on their backs. Each tag communicates with a network of satellites to fix the location of the animal.

By discovering the routes animals take during migration, scientists can assess the threats they face, like regions affected by habitat loss or the activities of hunters. But the movements of tagged creatures are no longer followed solely by the eyes of experts. For the rest of us, the increasing availability of visualisations of their journeys makes the world a more complicated and wondrous place. I'm able to sit at my computer and watch how great white sharks tagged in Californian coastal waters migrate over a thousand miles to spend their winters in a remote part of the Pacific Ocean now known as the White Shark Café, read of how Amur falcons might survive on their journey over the ocean between India and Africa by following swarms of dragonflies making the same trip and feasting on them in flight.

There are many websites on which the public can name, sponsor and follow tagged animals. I regularly visit one run by the British Trust for Ornithology, which tracks the annual journeys of individual cuckoos between Britain and Africa as part of a larger project investigating the species' rapid population decline in Britain: more than half have been lost since the 1980s for reasons that are still unclear. Today the internet informed me that a cuckoo called David has reached his home in Wales, though it's hard to know what home means to a cuckoo, for the project has shown that some spend only 15 per cent of their lives in their countries of origin. I click on David's photograph, and then those of sixteen other tagged cuckoos, nervous, golden-eyed bundles of grey feathers held in scientists' hands, so different from the fast-flying,

sharp-winged silhouettes that flicker between trees near my house in spring. Each
cuckoo's current position is represented on
screen by a clickable icon on a Google Earth
map. Coloured lines trace their flights from
England across Europe and North Africa,
over the Sahara and into the humid forest
zone where they spend their winters. The
default satellite view on the website has no
overlays indicating cities or countries. It
encourages me to see the world as an animal
does: a place without politics or borders,
without humans at all, merely a series of
habitats marching climatically from cool
northern mountains to the thick rainforests
of Angola and Congo.

Projects like this give us imaginative access to the lives of wild creatures, but they
cannot capture the real animals' complex,
halting paths. Instead they let us watch
virtual animals moving across a world of
eternal daylight built of a patchwork of
layered satellite and aerial imagery, a flattened, static landscape free of happenstance.
There are no icy winds over high mountain
passes here, no heavy rains, soaring hawks,
ripening crops or recent droughts. Despite
these simplifications, following a tagged
animal on a map is an addictive pursuit. It's
hard not to become invested in its fate. The

bird might die, the tag might fail. You do not know where it will travel next. The bird is unaware of the eyes that watch its progress, and you veer from a sense of power at your ability to surveil at a distance to the knowledge that you are powerless to influence what happens next.

The more you watch, the more you feel that you are somehow also taking the cuckoo's journey, are engaged on a virtual exploration of the globe. The fantasy of a borderless world is quickly replaced by visions of heroic exploration. You take up the part of a lone traveller engaged on an arduous quest to cross countries and conquer unknown spaces on the map. Because satellite tracking is expensive, we can follow the progress of only a few named animals. You become attached to them as they make their astonishing journeys. You watch young cuckoos find their way to Africa with no parental help, see loggerhead turtles swim seven and a half thousand miles from feeding grounds off Mexico to the beaches of Japan; discover bar-headed geese migrating over the Himalayas, in doing so enduring extreme and sudden changes in elevation that would disable or kill a human. You can marvel at the bar-tailed godwits that make a nine-day, eleven-thousand-kilometre non-stop flight from Alaska to New Zealand across the Pacific Ocean. To us, these appear remarkable feats of physical endurance. We cannot help measuring the capacities of animals against our own.

Our unconscious desire to see ourselves in the lives of animals is shared by the scientists engaged in these projects, who often think of the tagged animals as colleagues and collaborators. Tom Maechtle, a biologist and environmental consultant who has worked on raptor migration at the University of Maryland, has spoken of how satellite tracking 'turns the animal into a partner with the researcher' and suggested that you can think of tagged falcons as biologists who have been 'sent out to find and sample other birds'.

Increasingly, animals are seen not only as proxies for scientific researchers but also as scientific-research equipment functioning like sensors or probes. In one project studying climate change in West Antarctica, for example, elephant seals with tags glued to their foreheads collect and transmit data on ocean conductivity, temperature and depth that is used for weather forecasting and climate research. This notion of autonomous biological-sampling devices confuses the distinctions between technology and living organisms, quietly erasing the animal's agency.

Tagged animals carry more than human technology; they carry human ways of visualising the world. Hybrid beasts, they perfectly fit our modern conception of the planet as an environment under constant watch, where eyes in the sky track animals moving from one country to another and plot them on a map just as they do moving ships and aircraft; a world where Defense Department researchers in the US are working on autonomous flying robots that mimic the flight of hawks and insects, where scientists fit electronic backpacks on giant flower beetles that enable them to be flown and steered by remote control.

Early pioneers in the remote tracking of animals sought military funding for their efforts and suggested that bird-migration studies could be used to improve navigation and missile-guidance systems, and the development of technology suitable for animal surveillance came from a microelectronics industry with strong early links to the military. In our age of drone warfare, it is hard not to see each animal being tracked across the map as symbolically extending the virtues of technological dominance and global surveillance.

If the stuffed *pfeilstorch* in the German museum is the iconic bird of early animal-migration science, I think today's equivalent is another stork, a young bird called Ménes that was satellite-tagged in Hungary in 2013 as part of an avian-migration tracking project sponsored by a European cross-border cooperation programme. After leaving his nest, Ménes travelled south across Romania, Bulgaria, Greece, Turkey, Syria, Jordan and Israel, landed in the Nile Valley in Egypt, and was there captured by a fisherman and taken into police custody. The stork, carrying a 'suspicious electronic device', was suspected of being a spy.

I've spent a long time looking at photographs of Ménes behind bars, half in shadow, beak lowered and toes spread upon concrete, a mournful casualty of a country in the grip of the deepest political tensions. Security experts cleared the stork of espionage, and he was released, only to be later found dead on an island near Aswan, a draggled corpse of a stork that had become a poignant avatar for human fears and conflicts. Media reports of his plight cast his story as one of almost comical paranoia. But although the stork was innocent – an unwitting player in a geopolitical game of surveillance and intelligence – the hybrid being made of the stork and device was far less clearly so.

ASHES

On a dank January day in the mid-1970s, I stood on an English hillside with my mother and watched men with chainsaws cutting up wrecks of trees and tossing brushwood on to fires. I was five years old, amazed by the roaring blades and drifting smoke, and troubled too.

'Why are they burning them?' I asked her.

'It's Dutch elm disease,' she said, pulling at the knot of her headscarf. 'All the elm trees are dying of it now.'

Her words confused me. I'd assumed until then that the countryside was an eternally unchanging place. At that time, Dutch elm disease was spreading across continents, blight had killed four billion American chestnuts, and catastrophic new tree diseases were to follow. Last week that cold hillside of my childhood came to mind as I drove through rural Suffolk, past painted farmhouses and arable fields sloping under a haze of summer clouds. The ash trees on this stretch of road were obviously dying. Their once-luxuriant crowns had thinned to an eerie transparency; instead of a shifting canopy of pinnate leaves, bare twigs showed stark against the sky.

It was my first sight of ash dieback disease, a new and virulent fungal infection that has spread westward across Europe and will likely kill nearly all the ashes in Britain. In America, the effects of the invasive emerald ash borer beetle have been just as devastating. Globalisation is the culprit. While there have always been outbreaks of tree disease, about as many have appeared since the 1970s as in all recorded history. The accelerating scale and speed of international trade has brought numerous pathogens and pests to species with no natural resistance to them. If you are a tree, death comes hidden in wood veneer, in packing material, in shipping containers, nursery plants, cut flowers, the roots of imported saplings.

Later that night, I compulsively searched for images of elms on the internet, seeking their buoyant, ragged silhouettes in snapshots of village fields or half-hidden behind actors in 1960s films. I saw trees like frozen cumulonimbus clouds towering over cricket matches at English public schools; postcards and photographs of elm avenues in Massachusetts and coastal Maine, lofty branches shading summer streets and suburban Oldsmobiles. These trees were the ghosts of half-remembered landscapes, and looking at them I realised that living trees could haunt you, too. That drive in Suffolk had changed the meaning of ash trees for me. From now on, each one I saw would mean death, no matter how healthy it might be.

But should they contract a mortal disease, trees cope better than we do. Many can regenerate. The vast Appalachian chestnut forests crowned with white flowers have all but disappeared, but fallen trees still sprout new shoots from their roots. As soon as they reach a certain height they again become susceptible to blight and die. Chestnuts and elms living in this endlessly youthful state are less fruitful than mature trees, and they trouble us because they are not what we think trees should be. We use trees to measure our own lives, to anchor our notions of time. To most of us, they represent constancy and continuity, living giants that persist through many human generations. We want them to achieve maturity; we want them to tower above us.

The spectral elms on the internet were images of a different kind of extinction from that of the passenger pigeon or dodo: the extinction of a landscape. For days afterwards, I found myself looking out at the blank brows of local hills, imagining there the billowing shapes of elms. I was preparing myself to think about what it would look like here when all the ash trees were gone. It was painful to force myself into a kind of anticipatory *solastalgia,* a term coined by the Australian environmental philosopher Glenn Albrecht to refer to people's emotional distress when their home landscapes become unrecognisable through environmental change. He was speaking of the effects of drought and strip mining in New South Wales, but solastalgia can arise in landscapes as varied as melting tundra and south-western states stricken by wildfire. Like droughts, tree diseases bring economic loss and ecological impoverishment while at the same time stripping familiar meaning from the places we live in. Writing about the slow death of American forests from a hundred years of tree diseases in his book *Nature Out of Place,* the writer Jason Van Driesche found himself almost mute: 'This is my home. How can you put something like this into words?'

But there are trees that can offer solace. I looked for photographs of them on the internet, too: the last few big American chestnuts, some of which have been given names. The Adair County Chestnut, found in 1999 in Kentucky, for instance. Rounded in form, it does not much resemble the gigantic, spiralling cathedral-columns of ancient Appalachian trees, but it is beautiful, spreading dark limbs and long, serrated leaves towards the sun. Around five hundred are left: the Hebron Chestnut in Maine; an unnamed chestnut in Ohio. People seek out these singular chestnut trees that have cheated death; some even steal leaves and pieces of bark from them as mementoes. The precise location of these trees must often be kept secret – encountering one, it is said, is an experience akin to finding Bigfoot.

Dedicated scientists, volunteers and nursery workers have spent many decades trying to restore the American chestnut with the aim of recreating the landscapes we have lost. Some organisations, like the American Chestnut Foundation, are backcrossing American trees with resistant Chinese varieties to produce seedlings that resemble American chestnuts but have sufficient Chinese qualities to survive the effects of blight. Others, like a team at the State University of New York College of Environmental Science and Forestry, insert genes from wheat and other plants into chestnut embryos to change their chemistry and make them more resilient to attack. Despite the increasing success of projects like these, some commentators regard them as a diversion, believing instead that it would be better to put resources into preventing new diseases than attempting to cure old ones. Their position makes sense if you think our reasons for wanting to restore the trees are merely ecological. Of course, they are not. They shape the landscapes of our lives and are a matter bound up with our sense of identity.

Increasingly, knowing your surroundings, recognising the species of animals and plants around you, means opening yourself to constant grief. Virulent tree diseases hit the headlines, but smaller, less visible disappearances happen all the time. The flycatchers that nested in my neighbourhood a decade ago have vanished; meadows in my hometown that were full of all kinds of life have become housing developments full of nothing but our own. People of a certain age tend to look back elegiacally at the things that have gone: the shop you used as a kid that closed, the room that became a memory. But those small, personal disappearances, however poignant, are not the same as losing biodiversity. Changes to city skylines are not the same as acres of beetle-blasted trees: though they are caught up in stories about ourselves, trees are not ever just about us. They support complex and interdependent communities of life, and as forests slowly become less diverse, the world loses more than simply trees. It has been suggested that the rise of Lyme disease in many parts of North America and Europe is in part because less diverse forests favour the ticks that carry it.

I am old enough to remember elms and the landscapes they made; people only a few years younger than me do not, and to them the elm-free fields are reassuringly normal. Are we now becoming inured to a new narrative of nature, in which ecosystem-level change in accelerated timescales is part of the background of everyday life? Children who are growing up watching glaciers retreat and sea ice vanishing, villages sinking, tundra wildfires raging and once-common trees disappearing – will they learn to regard constant disappearance as the ordinary way of the world? I hope it is not so. But perhaps when all the ash trees are gone and the landscape has become flatter and simpler and smaller, someone not yet born will tap on a screen, call up images and wonder at the lost glory of these exquisite, feathered trees.

A HANDFUL OF CORN

White-haired, soft-featured, and in possession of a faintly aristocratic glamour, Mrs Leslie-Smith lived alone in a wooden bungalow full of books and glossy houseplants a few doors from my childhood home. On a warm autumn evening more than thirty years ago, she invited my mother and me to watch her nightly ritual. She ushered us to chairs set before glass doors into her garden, picked up a biscuit tin, prised open the lid, then went outside to scatter handfuls of broken biscuits on the flagstones of her patio, where they glittered dustily under the light of an outside lamp. Back in the darkened room we sat and waited. We didn't talk; the event had all the hush and ceremony of theatre. From the edge of the illuminated lawn, a striped black-and-white face appeared and then retreated into darkness. Soon afterwards, two badgers trundled across the grass out of the night to crunch

314

up the cookies, so close to us we could see the curves of their ivory teeth and the patterned skin of their noses. They weren't tame – if we had turned on the light, they would have bolted – but they were so close I had an urge to press my hands to the glass to make them understand I was there. The space between us in the house and these wild creatures in the garden was filled with unalloyed magic.

We didn't feed badgers in our childhood garden, but we fed the birds. So do a fifth to a third of all households in Australia, Europe and the United States. Americans spend over three billion dollars each year on food for them, ranging from peanuts to specialised seed mixes, suet cakes, hummingbird nectar and freeze-dried mealworms. We still don't clearly understand how supplementary feeding affects bird populations, but there's evidence that its enormous increase in popularity over the last century has changed the behaviour and range of some species. Many German blackcaps, for example, soft grey migratory warblers, now fly north-west to spend the winter in food-rich, increasingly temperate British gardens rather than flying south-west to the Mediterranean, as their ancestors had done, and feeding may be behind the northward spread of northern cardinals and American goldfinches.

Putting out food for birds in your back garden can attract predators, and virulent diseases like trichonomosis and avian pox can be spread through contaminated feeders. But even if its impact is not always positive for wildlife, it is for us. We give food to wild creatures out of a desire to help them, spreading cut apples on snowy lawns for blackbirds, hanging up feeders for finches. The writer Mark Cocker maintains that the 'simple, Franciscan act of giving to birds makes us feel good about life, and redeems us in some fundamental way'. That sense of redemption is intimately tied with the history of bird-feeding, for the practice grew out of the humanitarian movement of the nineteenth century, which saw compassion towards those in need as a mark of the enlightened individual.

In 1895, the popular Scottish naturalist and writer Eliza Brightwen gave instructions on how to feed and tame wild red squirrels to become 'household pets of their own free will'. In Britain, garden feeding was popularised by the formation of the Dicky Bird Society, a late-nineteenth-century children's organisation that required its members to take a pledge to be kind to all living things and to feed the birds in wintertime. The society was highly influential, even receiving letters from workhouse children explaining how they carefully saved crumbs from their own meals to feed the birds outside.

In the United States, one of the most significant figures in the new movement was the Prussian aristocrat Baron Hans von Berlepsch. A book detailing his ingenious bird-feeding methods, *How to Attract and Protect Wild Birds,* described how you could pour melted fat mixed with seeds, ants' eggs, dried meat and bread over conifer branches for birds to feed from in winter. 'Kind-hearted people,' he wrote, 'have always taken pity on our feathered winter guests.' During the First World War, feeding American birds became something of a patriotic duty, for it helped them survive the winter so they could go on to eat insects that threatened agricultural production. By 1919, the nation's garden birds were to be considered, according to the ornithologist Frank Chapman, 'not only our welcome guests but our personal friends'.

Today, the opposite is true: close and intimate contact with animals is increasingly rare. We permit only a few types of animals to enter our homes as pets; interactions with wild animals tend to be restricted to experts like biologists or park rangers. But gardens and backyards are special trading zones that span the imaginary boundaries between nature and culture, domestic and public space. They are shared territory, places that both humans and wildlife consider home. Even so, when we feed animals, we want it to be on our terms, not theirs. We expect them to respect their place in an unspoken social order. When a wary squirrel or bird trusts you sufficiently to take food from your hand, it's gratifying and special, a reaching across the border between us and them, wild and tame. But if a squirrel runs unbidden up your arm demanding food or a seagull snatches a sandwich from your hands, it often generates an emotion close to outrage. Back in the early days, proponents of bird-feeding had to fight against the conviction that animals would become 'spoiled' by artificial feeding and would 'no longer do their work in nature's household'. Even today, it's hard to read articles giving advice on wildlife feeding without suspecting that they might be about something else entirely. We're told to feed foxes sporadically, so as not to cause dependence, for example, and we're warned that feeding them can make animals lose their 'natural respect' for us.

There are acceptable animals and unacceptable animals, as there have been deserving and undeserving poor, and the lines of respectability are drawn in familiar ways, through appealing to fears and threats of invasion, foreignness, violence and disease. As usual, animals reflect back at us our own assumptions about the natural structure of the world. 'Feeding foxes is one of those things you don't talk to people about,' one blogger confessed online, worried that her neighbours would find out her secret. To purposely feed the wrong animals – sparrows, pigeons, rats, raccoons, foxes – is an act of social transgression that's liable to get you reported to officials by whistleblowers who are concerned with mess, or health, or noise, or are powered by sheer indignation. Of course, with sufficient social capital, you can get away with whatever you like. Actress Joanna Lumley not only feeds tame wild foxes in her London garden but lets them into her house; newspapers have printed photographs of one fast asleep upon the cushions of her living-room sofa.

Feeding animals can be a deep solace to those who, for reasons of social or personal circumstance, find contact with others difficult or impossible. People who feed urban pigeons tend to be isolated and socially marginalised: older people, lonely people, homeless people. Sociologist Colin Jerolmack has memorably described such encounters with pigeons as ephemerally dissolving people's solitude, and some of the saddest wildlife reports in the media are those about individuals who have been fined or jailed because they refuse to stop feeding birds in their gardens. 'They are my whole life, because all my relatives are gone,' explained Cecil Pitts, a sixty-five-year-old fined five hundred dollars for repeatedly feeding large flocks of pigeons at his home in Ozone Park, Queens, in 2008. He is one of many people who have come to identify with the unloved denizens of their neighbourhoods, creatures that are ignored or despised, living behind the visible workings of the modern city.

Growing up with bird tables outside my window taught me a lot about animal behaviour – context gave meaning to the aggressive flicking of a squirrel's tail, the precise posture of a courting robin – but it taught me, too, that curious blend of familiarity and otherness that we see in wild creatures. Animals are not human, but they are enough like us to grant us a strange and strong sense of kinship. Mrs Leslie-Smith's badgers brought her the company of many guests keen to see these rare creatures at close quarters, but the company, too, of wild animals that chose to spend time at her house. This morning, as I filled the feeders in my garden, a flock of small passerines hopped about in the hedges while three jackdaws perched expectantly on the eaves above. One looked down at me, shook its dusky feathers and yawned, and I found myself yawning, too, in a moment of contagious fellowship. The birds that choose to come to my garden make my house a less lonely place. And that is why many of us feed animals – not merely because it's satisfying to feel we have helped them, but because it surrounds us with creatures that know us, are able to forge bonds with us, have come to regard us as part of their world.

BERRIES

On the first of December, I dragged my old artificial Christmas tree down from the attic and plugged it in. Instantly it glowed with light. On went my collection of odd Christmas baubles: a bescarfed tweed sausage dog, a golden stegosaurus, a crystal stag, a small ceramic robot and a handful of glass spheres dusted with glitter. The whole thing took less than five minutes, which left me feeling obscurely cheated by the ease of my seasonal effort. So later that afternoon, the light dying and the air outside thick with woodsmoke, I went out with a pair of secateurs to collect greenery from the big holly tree near my front door. It's tall, wreathed in ivy, and this year heavy with fruit. I shook each cut branch to rid it of wintering insects, dragged the whole lot inside and started laying down boughs on sills and mantels. The gloss of lamplight on the leaves and the gemlike clusters of berries made the house look spectacularly festive, but I felt a pang of guilt at bringing the outside in: those berries were meant for birds, not for me.

Berries grow to be eaten, not used for interior decoration. Most, packed with fats and carbohydrates around the seeds at their hearts, have evolved as vegetable offerings to birds; some even contain alkaloid compounds toxic to mammals. Passing through avian digestive systems, the seeds are carried far and wide before being deposited in droppings to take root and flourish. The little lights of haws, the fat dusty globes of sloes amongst blackthorn needles; hips like miniature lamps, the tiny-apple handfuls of rowans and whitebeams; and then the weirder berries like the pale, gelid orbs of mistletoe or spindleberries, the last looking as if Pucci decided to make tiny popcorn ornaments out of pink and orange wax. Blackcaps, plump little warblers, adore mistletoe berries. They pick away at their sticky flesh until their beaks are covered in goo then clean them on branches, where the seeds adhere and grow. In recent years German blackcaps that have started spending winters here rather than in Africa may be directly responsible for spreading mistletoe to new areas of the British Isles.

In early winter, mistle thrushes turn full Smaug: they'll claim possession of particularly fine yew trees, hollies, mistletoe clumps or bushes full of berries and defend them against intruders, chasing them away with strident, football-rattle calls of fury: the better they defend their hoard, the earlier and more successful their breeding attempts tend to be the following spring. But not all birds are so territorial. At this time of year our local blackbirds are joined by small flocks from Scandinavia and other parts of Northern Europe, and they'll feast on berries together. In the presence of such bounty they'll tolerate, if not entirely welcome, each other's presence.

With exceptions like dogroses and brambles, most shrubs and trees flower and fruit on that year's new growth, so the traditional yearly trim of hedgerows in autumn will deprive a whole community of valuable winter foodstuffs. But increasingly, as hedgerows become valued for wildlife rather than simply as stock barriers, they are cut on two- or three-year rotation, which ensures a supply of berries through the coldest months. Some berries are more palatable than others. Autumn blackberries disappear fast; by winter they've gone except for furry, frost-dried knots. Hawthorn and blackthorn, too. By late winter, few berries are left. Wood pigeons feast on the black fruits of ivy, clambering awkwardly on thin twigs and later depositing bright purple droppings under their roosts. As winter progresses, some berries ferment and become alcoholic, and it's not uncommon to see faintly disoriented birds wandering around beneath affected shrubs.

Among the last berries to be eaten in winter are those on ornamental shrubs and trees, either because they are relatively unpalatable or because they're coloured so unusually that many native birds do not recognise them as edible. It's these berries that become the targets of the unpredictable visitations of a bird that more than any other means winter's wonder to me. The last time I saw them was five years ago in a small pedestrian precinct in Alton, Hampshire. It was a bitter February day, everyone hooded and hatted, heads down, trudging stoically between shops. I was asking my mother where she'd like to meet for coffee after our errands were done when I heard an unearthly trilling noise, like a carillon of silver bells, and like a gravity-stricken whirlwind a pack of fat birds swirled down from the blank sky on to a slim twelve-foot sorbus tree right above us. They were waxwings, irregular visitors from the far north. They're neither pink nor grey nor brown but something in between that's no colour the way winter skies are no colour. They glommed on to the tree and began stuffing their maws with white berries, every so often rising en masse to the sky before resettling on the branches in a slightly different arrangement. They had elegant crests, bandit-black masks and flashes of russet, their black tails and wings patterned with daffodil yellow; and on their wing coverts, rows of the bizarre ornaments for which they're named, small waxy red protuberances that look exactly like the heads of matches. They're both highly classy and fantastically trashy to look at; no Christmas decoration could ever approach their absurd, animate beauty. Their magic isn't simply in the surprise of their comings and goings – some years they appear, often they don't – but where they're most often seen. They are particularly drawn to the fruits of tree cultivars beloved of town planners, so every winter there'll be reports of waxwing flocks on the internet that read something like: *Twenty birds, Aldi car park,* or *small flock behind PC Warehouse!*

My mother and I stood entranced. No one else noticed them, even though the nearest bird was two feet from our faces – they're so unconcerned by people they will even feed from apples held out in one's hands if they're hungry enough – and a few seconds later the winter vision swirled upwards again like leaves and was gone, leaving a bare tree and faint trills over the shopping-centre roofs.

CHERRY STONES

Autumn 2017 has seen an unprecedented invasion from Europe. It's been reported all over the British press and set internet message boards on fire. People have left their homes expressly to search for the immigrants and some have set up microphones to detect their calls at night. Between mid-October and mid-November, fifty passed through Greenwich Park in London and more than a hundred and fifty were seen at one location in East Sussex. They've made their way to Britain because of food shortages in their countries of origin, and there's a general hope among those who look for them that they'll find what they need here, settle in and stay.

The immigrants are hawfinches, starling-sized finches on steroids dressed in tones of salmon pink, black, white, russet and grey. Their enormous, cherry-stone-cracking beak resembles a pair of side-cutting steel pliers and is quite capable of severing a human finger. With coppery eyes set in an ink-black bib and mask, overall their appearance always reminds me of an exquisitely dressed pugilist. They're rare and declining in Britain – around eight hundred pairs breed here. The first time I ever saw one was on a winter's evening in the late 1990s while driving through the Forest of Dean in a rainstorm at dusk. As I rounded a corner, a single bird flew up from the verge. Caught in my headlights, its pied wings strobed through bright lines of falling water before it disappeared back into the dark. The encounter was every bit as ghostly and strange as the species' reputation among British birdwatchers, for hawfinches are legendarily mysterious, secretive and difficult to see. Local populations frequently disappear completely for a number of years before reappearing in their old haunts for no obvious reason. They're most often detected by their call alone: a short, metallic, emphatic *szick*! They're easier to locate after the leaves have fallen, but are so skittish that most of my sightings have been tiny silhouettes set on the topmost branches of distant winter trees.

But things are very different in mainland Europe. Walking through Berlin's Volkspark

Friedrichshain on a cold spring day some years ago with a friend who lived in the city, I stopped in frank astonishment under a cock hawfinch singing on a lime twig a few feet above my head. *It's a hawfinch!* I breathed. 'Yes, there's loads of them here, all over the place,' she said, casually, and shrugged. I waved my hands in frustration as the bird continued to sing. Faced with this absurdly tame creature, as much at home in the city as a feral pigeon, there was no way I could explain to her how enigmatic hawfinches were supposed to be.

The recent influx to Britain is likely to have been spurred by a failure of the hornbeam crop across Eastern Europe, though some blame it on unusual weather. One British Trust for Ornithology spokesman suggested that warm air pulled north-west by one of this year's biggest storms, Ophelia, has brought the hawfinches here. Whatever the cause, this unprecedented irruption of avian refugees fascinates me partly because it speaks so obviously of current issues – it's a truism that birds know no political borders – but also because it reminds me of how closely human concerns inform our understanding of nature. Today, our small population of resident hawfinches lives mostly in ancient woodlands or as small colonies in the forests and parklands of stately homes, to such an extent that I once heard a birder call them National Trust finches, after the heritage conservation charity that administers so many of Britain's most magnificent historic estates. So closely are hawfinches tied to these symbolic British landscapes that for years I assumed they were the last remnants of a native, much decreased ancient population whose present-day rarity was a function of modernity. My mind was blown when I found out that Britain had no breeding hawfinches until the mid-nineteenth century, when a number of prospecting pairs from mainland Europe started a nesting colony in Epping Forest. They spread from there until fifty years later there were birds in almost every English county taking advantage of apple orchards and leafy deciduous woodlands full of their favourite food sources: hornbeam, beech, maple, elm, yew, hawthorn and cherry. British hawfinch populations reached their peak in the 1950s, after which they went into precipitous decline.

The history of hawfinches in Britain reminds us how seamlessly we confuse natural and national history, how readily we assume nativity in things that are familiar to us, and how lamentably easy it is to forget how we are all from somewhere else. The loss of suitable habitat is one important factor in the decline of British hawfinches, but another is nest predation by grey squirrels, commonly seen as unwanted foreign invaders. Ironically, they appeared in the British landscape at about the same time as hawfinches.

Perhaps the immigrant finches will stay and raise young here. That's what a lot of people are hoping. I certainly am. But for now, what is most joyous to me about this once-in-a-lifetime influx is that birds renowned for their attachments to ancient woods and country estates are turning up in unexpectedly everyday places. They're clambering about yew branches in local churchyards and foraging in the leaf litter of suburban parks. In late November, eight were spotted at Mill Hill Sports Centre in London. 'At last!' wrote Ms Sue Barnecutt Smith in a comment to one newspaper article about the invasion. 'I couldn't work out the identity of a bird my son spotted at my allotment last week (near Putney Bridge, west London). Now we know.' These spectacular refugees have eschewed the venerable treetops of stately homes to spend their time instead with sparrows, feeding happily upon sunflower hearts and peanuts scattered on garden bird tables.

Birds, Tabled

The strangest thing about the Bird Fair, Britain's premier birding event, is that there are no birds there. 'Yes there are!' hissed the man in the entry line behind us, though I'd been speaking only to my mother. 'There are *ospreys.*' It's true that wild ospreys live on the lakes at Rutland Water, the site where the Bird Fair is held, but there are no birds at the Bird Fair. What there are instead: thousands of people, the sweet scent of trampled summer grass, shaded marquees inside which are tables and touts for bird tours to every part of the Earth. Binoculars and spotting scopes. Books. A refreshment tent. An art tent. Tents for lectures. Every time I go to the Bird Fair I see people I know and love. But no birds.

A few years ago I drove to the West Midlands with my boyfriend, a birdkeeper, to visit a different kind of bird fair: a bird show. We parked in a Staffordshire field beside two hangar-like halls. The men walking past us looked nothing like the men at the Bird Fair, who tend to be pale and urgent of face and dressed in hiking boots and technical trousers. These men were laughing as they lugged boxes and cages and the tops of trestle tables. They wore rugby shirts, lumberjack shirts, hooded tracksuits, fishing waistcoats. There were tattoos and many baseball hats. There were no binoculars at all.

But there were a lot of birds. The halls were full of show cages. Far smaller than the cages and aviaries these birds lived in at home, they were designed to display the beauty of the creatures within. There were hooped wire ones like tabletop Victorian aviaries inside which hopped stout canaries; vertical stacks of wooden boxes fronted with the tiniest gauge wire for minute owl-finches and waxbills; bigger cages for pigeons and chickens and quail. A few tables of huge-headed, feather-perfect show budgerigars with spotted gorgets, birds that looked far more artificial than the plastic feed trays in their cages. I watched in awe as a man walked past holding a tight-feathered white pigeon the size of a baby. He told me it was a Hungarian Giant House Pigeon, and instantly my own house seemed the poorer for not having one.

An industrial propane heater roared in a corner and the halls echoed with Tannoy announcements instructing exhibitors to ensure that water and feed bowls were filled and their birds weren't too hot, or too cold, and showed no signs of distress. Wandering about from table to table I sneaked photos on my phone using all the tactical guile my father taught me from his years as a photo-journalist. Keeping the phone low at my hip, maintaining eye contact and smiling with stallholders, I took a series of blurred and tilted shots using one thumb. Birdkeepers are wary creatures. I didn't want them to know what I was doing, for if the culture of watching wild birds has all the social acceptability of drinking wine, birdkeeping feels more like legalised cannabis use. Both involve a deep love of birds and displays of natural-historical connoisseurship, but bird-keeping is considered by many to be mor-ally dubious and, at its fringes, prone to lawlessness.

Thankfully, all the birds at this fair were domestically bred. Legislation in the 1980s made the keeping of wild-trapped British birds illegal, and the international trade in wild birds has declined by 90 per cent since the European Union banned imports in 2005. That was a trade made entirely of heartbreak – I will never forget looking up at the window of a warehouse in West London's Cromwell Road as a child and seeing the flurried wingbeats of scores of distressed, disoriented, recently arrived cockatoos.

One section of this bird show was dedicated to what birdkeepers call *British:* native species, the same kinds as those that sing in our woods and gardens and forests and fields. Insectivorous and fruit-eating birds like blackbirds and thrushes were displayed in cages painted white inside, often with embellishments that hinted at their natural habitat, such as rocks for wheatears or a sheet of forest bark for redstarts. The show cages of British finches had glossy black exteriors and were painted inside with Bro-lac Georgian green, a mossy tone particularly favoured by interior designers in the eighteenth century. Inside them were goldfinches, linnets, redpolls, siskins, bullfinches, hawfinches.

One of these cages was attracting considerable attention. Inside it was a pied goldfinch, its plumage broken with freakish patches of white. Unusual colour mutations like these are highly prized among British

337

bird aficionados – goldfinches with a white spot under their chin are called peathroats; those with an entirely white throat, cheverals. A group of Irish Travellers clustered around this cage, engaged in animated discussion about the merits of the bird while a pile of twenty-pound notes was counted out upon the table. *Seven-colour linnets*, they call goldfinches; it's a very old name, hardly ever used by birdwatchers. This one was likely destined to breed mules, a kind of bird beloved by Romani and Traveller birdkeepers. The offspring of a wild finch (usually a male goldfinch or linnet) mated with a domesticated canary, they're known as mules because like the offspring of a horse and a donkey, they're sterile. They're treasured for their intensely beautiful songs, which combine sweet, wide-ranging canary trills with the varied, sharp, metallic notes of their wild fathers.

A few years ago I spoke to a man who confessed to me that he used to trap wild goldfinches when he was younger, despite knowing it was illegal. 'I didn't keep them – I was catching hormone-addled males for muling,' he said. 'I'd pop them in a cage with a female canary, long enough for them to mate, then let them go. They'd be in the trap, in my hand, in the cage, for only a few minutes. Where was the harm in that? The problem is,' he said darkly, 'they don't like us keeping British at all.'

His use of the term *they* helps us understand one aspect of the difference between the Bird Fair and the Bird Show: that our attitudes towards nature are shaped by history and class and power. These two events mirror a longstanding division in the ways we relate to the natural world. One view is that nature is something pristine out there that should only be observed or recorded; the other sees it as something that can be brought into interior spaces and closely interacted with. It runs along the same lines as the division between field scientists and lab scientists, or between hunters and farmers. Such divisions are freighted with social meaning. Like so many battles about nature, at heart they're about who has the right to define what a creature is, who has the right to interact with it, and how.

Birding, along with similar forms of observational nature-appreciation, has near-universal cultural acceptability in the present day – there's considerable media coverage of the Bird Fair, for example – but the keeping of small native birds does not. It has long been a hobby associated with working-class and minority communities, like miners, immigrants, East End Londoners, Romani and Irish Travellers. The last long conversation I had about birdkeeping was with a Romanian taxi driver on the way to an airport very early on a Sunday morning. In the darkness the screen of his iPhone glowed with a photograph of a bird with a black cap, a pugnacious beak and a chest the colour of young red wine. I told him I thought it was a beautiful bullfinch, and he was beside himself with delight: *You know what it is! This is my bird!* And we talked about his birds for the rest of the journey. He'd got into it late, he said. When he was a young man he had no idea how perfect birds were: like precious stones, but alive. And their songs! He explained that his birds are his life, and they are like children in two ways: because he loves them and because he cannot remember the person he was before them.

The great anti-cagebird campaigns of my childhood were in part the crusade of bird lovers like Peter Conder, then Director of the Royal Society for the Protection of Birds, who had spent years behind wire in German prisoner of war camps. But that's not the only reason we don't like to see birds in small cages. Those cages radically attenuate the possibilities of a bird's life. I can't look at birds in them without my heart aching fit to burst, even if those birds look otherwise healthy and happy and well-adjusted. But we limit the lives of captive animals in myriad ways, and don't always judge their impacts according to the needs of the creatures involved. The high-density broiler operations of chickens kept in locked sheds, for example – birds bred to gain weight so fast that after only a few weeks many find it difficult to walk – are something hardly any of us see, and are thus easy to ignore. Moreover, we often fail to see many of the other cruelties we visit on animals because we don't consider what an animal's world ought to contain – the lives of single rabbits kept in cramped garden hutches have always broken my heart, no matter how beloved those animals might be.

Nearly every year I read news reports of the arrests of working-class men who have been keeping illegally trapped British finches. Their depredations must have a negligible impact compared to the ravages of habitat loss and agricultural chemicals on bird populations, but that's not the point. What they have done is not simply illegal, but considered highly immoral. Species perceived as animate elements of the British countryside have been deprived of their freedom and confined to cages for the delight of the working classes, for whom these birds possess very different meanings. There's a tender domesticity attendant to birdkeeping that cuts through familiar stories about working-class masculinity. Cages are cleaned, babies are tended, droppings are scraped, food is weighed, and birds are held quietly in the hand to be minutely and lovingly examined, activities that mirror the cleaning and housekeeping, cooking and child-keeping roles more familiarly ascribed to women. It's always struck me that people who keep and breed goldfinches, for example, have a far more detailed knowledge of their habits, their intraspecific variations, their breeding behaviour and songs than that of most birdwatchers, to whom goldfinches tend to be birds clinging to feeders in suburban gardens, or flocks that rise from stands of seeding thistles. I grew up watching birds, not keeping them. To me, redpolls have always been delicate and distant entities, small dots flitting around the tops of alder trees. I would never have known that redpolls are a thousand times more charismatic and full of personality than goldfinches had I not had the experience of seeing both kinds of birds close up in aviaries and cages.

It's not birdkeeping per se that is the problem. Some forms of it have almost entirely escaped censure because they have traditionally been the province of those of high social status. You can keep a singing goldfinch in the smallest of caravans, but you need money and land to keep lakes of swans and diving ducks. Waterfowl luminaries have included the aristocrat Lord Lilford; the artist-conservationist Sir Peter Scott; and the eponymous founder of British department store John Lewis, who maintained an enormous collection of ducks and geese on his Hampshire estate. It's still legal in Britain to ask a vet to pinion a young duck or goose or swan, to cut off the last joint of one wing so that forever afterwards it can walk and swim but never fly, a literal amputation to the nature of a migratory species whose wild cousins fly thousands of miles over tundra and ocean every autumn and spring. I have always wondered if a pinioned goose on the lake of a stately home might be experiencing hardships of the same order as that of a goldfinch confined to a cage.

Unlike finches inside houses, the waterfowl in such collections are not treated as an intimate part of the household, but as part of a wider demesne, as landscape-scale additions to an estate. Captive ducks swimming on a lake look pleasingly wild, even if they have had the end of one wing cut away to stop them escaping. An enormous amount of work is involved in creating this elite version of nature, which, as in the eighteenth-century landscape-garden tradition, is designed specifically to look untouched, eternal, natural and unaffected by human artifice, even though that is exactly how it has been made.

Conversely, as journalist Henry Mayhew wrote in the mid-nineteenth century, 'The buyers of singing-birds are eminently the working people.' He went on to describe the species that various classes of tradesmen and artisans preferred to keep – blackbirds and thrushes, for example, were favoured by grooms and coachmen. 'The fondness of a whole body of artificers for any particular bird, animal, or flower, is remarkable,' he concluded. It's the term *artificer* that sings, here, and of a matter that is at the heart of the class system: taste. Keepers of small birds love them not only as individuals but as possibilities and potentialities; over the years they design complex strategies of pairing and selecting to breed birds of particular shapes and patterns and colours and songs. Birdkeeping gestures towards the future as much as it does to those moments in the present when a goldfinch mule raises its head, puffs out its throat and pours forth song. It is, in ways that are not trivial, a deeply creative art. Obvious artifice is the issue: unlike the carefully constructed apparent naturalness of waterfowl kept on country estates, working-class birdkeepers delight in artificiality, creating hybrid finches and thrushes whose beauty is judged in how richly and elaborately it deviates from naturalness.

'Mine!' says the birdkeeper, of the goldfinch. 'Mine!' says the birder, of the same. 'Mine!' says the estate owner, of his flock of pinioned European geese. Outside the bird show, I hear a goldfinch singing from the top of a sapling behind me. While my boyfriend walks on to the car, I stop and listen for a while to a bird that is calling a claim to the whole of its life. It sings of seeds and thistledown, of mates and flights and the fragility of eggs in a moss-and-cobweb nest, and of territorial battles and parasites and sparrowhawks and scarcity and stress.

HIDING

A wildlife hide: a building whose purpose is to make one disappear. This one is a rustic wooden box with bench seats and narrow slits along one side. Walking up to it, it looks almost exactly like a small, weather-beaten garden shed.

I've made myself disappear in hides for as long as I can remember; structures like it are found in nature reserves all over the world, and they seem as natural a part of these places as trees and open water. Even so, a familiar, nervous apprehension flares up as I reach for the door, so I pause for a few seconds before opening it. Inside the air is hot and dark and smells of dust and creosote.

There's no one else here. I swing my legs over the bench-seat and lower the wooden window blind to create a bright rectangle in the darkness; as my eyes adjust, the space before me resolves into a shallow lagoon under streets of cumulus clouds. Almost automatically, I scan the scene with binoculars, ticking off species – three shoveler ducks, two little egrets, a common tern – but my mind is elsewhere, puzzling over that odd sense of apprehension, trying to work out what causes it.

Wildlife hides are not innocent of history. They evolved from photographic blinds, which in turn were based on structures designed to put people closer to animals in order to kill them: duck blinds, deer stands, tree platforms for shooting big cats. Hunting has shaped modern nature appreciation in myriad unacknowledged ways, including the tactics used to bring animals into view. As hunters bait deer and decoy ducks, so preserve managers create shallow feeding pools that concentrate wading birds near hides, or set up feeding stations for wary nocturnal mammals. In the Highlands of Scotland, one celebrated hide gives visitors a 95 per cent chance of seeing rare pine martens – lithe arboreal predators – munching on piles of peanuts.

What you see from hides is supposed to be true reality: that is, wild animals behaving perfectly naturally because they do not know they are being observed. But the side-effect of turning yourself into a pair of eyes in a darkened box is to distance you from the all-encompassing landscape around the hide, in so doing reinforcing a divide between human and natural worlds, encouraging us to feel that animals and plants should be looked at, never touched. Sometimes the window in front of me resembles nothing so much as a television screen.

You don't need to be invisible to see wild animals behaving entirely naturally. As scientists studying creatures like meerkats, chimps and the small brown birds called Arabian babblers have long known, with time you can habituate them to your presence. But hiding is a habit that is hard to break. There is a dubious satisfaction in the subterfuge of watching things that cannot see you, and it's deeply embedded in our culture. When wild animals unexpectedly appear close by and seem unbothered by our presence, we can feel as flustered and unsure about how to behave as teenagers at a dance.

A few years ago, I was walking with my friend Christina through a park in a small English town when characters I've only ever seen in bird hides began to appear: camouflage-clad photographers with 300-millimetre lenses and expressions of urgent concentration. We looked where the cameras were pointed. Three yards away, two of Britain's most elusive mammals were swimming in the shallow river running through the park. Otters! They didn't seem to see us; they certainly didn't care. Their wet flanks gleamed like tar as they rolled in the water. They broke the surface to crunch fish with sharp white teeth, showering droplets from stiff whiskers, then slipped back beneath the surface to swim down the river, the photographers chasing them like paparazzi and intermittently running backwards because the lenses they'd brought were the wrong ones for such close views. It was thrilling. We followed the otters downstream and stopped by a woman with a toddler and a baby in a pushchair, who were watching them, too. She told me she loved the otters. They were part of her town. Part of her local community. They'd eaten all the koi carp from the fishpond in the big house, she said, amused. 'Drove them bonkers, the people that lived there. Those fish were really expensive!' Then she tilted her head at the photographers. 'Aren't they weird?' she asked. Outside a hide, they did look ridiculous; so accustomed to their binoculars, camouflage and high-zoom lenses, they were compelled to use them even when they were entirely unnecessary.

While hides are places designed for watching wildlife, they are equally rewarding places to watch people who watch wildlife and to witness their strange social behaviour. One of the reasons I hesitated before entering the little hide is that I was worried there would be other people in it. Walking into a crowded hide is rather like arriving late at a live theatrical performance and trying to find your seat. There are unspoken rules in hides. As in a theatre or a library, you are required to be silent, or to speak in a low murmur. Some rules are ostensibly in operation to prevent animals detecting your presence – there's a general prohibition on telephone calls, slamming the door too hard, extending your hands out of the window. But others are more curious and they stem from a particular problem: your job in a hide is to pretend you are not there, so when there is more than one person in the hide, the sense of disembodiment the trick relies on is threatened. Regular visitors to hides often solve this conundrum spatially. When she started visiting hides for the first time, Christina – who is from Melbourne – wondered why people chose to sit at the far edges, leaving the seats with the best view unoccupied. 'I thought it was self-sacrificing English etiquette,' she said, 'before I realised that people sat at the far sides of the hide because they wanted to be as far from everyone else as possible.'

There's a constant monitoring of others' expertise in the hide as its inhabitants listen to one another's hushed conversations about the things they can see outside. It's an agony when people get things wrong. I remember the chill in the air one spring day in Suffolk after a man confidently told his companion that what he was watching was a water vole. Everyone else in the hide knew this lumbering creature with a long tail was a large brown rat. No one said anything. One man coughed. Another snorted. The tension was unbearable. With impeccable British reserve, no one felt they could correct his mistake and lessen him in the eyes of his friend. A few people couldn't bear the atmosphere and left the hide.

The uses of hides are as various as their inhabitants. You can sit with a camera hoping for the perfect shot of a passing harrier or owl. You can sit with a proficient naturalist and hear whispered identification tips, or use it as a place to sit down midway through a long walk. Most people sit and scan the view with binoculars for a few minutes before deciding there is nothing of sufficient interest or rarity to keep them there. But there is another kind of hide watching that I am increasingly learning to love. It is when you embrace the possibility that you will see little or nothing of interest. You literally wait and see. Sitting in the dark for an hour or two and looking at the world through a hole in a wall requires a meditative patience. You have given yourself time to watch clouds drift from one side of the sky to the other and cast moving shadows across ninety minutes of open water. A sleeping snipe, its long bill tucked into pale-tipped scapular feathers and its body pressed against rushes striped with patterns of light and shade, wakes, raises its wings and stretches. A heron as motionless as a marble statue for minutes on end makes a cobra-strike to catch a fish. The longer you sit there, the more you become abstracted from this place, and yet fixed to it. The sudden appearance of a deer at the lake's shore, or a flight of ducks tipping and whiffling down to splash on sunlit water, becomes treasure, through the simple fact of the passing of time.

EULOGY

By nine the sun has set behind the King's Forest. The sky is a soft Tiffany blue, darker above us, and there's not a breath of wind. Judith knows the place well, leads us through deep woodland to a few acres of open land, a block of head-height young pines growing through grass and brambles, surrounded by walls of mature trees.

We're waiting for something that won't happen until the light is nearly gone, so we amble for a while along the sandy paths. As night falls, our senses stretch to meet it. A roebuck barks in the distance, small mammals rustle in the grass. The faintest tick of insects. The scratchy, resinous fragrance of heathland grows stronger, more insistent. As we pass clumps of viper's bugloss we watch the oncoming night turn their leaves blacker, their purple petals bluer and more intense until they seem to glow. The paths become luminous trails through darkness.

White moths spiral up from the ground, and a cockchafer zips past us, elytra raised, wings buzzing.

Soon all colour will be gone. The thought is a hard one. Over the last few weeks I've spent much of my time visiting Stu in a local hospice. He and his partner Mandy are among my dearest, closest friends. I first met him in the 1990s on a raw December morning at a falconry field meet in the East Anglian Fens. He was a giant of a man with curly hair and a huge old goshawk and he was formidable and faintly scary. But as I watched him handle his hawk and his dogs, I saw there an extraordinary gentleness and care. So many of my memories of Stu are of this gentleness; the way he'd look at his family, the expression on his upturned face as he followed his falcons' flight, the tender way he'd clean their hooked beaks between finger and thumb. He was a strong man, a strong-willed man, who carved his own, inimitable path through life, and he had an astonishing capacity to reassure, to teach, to inspire.

Stu was so ready to see magic in the world. He told me once, shaking his head in wonderment, that he'd watched a white stag stepping across the road at midnight like something out of a medieval legend. About the time he caught a bat in his motorcycle leathers while biking at top speed, and how he was so amazed and delighted he put it in his pocket and brought it home to show everyone before letting it go. And how, after he had been diagnosed with the illness that he knew would take him, he'd been walking with his pointer dog Cody across fields when she'd found two just-born leverets, twin baby hares, tucked in the grass. Stuart was the strongest of men, but he told me about them with tears in his eyes. They were so small. So new.

Now, watching the slow diminishment of sense and detail around me, I'm thinking of Stu and what is happening to him, thinking of his family, of what we face at the end of our lives' long summers when the world parts from us, of how we all, one day, will walk into darkness. Then the sound begins. It spools out from the trees behind the sapling pines, and I catch the flash of a smile on Judith's face in the gloom. The noise resembles a sewing machine running at top speed, or an unspooling fishing reel, but such mechanical analogies fail to capture its rich musicality. It's a deep and beautiful *churring* that lasts for four or five seconds before the creature that's making it breathes in, briefly lowering the pitch, and then starts up again. Judith cups a hand behind each ear and turns her head to pinpoint the source. She gestures out in front of us, a little to our left. Somewhere in that direction, sitting lengthways on a branch, his throat puffed out to raise this strange song to the night, is a nightjar.

Imagine a slim bird as long as your hand from wrist to fingertip, and with huge, black-ink anime eyes. Imagine its plumage is patterned with all woodland things rolled together: bark, rotting wood, the tips of dry fern fronds, cobwebs, the bright ends of broken twigs, dappled shadows, dead leaves. Nightjars are cryptic beasts for whom subtlety is safety; during daylight hours they rest and nest upon ground that so perfectly matches their feathers they are almost impossible to detect, even from a few feet away. Their neat beaks look ordinary enough until they open their mouths into a huge, froglike pink gape surrounded by bristly feathers that help them catch their flying prey: moths, beetles, other insects. The bird we're hearing spent his winter in Africa, has come here to mate and rear young in this chequerboard landscape of coniferous forest and heath before he heads back south in late August or September. Another *churr* begins, then another. Five birds, six? It's hard to tell, but they're calling all around us. It's exquisite music, but I'm hoping we get something more.

We do. There's a soft call, a different call, the one they make in flight. I whistle something like it back into the darkness. The call comes again, closer now, and as I strain my eyes into the noisy black I see the barest suggestion of a bird flying towards me, wings as thin, wavering lines appearing and disappearing over the distance between the noise and my upturned face. And then, sailing out just above our heads, dark against the sky, is a nightjar. It's remarkably odd, the shape of a skinny falcon, but somehow the quality of its flight makes it look like a paper aeroplane. It's so light in the air it seems to have no weight at all, and there's something mothlike about it too. I can just make out the barring of the underside of its wings, the lack of white near their tips – it's a female – and we watch as she hunches herself in mid-air, curls down to the left and hovers, briefly. A male joins her, white wing-patches blurring; they circle for a few seconds before breaking apart and disappearing into darkness. We hear a quick, flat clapping noise as the male slaps the top of his wings together in flight, a display that sounds like quiet applause, and then they are gone, slipping back into the nothing around us.

For years, on and off, I have woken in the dark, shouting out loud, stricken with horror at the impossible fact of death. It has been my most abiding and paralysing terror but it was Stu who banished it from me. At the hospice he looked me in the eye, very seriously, very quietly, and said, of what was happening to him, *It's OK. It's OK.* I knew it was not, that what he was doing was reassuring me, and it was an act of such generosity that for a while I couldn't find anything strong enough inside me to reply. *It's OK,* he said. *It's not hard.* Those are the words I am remembering as we walk onward, as the minutes pass, until night thickens completely and there is starlight and dust and the feel of sand underfoot. It's so dark now I cannot see myself. But the song continues, and the air around us is full of invisible wings.

RESCUE

My friend Judith cuts the head off a dead cricket with a pair of nail scissors and discards its leggy, thorny thorax before dropping the abdomen into a small china bowl on the kitchen table, the kind of bowl that you'd use for olives or pretzels. The cricket's insides are as white and creamy as soft cheese. Outside, sparrows squabble in the garden, and their chirruping calls back the crunching scythe of blades through chitin and the wet patter of insect parts dropped one by one into the pile. Next to the bowl is a plastic washing-up tub. When I lean over to look inside it, dark eyes stare up at me from a huddle of pale-fringed faces.

The tub is full of baby swifts. Adults might be renowned for their aerial grace, but the baby ones in front of me resemble a cross between subway mice and a pile of unexpectedly animate kindling. Their clawed feet are so tiny that they cannot walk, only shuffle, and their impossibly long wings stick out at a variety of unlikely angles. Judith, a gentle and deliberate woman with silver hair cut in a practical bob, lifts up one of the nestlings and sets it upon a tissue-covered towel. Plucking a lump from the bowl, she touches it to the tip of its tiny beak, which opens into a huge pink maw that swallows the tip of her finger. The cricket vanishes down the bird's throat. Another follows.

Frowning with concentration, Judith feeds her birds with the calm assurance gained from long experience. Seventeen years ago she spotted what she thought was a pile of feathers by the side of the road while walking her dog. It was a swift chick. She picked it up and brought it home. Numerous experts told her that it would be too difficult to raise and would die. 'Of course it didn't,' she said. 'It survived. But it was a steep learning curve.'

She's now so renowned for her swift-rearing skills that orphans are brought to her from all over eastern England. Some arrive from vets, others from members of the public who have found her name on the internet having come across birds that have fallen from their nests. She's had around

360

thirty in her care this year, and has raised them all on a diet of crickets and wax-moth caterpillars dusted with powdered vitamins. While some don't make it – usually because they've been given unsuitable food by their initial rescuers – most are successfully returned to the wild, triumphing over death. And the chance to observe that particular triumph is why I'm sitting in her small bungalow in a village near the American air base in Suffolk where she used to work in communications and public affairs. If the wind drops later this morning, we'll set some of her young birds free. 'It can be very tiring,' she says. 'The early mornings! But when you let one go, it's just sheer magic. And sometimes I'm in the garden in the evening, and I might see twenty, thirty, forty swifts in the air, and I think, *I know they're not, but they could be all mine.*'

We tend to physically touch wild animals only when they're hunted, studied or in serious trouble, and the latter is usually our fault. We dislodge nests, soak seabirds in oil, hit hares and foxes with cars, pick up casualties from beneath glass windows and power lines. When I was twelve I reared a brood of baby bullfinches brought to me by a neighbour who had felled their nest tree. When those chicks flew free, there was a strong

361

sense of having righted a wrong that humans had perpetrated on the world.

Against a backdrop of environmental destruction and precipitous species decline, our social anxieties about the impact we have on the natural world are often tied to tragedies suffered by individual animals. Tending injured and orphaned creatures until they are fit to be returned to the wild can feel like an act of resistance, redress, even redemption. Rearing a single nest of finches in the 1980s didn't halt the decline of British songbird populations. But my simple sense of the justice of saving them was magnified by coming to see things about them I'd never otherwise have known: how they slept, how they communicated with each other, their myriad bewitching idiosyncrasies.

'We feel responsible,' says Norma Bishop, executive director of Lindsay Wildlife Experience in Walnut Creek, California, which operates America's oldest wildlife rehabilitation centre, founded in 1970. 'It's a little like the story of Noah rescuing the animals.' Rehabbers stress that their animals are never pets, and that their role is to return them to the wild as fast as possible, but inevitably they forge emotional bonds with their charges. British regulations allow individuals to tend to animal casualties themselves provided they adhere to established welfare guidelines. In America, wildlife rehabilitation is confined to licensed experts, often working for charitable institutions. But whatever the rehabber's position, the dedication involved is immense: keepers of orphaned elephants in Kenya, for example, sleep next to the animals every night, but they take turns with others because too great an attachment to any one keeper risks the baby elephant being overcome by grief when he or she takes the night off.

Why do people rescue wildlife? The eminent veterinarian John Cooper thinks 'there's something inside humans when they're faced with a helpless creature. We have an imperative. A duty.' Bishop agrees: 'I believe most people, especially children, simply cannot see an animal suffer.' The Lindsay rehab centre receives everything from bobcats to snakes, ducklings to songbirds, brought in by concerned members of the public who may have driven many miles to deliver them. Los Angeles-based hummingbird rehabber Terry Masear thinks that rescuing animals draws out 'raw emotions that unleash our deepest insecurities about our humanity, mortality and place in the natural world'. These insecurities often lead to mistaken attempts at rescue: most 'lost' fledgling birds in trees or sleeping fawns in long grass are not lost at all, but are still being fed by their parents.

Rehabbers are often criticised for being too sentimental, their work dismissed as acts of compassion for individual animals with little or no conservation benefit. It's a reasonable view, but one that misses the point. It's hard to feel a meaningful connection with creatures whose lives in the wild hardly coincide with our own. Bats are things of unnerving mystery to most of us, flickering aerial presences briefly and surprisingly appearing out of the night. But holding a little brown bat, staring into its bleary eyes from a few inches away, seeing its uptilted snout and delicate, mouse-like ears – that turns it into something much easier to love. The way rehabbers talk about what they do evokes in me precisely the feelings I've had about rescue animals in my own life: an intoxicating process of coming to know something quite unlike you, to understand it well enough not only to keep it alive but also to put it back, like a puzzle piece, into the gap in the world it left behind.

Judith has no truck with accusations of sentimentality when it comes to swifts, whose numbers in Britain have fallen by more than 35 per cent over the last twenty years. Each bird she saves, she tells me, may truly be precious to the species' fortunes. Increasingly, people are blocking up holes in the eaves of old buildings where swifts nest, and modern buildings often have nowhere for swifts to nest at all. Similar problems face chimney swifts in North America as defunct and crumbling chimneys are removed. Many renovators do not know about the swifts' reliance on our buildings, do not know they are destroying their homes, because they simply don't know they are there. Seeing a rescued swift can change all that. 'Once people have seen a swift in the hand, they're in awe of them,' Judith says. Her kitchen is full of cards from well-wishers and people who have brought her swifts, and rescuers drop by to see how their chicks are faring. Some of them have been motivated to build and fit swift nest-boxes under their roofs, welcoming these birds into their homes.

The wind has dropped, and the sky above the house is a widening pool of blue. Judith has put seven swifts into a paper-towel-lined pet carrier, where they clump together in a feathery mass. One has reached across to gently preen the mantle feathers of a nest-mate. Watching them I realise I've never seen baby birds so desperate to snuggle. It's as if they've been magnetised to press themselves against each other, wing upon wing.

It's a short drive to Judith's favourite release site, the village cricket field. We arrive just as a local match is beginning, but after brief, good-natured negotiations, the cricketers stop playing and watch. Judith takes a swift from the box, plants a quick good-luck kiss on its feathery crown and hands it to me. People often presume that the way to release swifts is to throw them high in the air, but this can result in serious injury if the bird isn't ready to go. The right method is to hold the bird on your raised and outstretched palm, turn so it faces into the wind, and wait. In the bright air the swift looks a weird, unearthly creature, a delicate construction of scalloped feathers and ungainly wings. Hunched into itself, its miniature claws grip my fingers, its deep eyes like reflective astronaut visors. I wonder what it can see: lines of magnetic force, perhaps, rising air and flying insects and the suspicion of summer storms. The flat green beneath it has nothing to do with it at all. I lift my hand higher. All I can do now is wait.

It stares into the wind for a while, then starts shivering. Anticipation. I think. Functional explanations: this bird is warming up its pectoral muscles ready for flight. Emotional explanations: anticipation, wonder, joy, terror. The sensitive filoplumes growing between the feathers of its wings and sleek sides are being brushed by the breeze, feeling their element for the first time.

Nothing has visibly changed, but something is happening, like an aircraft avionics system coming online as it powers up. Blinking lights, engine check. *Check.* That doesn't work, though, not quite, as an analogy, because what I am watching is a new thing making itself out of something else. There is no doubt in my mind that this is as much a transformation as a dragonfly larva crawling from water and tearing itself out into a thing with wings. On my open palm a creature whose home has been paper towels and plastic boxes is turning into a different creature whose home is thousands of miles of air.

Then the swift decides. It tilts the pug-sharp tiny tip of its beak upwards, arches its back, and drops from my flattened palm, making an aching series of stiff and creaky wingbeats. For five or six seconds everything feels wrong. The bird is a mere foot above the grass, and my heart is beating fast. 'Up! Up! Up!' calls Judith. Nothing is broken. We are just watching a bird learning to fly. Hitching as if pulling into gear, the swift starts to ascend, flickering up and up into a sky streaked with evening cirrus. It describes one careful circle above our heads, then lifts even higher and straight-lines it to the south. The cricketers applaud. I look down at my palm. There's a little scratch on the meat of my thumb where its claws had gripped tight before letting me go, gripped tight to the hand that was the last solid thing the bird would touch for years.

GOATS

As a child I discovered a simple game that's good to play with goats. You lay your hand flat on a billy goat's forehead and push, just a little. You push, and it pushes back, and you push harder, and it does too, and it's a little like arm-wrestling, but much more fun, and the goat always wins.

I told Dad about my love of pushing goats once, just as an aside while we were talking about something else. He must have filed this information away, because about a year later, he came home very crossly, and he was cross with *me,* and that was a very rare thing. In his capacity as a press photographer, he'd spent the day at London Zoo taking photographs for their Annual Animal Census, and at one point he happened to be standing with the rest of the press pack in the petting zoo.

And there he sees a goat.

And he says to everyone, *Watch this.*

I hadn't explained the activity very well. Because he puts his hand against the goat's forehead, with everyone watching. Then he pushes.

He pushes really hard.

And the goat falls over.

There's a long silence broken only by the sound of photographers and journalists saying, '*Jesus*, Mac!' and, 'What the *fuck*?!'

The goat gets up, stares at him and runs away. And the press pack never let him forget the time he pushed a goat over in front of all of them and it was all my fault.

DISPATCHES FROM THE VALLEYS

There was a TV reality show a decade or so ago called *Victorian Farm*. I used to watch it with nostalgia and remember what life was like in the winter of 1997. Those were the days. I'd walk up the hill to the house at lunchtime, check the sheep, bring them hay, feed the hens, break the ice on the water troughs and drinkers, fill the scuttle in the outhouse, trudge inside to load the Rayburn range with coal, and then walk back down to the office along a country lane rutted with refrozen snow.

It was the age of *The X-Files* and *Friends,* Beck and The Prodigy, Dolly the Sheep and the death of Diana. I'd just graduated from university and had quite enough of libraries and the half-light of college refectories and university bars full of would-be poets. I was young, self-important, extremely self-absorbed. I wanted to *live,* wanted a real job in the real world, working with real and sensible people. So when I was hired by a falcon conservation-breeding farm in rural Wales, I was convinced I had found my perfect career.

I don't think of those times often. But they always come to mind if I'm watching a sci-fi movie in which an ill-matched crew with personality issues is stuck on a ship in deep space with nowhere to go. That's what it was like, although sometimes we all got in a car and went shopping in Swansea. We worked seven days a week, which was not good for our mental health, but at least we were doing what we loved, I'd tell myself, sometimes out loud in incantation, like after I heard the local builder muttering, 'They should tear this house down, it's a wreck,' outside our kitchen door.

The property belonged to our boss and his wife. A pebble-dashed box streaked with green algae, it had a pine-panelled kitchen and a low-ceilinged sitting room with the Rayburn, a brown vinyl sofa and eye-bending 1970s carpets that did bad things to you when you were drunk. I liked the house because it was home, even though towards the end of my stay bead-curtains of water pattered on to the carpet from the ceiling when it rained, and once I stood nonplussed as a rat ran out of the oven when someone opened the door. It could be idyllic in the summer, when swallows chattered and preened on the telephone wire outside my bedroom window, but it was often cold enough in winter that I'd need to train a hairdryer into the cave of my duvet to make it sufficiently warm inside that I could sleep. It was not a dry house. I wasn't allowed to bring falcons back home, the boss told me, because it was unlikely their delicate respiratory systems could cope with the atmosphere the staff lived in.

The house stood in rough pasture at the top of a steep mudstone valley. Behind us were dark woods and tussocky fields where the boss ran a small herd of mixed-breed steers that grew increasingly wild as the months went by. We lost them sometimes. Lost them in that they literally wandered off through gaps in the hedges. None of us were farmers, but we tried our best. In the evenings we'd make the long trek out to the pub for beer and pool and walk back in the small hours until the landlord barred us, as he'd barred everyone else that ever went there, and the pub closed down. At least, I think that's what happened. A lot of what happened back then has the quality of a fairy tale.

■ ■ ■ ■

Hawk-obsessed volunteers flocked to us every summer of the four years I worked there. Among them were an aristocratic Mexican veterinary student, a kickboxing champion from the Kyrgyz Republic, and a lad who spent so much time jerking off in the bathroom we used to hammer on the door and yell at him to stop. All of them were men. And apart from a biologist who left a few months after I arrived, so were the permanent staff. In the office with me was a lanky dark-haired northerner studying for his part-time Ph.D. who ended up in a relationship with me. Everyone else was outside with the birds. There was the enthusiastic Geordie who explained to me that the correct mindset for running out on to a rugby pitch was, *Let's break arms!;* the wiry ex-Marine who managed the breeding programme and while expert at the complexities of falcon artificial insemination and incubation was repeatedly dismayed by his inability to cook rice without it sticking together; and a skinny lad who'd grown up on a caravan site and spent his days jet-washing shit-splattered aviaries with re-signed good humour – he told me once that if he ever won the National Lottery, he'd buy himself a brand-new Ford Fiesta. There was the ebullient son of a white Zimbabwean tobacco farmer who stomped around in wellingtons and shorts and opined that accepting homosexuals was the symptom of a decadent and doomed society, and a quiet South African who'd make us *bobotie* and liked Hungarian folk music. He rebuilt the stone walls, cared for a kit of roller pigeons, and eventually acclimatised to our spartan life, though he spent his first night literally hugging the Rayburn to keep warm. This was the real world; these were the sensible people I'd left academia for.

Once, when it got really cold – the snow heaped high against the hedges and the fields littered with weak, emaciated arctic thrushes – I snapped with whatever the equivalent of the red mist is when you're just too frozen to deal. I filled the range as full as I could, eventually cramming lumps of coal in with my hands, opened up all the air vents as wide as they'd go and went back to work. A part of me knew this was not wise, and it was not. When I got home from work the house was full of smoke from the wallpaper burning away around the flue. But the Rayburn was our friend. It heated our water to Venusian temperatures, and saved us when the electricity went out, which it did from time to time, and we cooked chickens in it, often our own, young, poorly plucked, gristly cockerels bristling with filoplumes, which we chewed stoically by candlelight.

The office had a couple of hulking grey PCs and an internet connection so attenuated it took three days to download a sound file. The work we did there was fascinating and sobering. The recent collapse of the Soviet Union had opened up the breeding range of saker falcons to organised trapping and smuggling gangs, and falcon populations were in free fall. We ran field teams across their range to monitor their decline, ran sustainability education programmes, and sought to undercut the traditional market for wild-caught falconry birds in the Gulf States by sending out hundreds of home-bred falcons every autumn. I travelled out with them. I remember sitting in the night-illuminated cockpit of a 747 with a pilot who handed me a pink rose while explaining to me that aircraft greet each other in the darkness by flashing their lights. He let me throw the switches to do this, my heart lifting thousands of feet at the distant, impossible reply. Abu Dhabi itself was pale and dusty and in the midst of its mutation from coastal desert town to sci-fi high-rise metropolis, and my rooms on the Corniche looked out over one of the oldest buildings in town, the low concrete bulk of the 1972 British Embassy.

I treasure the times I spent in the UAE talking hawks and heritage with Emirati falconers. But the opportunity to spend time in the Gulf States wasn't what kept me at the farm. The birds did. They kept all of us there. As racehorse trainers know, young people will put up with almost anything to work with the objects of their passion. Every year we'd hand-rear a few falcons and raise them in the office. I'd find fledglings fast asleep on my keyboard, squeaking irritably and sending feather dust into the air when I gently nudged them awake and asked them to move so I could type. Sometimes I'd roll scrunched-up paper balls to them across the laminate floor and they'd run, stumpily, unsteadily, wings half-open, grabbing at their rolling targets with feet that weren't yet entirely coordinated, chittering with high excitement. Their presence made the office a much better place. But the breeding season was brutal for the bird staff. They slept in shifts to feed hatchlings through the night, and as the weeks went by became so exhausted they'd fall asleep in the middle of eating lunch, heads on folded arms, or pass out on the sofa and drool silently into the cushions. All spring they lived on pints of instant coffee and junk food and their lives were spent mincing frozen quail, changing paper towels, checking brooder temperatures, filling small falcon mouths begging for food again and again and again.

I learned a lot on the farm. Raptor biology, falcon breeding, for sure. But also how to work in a tight crew and love it; how to enjoy watching Premiership football matches on pub televisions, including the precise nature of the offside rule. I learned that counting sheep is harder than it appears, and that some sheep really are better looking than others. That the wet grass at the bottom of the field opposite the house was where the snipe were, and in deep winter, woodcock sifted down into the valley woods, their backs patterned like thumbprints and bracken fronds. I knew I'd leave the farm one day, but for a long time it was as vague and unexamined a notion as that of getting married or having children. What brought that intimation into focus was not my growing sense of dissatisfaction with this life, but the dreadful incident with the ostrich.

For there were ostriches. The wet valleys of West Wales were an unlikely place to find them, but the boss and his wife had repurposed a portion of their grazing land as an ostrich farm. It was the time of the Great British Ostrich Bubble, when ostrich steaks were heralded as the health food of the future and fertilised eggs were selling for £100 each. Soon this breeders' market would saturate and prices collapse along with most of the farms. Disaster was already in the air: I shiver at the memory of the Welsh ostrich farmers' social event we attended one night, where tables of former sheep farmers chewed sadly at ostrich steaks and took heart pills while a man in a lounge suit played show tunes on a Casio organ.

Ostriches are unlike falcons in that they're genuinely dangerous, so the high wire fence surrounding their fields had a gap at the bottom that you could roll through if they chased you. I had as little to do with the ostriches as possible, but occasionally I was asked to check the fences along their field boundaries – I blush to admit that I used to pretend I was walking the electrified dinosaur containments in *Jurassic Park* to make the job more interesting – and I was in the

379

company of the boss's wife one morning doing just this when it happened. We saw a lump on the ground further up the hill that resolved, as we grew closer, into a female ostrich lying in a circle of trampled, blood-soaked mud. The poor bird had stuck a foot through the wire sometime the previous night, panicked, and had broken her leg trying to get free. She was still alive, somehow keeping her head off the ground though most of her neck lay flat in the dirt. The compound tibiotarsal fracture was so obscene, a chaos of torn red muscle and splintered white bone, that I went straight into full-on emergency mode. I searched my pockets and pulled out a miniature penknife branded with the logo of a local photographic shop. I unfolded it, picked up a big rock, hit the ostrich over the head to render it unconscious, then knelt down and cut its throat to put it out of its misery. Keychain novelty penknives are not sharp. It took a while. You do such things when there's no other thing that can be done. I got up, watching the bird's one good leg kick until it stilled, the blankness of sheer necessity receding then to leave a wash of simple, overwhelming sadness in its wake. This was so senseless. This bird shouldn't have been able to break her leg. She shouldn't have suffered like this all night. She shouldn't have been here at all. I watched my hands wipe streaks of bloody mud down the front of my jeans, then looked up and saw the stricken face of my boss's wife. I had forgotten she was there.

Oh, I thought.

The chain of command had fallen away. A bright, fierce sense of personal agency flared up, newborn of the grimmest necessity. My head pulled from the sand. We walked back in silence. I never felt the same about the farm after that morning; always a part of my heart flickered and beat and thrummed with the need to escape, a bird trapped in a locked barn. I handed in my notice a few months later. The date of my departure may have been hastened by my boss telling me he wanted to enroll me on a secretarial course at the local college, but what finally made me leave were the cattle on the hill.

It was a blank summer evening. Everyone else had gone drinking in town. I hadn't wanted to go but I didn't want to sit at home either, so I set off for a walk in the woods at the back of the farmhouse. I was bored with my life. I was so bored I didn't know I was bored. I needed to do *something.* Then I saw the herd of bullocks on the lee side of a slope in the far distance. They had been left alone so long they were now almost entirely wild, and that was when the plan gripped me. I made some mental calculations. The valley was dark. The shoulders of the hill were bright with rays of low sun. The wind was in my face. There wasn't so much cover that I couldn't do it. Was I going to do it? I was.

I slipped deeper into the birch thicket and began stealthing my way towards them. A little later I grabbed some bracken fronds, tore and twisted them until they came free and tucked them into my T-shirt so my head was half-obscured, my hands gritty with fern juice, and then I took a handful of mud and rouged my face with it. I went full-on Captain Willard from *Apocalypse Now.*

It was an epic stalk. Cover, concealment, camouflage. No sudden movements, everything slowed into certainty. When I was within three hundred yards of my target, I got on my hands and knees and crawled. When I was even closer, I got on my belly. I spent a lot of time utterly motionless, because keeping still for long periods was a crucial part of the manoeuvre. I had expected this stalk to be absorbing. I did not expect it to be a truly mind-altering experience. Every time I stopped moving the world dipped and swung and held itself in suspension around me. I felt myself then loosely scattered, hardly a singular being, just a thing of leaves and dirt and stones. I suppose I was incredibly uncomfortable, though I didn't feel it, because later I found there was blood down one arm from a laceration, cause unknown, and my right knee hurt for weeks. But I persevered. I got right up to the herd. I got almost *into* the herd. They were sitting amid the thistly grass, flipping their tails on to the dried mud of their flanks, chewing the cud, flicking their ears. There was the rich smell of cow – I had crawled through God knows how many cowpats en route – and I was close enough to see flies and eyelashes.

And then I did it. I leaped up from the ground, waving my arms, and *yelled*. Under a low Welsh sky, to a herd of surprised cattle, I was a home-made ghillie-suited, dancing, mud-smeared monstrous apparition out of nowhere. The herd scrambled to its feet, lowing in entirely understandable terror, and stampeded. The earth trembled under their serried hooves. It was *perfect*. I yelled and yelled at the beasts as they flung themselves pell-mell hell-for-leather up and over the hill until they were all gone, and I knew the entire time that this was, hand to

God, the most satisfying thing I had ever done in my whole life, and I limped back to the farm, with my mouth hurting from grinning, buzzing with thistle-prickles and adrenalin, and got myself in the bath, and lay there soaking away the mud, and as the adrenalin subsided, I realised I had absolutely no idea why I had done it.

Over the years I've told a few people that once I covered myself in mud and leaves and stalked a herd of cows on a hill. It makes me sound a little unbalanced, but then balance has never been my forte, and I had certainly been feeling the insulating blankness that accompanies certain forms of long-term depression. I almost never tell the story about the ostrich. A friend once told me it made me sound like a psychopath. 'No,' I countered, stung, 'the point of the story is the opposite: it shows how none of us are used to seeing death any more, let alone having to . . . Well, that's not really the point, the point is that no matter who we are, we can all do things that we don't think we can do, really hard things, if we have to.'

Their eyebrows rose. 'Like kill an ostrich with a rock and a novelty penknife?'

I tried to explain that when all options

have narrowed to *must,* there comes a point where you can't even think about alternatives. 'Yeah,' they said slowly, 'but that just makes you sound even worse.'

It's true that most of us these days haven't ever killed an animal much larger than a fly, though humans kill more animals today than ever before – sixty-five billion chickens each year, for example. And it's also true that all of us have the capacity to do things we think unimaginable until the moment they are not. But that's not the point of the story either.

The point is that I would never have fled the farm without the ostrich and the cattle.

On my travels I've talked to many strangers about grief, and birds, and love, and death. And many have been generous enough to share with me a meaningful encounter they have had with an animal. With ravens or owls or hawks or bears; herons or cats, foxes, even butterflies. Each encounter has heralded a subtle but tectonic shift in the way the person related to the world, and so often they have involved animals appearing at a time of great hardship for the witnesser, and in places they should not be. A woman told me that after the death of a beloved parent in a city hospital she heard a lone wild goose frantically calling for the rest of its flock in the small courtyard outside before it took off and disappeared over the urban roofline. A man told of a magpie that flew down to the coffin in the midst of a funeral, where it sat for a long while staring directly at the mourners. A veteran helicopter pilot denied their flight licence began to be visited daily by a wild black hawk.

For the longest time I assumed these meaningful encounters were examples of confirmation bias. That when something deeply affecting has happened, you'll find yourself searching for meaning in the things around you, and it's then you'll see animals that had always been there but you had never before noticed. But the more stories I heard, the more I began to feel restless with that explanation, and knew I should think more carefully about what animals can mean. I'm sure that the barn owl that turned its face to stare at a grieving son was merely momentarily surprised before flying on. But even so there was more to that exchange than an animal and a person looking at each other.

We have corralled the meanings of animals so tightly these days, have shuttled them into separate epistemologies that are not supposed to touch. You can consider the

Eurasian wolf as a social canid, or see it as an archetype with deep spiritual significance, but scientists aren't supposed to speak of magic, and New Agers tend not to bother with sustained research into animal physiology or behaviour. Of course we need science to comprehend the complexity of the moving world, and to help decide how best to conserve what there is still left. But there is always more. Perhaps one aspect of the sixteenth century is worthy of thinking about: the last great flowering of a form of emblematic natural history in which we could think of animals as more than mere creatures, each living species at the centre of a rich fabric of associations linking everything that was known about it with everything it meant to humans: matters allegorical, scriptural, proverbial, personal.

The ostrich and the cattle were living animals with their own life-worlds and deserving of their own stories. But they were also emblems to me, signs read by my subconscious mind to hasten me out of the quotidian incomprehension fostered by dismal circumstances. They were encounters with animals that resolved themselves into personal truths. And the nature of those truths were particular. They weren't hard-won through therapeutic dialogue. Nor were they revelations of divine intent. They were the kind of truths most akin, I think, to those offered by Tarot cards.

Like the I Ching, Tarot has a very peculiar sociocultural position. I've met many eminent people – scientists, writers, lawyers – who regularly turn to it, but they tend to keep this quiet because reading the cards is too *woo woo* to discuss in polite company. I've used Tarot too. Not often, but sufficient to know how little use the cards are in divining the future – and to see how unerringly the cards reflect my deepest states of being, emotions I'd not let myself feel at the time. I have no idea of the mechanism through which this could be possible, but even so I find myself inclined to trust that the Tarot can speak to us in ways to which we should pay the most careful attention.

Encounters with creatures are always with a real creature. But they are also built out of all the stories and associations we've learned about them throughout our lives. They are always already emblematic. And while we should honour their lived reality, and trust the science, I wonder if we might also be readier to accept what animals' emblematic selves are trying to tell us.

Sometimes the answers are simple. I understood what the ostrich had taught me almost instantly. But what the cows meant took me years. I was overtaking an animal transport truck on a motorway one afternoon when I glimpsed the wet pink nose of a cow pushed through its side. I felt pity, guilt, responsibility, sadness. I thought about the remorselessness of the system in which this creature had been caught up. And then I thought of the day I stalked the steers on the hill and it resolved into perfect clarity. For I had seen myself as one of those steers, one of a feral and uncared-for herd enjoying life in the middle of nowhere, not thinking about what would happen in the future, and not much worried about it, but knowing deep down that one day I was headed for the abattoir. There would be no escaping the deep sea for the shore. And my stalking and shouting was not mindless. It had been an inchoate attempt to knock them out of their contented composure. It had been a warning to make them run the *hell out of there,* because the valley we were all in was dark and deep and could have no good end.

THE NUMINOUS ORDINARY

The 1960s radio in my childhood home had a mahogany wood case, milled metal dials and a glass face printed with bands and frequencies. To find stations you moved the indicator through a gamut of squeals and static by turning a dial, which always felt a little as if I were a burglar unlocking a safe: *click, click,* hair-fine attention, feedback between the printed whorls of my fingertips and the slow beat of the sound-sensing hairs deep in my ears making me just a shorting arc between them, so that it was easy to feel that the voices were waiting for me alone to find them. LUXEMBOURG, BREMEN, STRASS-BURG, it said on the screen in fat capitals, BUDAPEST. BBC LIGHT. Polkas, waltzes, voices in unknown languages. That radio made Europe into an idea for me, and I loved it. But as I grew older my fascination with the 1960s radio ebbed and died and I spent far less time playing with it. It ended up on my bedroom bookcase tuned almost perpetually to BBC Radio 4.

But then, on occasional evenings in the early 1980s, I began noticing the strangest thing. Whatever the radio was playing – the news, perhaps, a discussion programme, a mystery drama – a melody would drift in behind the voices, fugitive as ash. Usually it was only barely discernible before burying itself again beneath the programme. But sometimes the music would come clear. Ten bell-like notes, rich with mystery, so plangent and eerie that I took to turning on the radio just in case they appeared. Decades later, after spending some time on radio enthusiast message boards on the internet, I worked out that in my small English bedroom I had been hearing the interval tuning signal of the All-Union Soviet station Radio Mayak. *Mayak:* Russian for lighthouse, beacon. The melody was from the famous Russian song 'Moscow Nights'. 'Речка движется и не движется,' runs the lyric. *River moving and not moving.* And ever since those days, certain unpredictable things will remind me of that ten-note melody – a photograph of thousands of bird skins laid out in open museum drawers, the dusty smear of the Milky Way, the details of spatter-coated samples in scanning electron micrographs, or the thin trails of summer meteor showers. I thought of it again yesterday while lounging on the sofa watching *Raiders of the Lost Ark,* hearing the amoral archaeologist René Belloq explain to Indiana Jones the nature of the Ark of the Covenant. 'It's a transmitter,' he says. 'It's a radio for speaking to God.' Somehow, the interval signal melody that slipped into the evenings of my everyday teenage life has become to me the music of the divine.

I was not raised in any faith. I was the child always surprised by grace before mealtimes at the houses of friends. The great authorities of my childhood were *National Geographic* and *New Scientist* magazines, though I wasn't ignorant of the Bible. My grandmother, a tall and striking woman with raven curls and stylish crimplene blouses, had given me *The Children's Bible* for Christmas before I could read. It was illustrated with scenes painted according to the aesthetic conventions of 1950s Technicolor Hollywood epics. The scenery mostly resembled southern Californian hillsides. There were scenes of hail raining upon dying cattle, men sweeping up frogs, an angel giving a shirtless Gideon the eye, and – my favourite because it was a bird I'd not yet seen – Elijah being fed lumps of meat by a raven. The Book of Revelation posed certain issues for the artists, who, faced with matters traumatically eschatological, opted for blue-toned abstraction.

Growing up living on an estate owned by the Theosophical Society didn't bring me to faith, but it widened my understanding of what it could be. Our neighbours believed in reincarnation, occultism, in mysteries at the heart of all the world's religious texts, and when I'd walk past the open door of the Liberal Catholic Church on my way to watch birds in the woods I'd sometimes stop to take deep breaths of sweet incense, though I don't remember ever venturing inside.

During my teenage years I didn't think much about religion except that I didn't have it, didn't need it and that people who did were sad, an unexamined contempt that was perhaps misdirected envy at the thought that some people could so easily feel unconditional love. But it was around then that I had a dream about God. It happened precisely once, and there was no question of what I was dreaming. *It* – for this was no He – was tall, roughly the shape of a human, lacking eyes and any kind of facial feature, and Its surface perfectly reflected everything around It. A slowly moving, purposive mirror that spoke things that weren't words that I could feel in my bones, deep subsonics. It burned unbearably hot and unbearably cold at the same time. I don't recall that It had any regard for me in particular, nor why It should have been in my dream, but then, I suppose, I was not supposed to, and that was perhaps the point. The dream didn't make me believe. Nor has anything since. But recently I've been thinking about religion again.

What has led me to it is largely a matter of craft. When I was writing my book about the death of my father and dealing with the matter of grief by training a hawk, I kept trying to find the right words to describe certain experiences and failing. My secular lexicon didn't capture what they were like. You've probably had such experiences yourself – times in which the world stutters, turns and fills with unexpected meaning. When rapturousness claims a moment and transfigures it. The deep hush before an oncoming storm; the clapping of wings as a flock of doves rises to wheel against low sun; a briar stem in the sun glittering with blades of hoarfrost. Love, beauty, mystery. Epiphanies, I suppose. Occasions of grace.

For a long while I tried to write about such things by borrowing from the extensive literature on the philosophical concept of the sublime. It got me some of the way there, but never far enough. Only recently have I found the language I need – in writings about forms of religious experience. Books written by people like William James and Rudolf Otto, books that investigate the nature of our intuitions of the sacred. The experience of the numinous, in Otto's account, is of a mystery outside the self that is both terrible and fascinating, in the divine presence of which 'the soul, held speechless, trembles inwardly to the furthest fibre of its being'. These are texts you're probably handed on your first day of studying theology, but all of them are new to me. Trying to think and write after reading them feels a little as if I'm trying to learn glassblowing on my own. Their concepts are hot, supple, incandescent, feel slightly dangerous, and I've not been taught anything about their tolerances, or what to do with them, and the things I will make of them will surely provoke pity and amusement from experts in this field. I'm a writer and historian, not a theologian or metaphysician. But even so I'm drawn to think about this stuff, to try to shape it, with all its burn and glow and texture.

■ ■ ■ ■

The natural world is not, to me, a fabric of stuff that gleams with revelation of a singular creator god. Those moments in nature that provoke in me a sense of the divine are those in which my attention has unaccountably snagged on something small and transitory – the pattern of hailstones by my feet upon dark earth; a certain cast of light across a hillside through a break in the clouds; the face of a long-eared owl peering out at me from a hawthorn bush – things whose fugitive instances give me an overwhelming sense of how unlikely it is that in the days of my brief life I should be in the right place at the right time and possess sufficient quality of attention to see them at all. When they occur, and they do not occur often, these moments open up a giddying glimpse into the inhuman systems of the world that operate on scales too small and too large and too complex for us to apprehend. What I feel is certainly the mysterious terror and awe of Otto's *numinous consciousness,* the sense of something wholly other that renders me breathless and shaking – and something else, captured in four lines from William Blake's *Milton:*

There is a Moment in each Day that
    Satan cannot find
Nor can his Watch Fiends find it, but the
    Industrious find
This Moment & it multiply, & when it once
    is found
It Renovates every Moment of the Day if
    rightly placed.

I am far from an industrious soul, except in my capacity, perhaps, to pay close attention to things. But these words speak exactly of how those moments seem to me. Not only do they renovate each moment of the day, but multiply into everything there is and will be. They break time itself.

Part of the numinousness in these experiences of nature is how unpredictable they are. There is no point in searching for them. In my experience if you go out hoping for revelation you will merely get rained upon. But as the music of Radio Mayak showed me, I've found it easier, over the years, to encounter numinousness in a different way – in those moments where mystery arises from the meeting of human art and unpredictable natural phenomena. The gift of the Radio Mayak interval melody was in how that melody reached me. It was carried to my ear on radio waves reflected from the ionosphere through a process called skip-propagation. From Moscow the signal rose high into the atmosphere, where it hit a layer of charged particles and was bounced back down towards me. I could never predict when the melody would ring clear and true because the ionosphere is always in flux, its conditions shifting according to the time of day, the season, even the stage of the eleven-year sunspot cycle, every alteration affecting the strength of the signal reflection. The sense of numinousness that interval signal gave me arose from the interaction of innumerable events – some chance, some law-bound. When I think of that melody now it contains the nature of space weather, regularities and irregularities in the shape of the world, the laws of electromagnetics, and the hope of unknown broadcasters in a distant Soviet radio station for listeners, for human minds that might attend to what they had sent into the air.

The most numinous ordinary object I own is a Sony BHF90 ferric-oxide cassette tape. Its black plastic casing is dented, its green label scuffed with age. It grinds and rattles when it plays. I've had it for nearly thirty years. It came into my possession mysteriously when I was a literature student spending a lot of time with friends in a college house in Cambridge. One of them was a tall man who possessed a kind of brooding softness, like a voice pitched *sotto* that makes you lean in and find yourself unexpectedly close. His best friend in the house had recently abdicated from manhood – not because he felt it failed to match his gender identity, but more that he had just worked out that the actions of men were mostly dreadful. He had a thing for Virginia Woolf, smoked roll-ups, wore his thick hair in a ponytail. Together they read Pasternak, and rejoiced in bizarre acts of motiveless violence against the house; they smashed chairs to the sound of Bartók string quartets, stuck cutlery into the plaster ceiling of the kitchen and left it there for its pleasing creepiness. Even so their company felt a safe harbour to me. Not many things did. I'd dropped out of college for a little while because I'd fallen in love with a married college professor, the kind of married college professor who much later told people I'd entirely made up our affair. It was a foggy summer, all late traces and contrails, grasshoppers singing in the thick grasses along the paths through the town commons where I'd walk for hours with no particular destination. I was very lost when the tape appeared.

There's only one track on it. It is a recording of Leonard Bernstein conducting Sibelius's Seventh Symphony. From the announcer's introduction, I think it was recorded from a radio programme in Japan. After it came into my possession I listened to it, rewound the tape and listened to it again. I listened to it hundreds of times. It wasn't soothing. The music was torqued at precisely the angle of the pain in my heart and it always felt too fast in places and far too slow in others and somehow the way that it flowed from one to the other felt like the way the human mind deals with the foreknowledge of death. The music coursed with every emotion I'd ever pushed away and pretended I didn't feel. But that was only a part of the recording's power. It wasn't a high-quality tape; the signal-to-noise ratio was poor. It stood even then for all the ways that age and distance corrode. Cosmic rays burying themselves in vaults of water. Rust on the tips of your fingers.

But these things alone didn't make the recording numinous. That was born of chance: it had been recorded from the radio during an electrical storm. The skies the signal had travelled through to reach the radio had been hot with potentiality, intermittent frequency overloads crackling and spitting and annihilating the broadcast with bursts of white noise. The lightning strikes were occasional at the beginning of the symphony, but towards the end they came so often it was hard to hear music at all, just scorching crepitation rampaging on and on, with faint strings behind it like crosscurrents on a sea. When the lightning obliterated the music, the noise was so loud it was like silence. It felt as if God had put thumbprints on the tape.

I knew it to be an unrepeatable event, fixed, for ever, on tape, so that it could be played again and again, and there was something so transgressive about this that listening to it felt like heresy. I'm still not sure how much of my need for this tape was refuge and how much a desire for obliteration. I think of the son of one of my mother's friends who became pathologically obsessed with C. S. Lewis's *The Voyage of the Dawn Treader* when he was a child and no one knew why, and it turned out that he had found out about a great family secret, one that could never be spoken out loud, so he cleaved to this book about the end of the world, about a boy whose sins could be cut from him like skin. Maybe the tape was something like that. Something impossibly heavy that held me in thrall, a scrap of the divine not good for my soul, a thing that should never have been fixed in place on tape to be repeatedly overheard, a thing that stood between me and the telling of secrets. It went on for months until I decided, quite suddenly one morning, that I didn't want to listen to it any more. These days that tape is somewhere in my house in a box, still hot with what it meant back then, and I have picked it up a few times and held it, surprised by its lightness, and how difficult it is even now to hold. It is a relic of a particular hour, of a long-past time, of the person I once was, and its power now is precisely in the knowing that I will never play it again.

WHAT ANIMALS TAUGHT ME

A long time ago, when I was nine or ten, I wrote a school essay on what I wanted to be when I grew up. I'll be an artist, and I will have a pet otter, I announced, before adding, *as long as the otter is happy.* When I got my exercise book back my teacher had commented, 'But how can you tell if an otter is happy?' and I boiled with indignation. Surely, I thought, otters would be happy if they could play, had a soft place to sleep, go exploring, had a friend (that would be me) and swim around in rivers catching fish. The fish were my only concession to the notion that an otter's needs might not match my own. It never occurred to me that I might not understand the things an otter might want, or understand much of what an otter might be. I thought animals were just like me.

I was an odd, solitary child with an early and all-consuming compulsion to seek out wild creatures. Perhaps this was part of the unfinished business of losing my twin at birth: a small girl searching for her missing half, not knowing what she was looking for. I upended rocks for centipedes and ants, followed butterflies between flowers, spent a lot of time chasing and catching things and not thinking much about how that made them feel. I was a child kneeling to extract a grasshopper from the closed cage of one hand, solemn with the necessity of gentleness, frowning as I took in the details of its netted wings, heraldically marked thorax, abdomen as glossy and engineered as jewellery. I wasn't just finding out what animals looked like, doing this, but testing my capacity to navigate that perilous space between harm and care that was partly about understanding how much power over things I might have, and partly how much power I had over myself. At home I kept insects and amphibians in a growing collection of glass aquaria and vivaria arranged on bedroom shelves and windowsills. Later they were joined by an orphaned crow, an injured jackdaw, a badger cub, and a nest of baby bullfinches rendered homeless by a neighbour's garden pruning. Looking after this menagerie taught me a lot about animal husbandry, but in retrospect my motives were selfish. Rescuing animals made me feel good about myself; surrounded by them I felt less alone.

My parents were wonderfully accepting of these eccentricities, putting up with seeds scattered on kitchen countertops and bird droppings in the hall with great good grace. But things weren't so easy at school. To use a term from developmental psychology, social cognition wasn't my forte. One morning I wandered off the court in the middle of a netball match to identify some nearby birdcalls, and was bewildered by the rage this induced in my team. Things like this kept happening. I wasn't good at teams. Or rules. Or any of the in-jokes and complicated allegiances of my peer group. Unsurprisingly, I was bullied. To salve this growing, biting sense of difference from my peers, I began to use animals to make myself disappear. If I looked hard enough at insects, or held my binoculars up to my eyes to bring wild birds close, I found that by concentrating on the creature, I could make myself go away. This method of finding refuge from difficulty was an abiding feature of my childhood. I thought I'd grown out of it. But decades later it returned with overwhelming force after my father's death.

By then I was in my thirties and had been

a falconer for many years. Falconry was a surprising education in emotional intelligence. It taught me to think clearly about the consequences of my actions, to understand the importance of positive reinforcement and gentleness in negotiating trust. To know exactly when the hawk had had enough, when it would rather be alone. And most of all, to understand that the other party in a relationship might see a situation differently or disagree with me for its own good reasons. These were lessons about respect, agency and other minds that, I am embarrassed to confess, I was rather late in applying to people. I learned them first from birds. But after my father's death, they were all forgotten. I wanted to be something as fierce and inhuman as a goshawk. So I lived with one. Watching her soar and hunt over hillsides near my home, I identified with the qualities I saw in her so closely that I forgot my grief. But I also forgot how to be a person, and fell into a deep depression. A hawk turned out to be a terrible model for living a human life. When I was a child I'd assumed animals were just like me. Later I thought I could escape myself by pretending I was an animal. Both were founded on the same mistake. For the deepest lesson animals have taught me is how easily and unconsciously we see other lives as mirrors of our own.

Animals don't exist in order to teach us things, but that is what they have always done, and most of what they teach us is what we think we know about ourselves. The purpose of animals in medieval bestiaries, for example, was to give us lessons in how to live. I don't know anyone who now thinks of pelicans as models of Christian self-sacrifice, or the imagined couplings of vipers and lampreys an allegorical exhortation for wives to put up with unpleasant husbands. But our minds still work like bestiaries. We thrill at the notion we could be as wild as a hawk or weasel, possessing the inner ferocity to go after the things we want; we laugh at animal videos that make us yearn to experience life as joyfully as a bounding lamb. A photograph of the last passenger pigeon makes palpable the grief and fear of our own unimaginable extinction. We use animals as ideas to amplify and enlarge aspects of ourselves, turning them into simple, safe harbours for things we feel and often cannot express.

None of us sees animals clearly. They're too full of the stories we've given them. Encountering them is an encounter with everything you've ever learned about them from previous sightings, from books, images, conversations. Even rigorous scientific studies have asked questions of animals in ways that reflect our human concerns. In the late 1930s, for example, when the Dutch and German ethologists Niko Tinbergen and Konrad Lorenz towed models resembling flying hawks above turkey chicks and saw them freeze in terror, they were trying to prove that these birds hatched with something like the image of a flying hawk already in their minds. Later research, however, suggested that it's likely young turkeys learn what to fear from other turkeys – and to me these 1930s experiments seem shaped by the anxieties of a Europe threatened for the first time by large-scale aerial warfare, when pronouncements were made that no matter how tight national defence, 'the bomber will always get through'.

Simply knowing that fragment of history and knowing that domesticated turkey chicks freeze when a hawk-like shape flies overhead makes them more complicated creatures in my mind than farmyard poultry or oven-ready carcasses. For the more time spent researching, watching and interacting with animals, the more the stories they're made of change, turning into richer stories with the power to alter not only what you think of the animal, but who you are. It has broadened my notion of home to think of what that concept might mean to a nurse shark or a migratory barn swallow; altered my notion of family after I learned of the breeding systems of acorn woodpeckers, where several males and females together raise a nest of young. It's not that creatures work as models for human lives — no one I know thinks that humans should spawn like wave-borne fish or subsist entirely on flies — but the more I've learned about animals the more I've come to think there might not be only one right way to express care, to feel allegiance, a love for place, a way of moving through the world.

Trying to imagine what life is like for an animal is doomed to failure. You cannot know what it is like to be a bat by screwing your eyes tight, imagining membranous wings, finding your way through darkness by talking to it in tones that reply to you with the shape of the world. As the philosopher Thomas Nagel explained, the only way to know what it is like to be a bat is to be a bat. But the imagining? The attempt? That is a good and important thing. It forces you to think about what you don't know about the creature: what it eats, where it lives, how it communicates with others. The effort generates questions that are really about how different the world might be for a bat, not just how being a bat is different. For what an animal needs or values in a place is not always what we need, value or even notice. Muntjac deer have eaten the undergrowth where nightingales once nested in the forests near my home, and now those birds have gone. What to my human eye is a place of natural beauty is, for a nightingale, something like a desert. Perhaps this is why I am impatient with the argument that we should value natural places for their therapeutic benefits. It's true that time walking in a forest can be beneficial to our mental health. But valuing a forest for that purpose traduces what forests are: they are not there for us alone.

For some weeks I've been worried about the health of family and friends. Today I've stared at a computer screen for hours. My eyes hurt. My heart, too. Feeling the need for air, I sit on my back doorstep and see a rook, a sociable species of European crow, flying low towards my house through greying evening air. Straight away I use the trick I learned as a child, and all my difficult emotions lessen as I imagine how the press of cooling air might feel against its wings.

But my deepest relief doesn't come from imagining I can feel what the rook feels, know what the rook knows – instead, it's slow delight in knowing I cannot. These days I take emotional solace from knowing that animals are not like me, that their lives are not about us at all. The house it's flying over has meaning for both of us. To me it is home; to the rook? A waypoint on a journey, a collection of tiles and slopes, useful as a perch, or a thing to drop walnuts on in autumn to make them shatter and let it winkle out the flesh inside.

But there is something else. As it passes overhead, the rook tilts its head to regard me briefly before flying on. And with that glance I feel a prickling in my skin that runs down my spine, my sense of place shifts, and the world is enlarged. The rook and I have shared no purpose. We noticed each other, is all. When I looked at the rook and the rook looked at me, I became a feature of its world as much as it became a feature of mine. Our separate lives coincided, and all my self-absorbed anxiety vanished in that one fugitive moment, when a bird in the sky on its way somewhere else sent a glance across the divide and stitched me back into a world where both of us have equal billing.

ACKNOWLEDGEMENTS

Vast thanks to my agent Bill Clegg, for his astonishing critical acumen, warmth, support, inspiration and wisdom. From our very first meeting I felt I'd known him for ever. I'm so happy to have found a home with the Clegg Agency. Thank you to all the staff there, who have been, and are, marvellous: Marion Duvert, David Kambhu and Simon Toop deserve particular gratitude, not least for putting up with my appallingly slow email replies.

Dan Franklin at Jonathan Cape is not only a legend in publishing but among the finest people the world has ever made, and I am honoured to count him not only as my editor but as a friend. Thank you, Dan, for everything. Huge thanks also to Bea Hemming, Rachel Cugnoni, Aidan O'Neill, Alison Tulett, Sarah-Jane Forder, Suzanne Dean, Chris Wormell, and all the other people who have worked to make this book a real live thing. It is a delight and an honour to work with you all.

Elisabeth Schmitz at Grove Atlantic is a marvel in so many ways it would take an encomium the size of a book to enumerate them all. I am so thrilled to work with her, and owe her so very much. Undying and very special thanks to you, Elisabeth. And enormous thanks also to all those I've been lucky enough to work with at Grove: Morgan Entrekin, of course; Deb Seager, John Mark Boling, Judy Hottenson, and so many more. Your offices in New York always feel like home.

To the booksellers, festival and event organisers and volunteers, and the readers, interlocutors and audiences I have met with over the last few years, thank you all. The conversations I have had with you over this time have enriched my life and thought beyond all measure. Special thanks to the refugee who met and spoke to me as part of Refugee Tales, an outreach project of the charity Gatwick Detainees Welfare Group, and the volunteer who accompanied him to our meeting. Neither can be named here, but I hope that the words that came from that meeting communicate the injustice of the hardships that the structures and strictures of the world visit upon those who do not deserve anything other than happiness.

Some of these pieces were written for friends, for the joy of exploring a subject, for piecing together a story or investigating something that troubled or fascinated me. Many began life as assignments for the *New York Times Magazine,* where I have had the joy of working with the truly brilliant editor Sasha Weiss. She has taught me so much about forging and fashioning pieces like these. I will never stop being grateful to her and her colleagues. Thank you, Sasha! Many of the other essays included here began life as meditations on seasonality for the *New Statesman:* thank you, Tom Gatti, for commissioning them and for putting up with my habitual last-minutery with such patience and good humour. Others were written for inclusion in anthologies (thank you, Tim Dee, Andy Holden, Anna Pincus and David Herd), for the online magazine *Aeon* (thank you, Marina Benjamin), or, in the case of 'Murmuration', to accompany the work of the wonderful artist Sarah Wood.

Deep love and thanks to my family: Barbara, Mo, James, Cheryl, Aimee, Beatrice, Alexandrina and Arthur, and my much-missed dad Alisdair – wherever he is, he's probably still cross about my telling him how to push goats. Deep love and thanks also to my BFF Christina McLeish, who has a brain the size of Jupiter and a heart of about the same size, and more than any other person has helped shape and test my thoughts about things. She is the only person who has ever video-called me to show me a bright green newly emerged cicada wandering around her open palm. That is how excellent she is.

This book was born of the inspiration, friendship, assistance and support of many, many people. My thanks to Thomas Adès, Christine Anders, Sin Blaché, Nathan Budd, Nathalie Cabrol, Casey Cep, Jason Chapman, Garry and Jon Chapman, Marcus Coates, Alan Cumming, Sam Davis, Bill Diamond, Sarah Dollard, Ewan Dryburgh, Abigail Elek Schor, Amanda and Stuart Fall, Andrew Farnsworth, Melissa Febos, Tony Fitzpatrick, Marina Frasca-Spada, Stephen Grosz, Meg and Larry Kasdan, Nick Jardine, Olivia Laing, Michael Langley, Hermione Lister-Kaye, Sir John Lister-Kaye, Toby Mayhew, Andrew Metcalf, Paraic O'Donnell, Fil OK, Stacey Reedman, Eamonn Ryan, Jan Schafer, Grant Shaffer, Kathryn Schulz, Pablo Sobron, Isabella Streffen, Cristian Tambley, Béla Tokody, Mukund Unavane, Judith Wakelam, Hilary White, Lydia Wilson, Jeanette Winterson,

Jessica Woollard. I am a lamentably disorganised person and very likely to have omitted some people from this list by accident. It's likely that I will, over the next few months, be waking in the small hours in a total panic as I remember them, one by one. My apologies to them in advance.

And while he cannot read, and is likely to shred this page into fragments should he get his beak to it in the future, I want to thank my parrot Birdoole for his feathery companionship and his ability to make long hours of writing less lonely. I love him very much, even when he sits on my keyboard and bites my fingers as I'm working to urgent deadlines.

ABOUT THE AUTHOR

Helen Macdonald is an English writer, naturalist and academic at the University of Cambridge. She is the author of *H is for Hawk,* which won the Samuel Johnson prize. This book is a depiction of the grief and depression she fell into after the sudden death of her father in 2007 and how she bounced back through falconry. *H is for Hawk,* which has just won the £20,000 prize, describes the year Macdonald spent training a goshawk. She writes about subsuming her grief in the relationship with the bird and trying to be like her: solitary, self-possessed, free from grief, and numb to the hurts of human life. Her book is the first memoir to win the prize.